special education and the law

and the

law

Second Edition

Second Edition
Updated With New **IDEA** Regulations!

special education and the law

and the

law

a guide for practitioners

allan g. osborne, jr. : charles j. russo

CORWIN PRESS
A SAGE Publications Company
Thousand Oaks, CA 91320

70.00

For information:

Corwin Press
A Sage Publications Company
2455 Teller Road
Thousand Oaks, California 91320
www.corwinpress.com

Sage Publications India Pvt. Ltd.
B 1/I 1 Mohan Cooperative
  Industrial Area
Mathura Road, New Delhi 110 044
India

Sage Publications Ltd.
1 Oliver's Yard
55 City Road
London, EC1Y 1SP
United Kingdom

Sage Publications Asia-Pacific Pte. Ltd.
33 Pekin Street #02-01
Far East Square
Singapore 048763

Printed in the United States of America.

Library of Congress Cataloging-in-Publication Data

Osborne, Allan G.
Special education and the law: A guide for practitioners/Allan G. Osborne, Jr.,
Charles J. Russo.— 2nd ed.
    p. cm.
Includes bibliographical references and index.
ISBN 978-1-4129-2622-5 (cloth)
ISBN 978-1-4129-2623-2 (pbk.)
    1. Special education—Law and legislation—United States. I. Russo, Charles J.
II. Title.

KF4209.3.O82 2006
344.73′0791—dc22   2005031748

This book is printed on acid-free paper.

07   08   09   10   11   10   9   8   7   6   5   4

Acquisitions Editor:	Elizabeth Brenkus
Editorial Assistant:	Desirée Enayati
Production Editor:	Sarah K. Quesenberry
Copy Editor:	Kristin Bergstad
Typesetter:	C&M Digitals (P) Ltd.
Proofreader:	Colleen Brennan
Indexer:	Nara Wood
Cover Designer:	Michael Dubowe
Graphic Designer:	Lisa Miller

Contents

Preface

In 1975 Congress enacted sweeping legislation mandating that eligible students with disabilities be provided with appropriate special education services tailored to their unique needs. Most recently reauthorized in 2004, this law, now known as the Individuals with Disabilities Education Act (IDEA), drastically altered the continuum of programs that educators must provide to students with disabilities. Over the years, the IDEA and its regulations have generated more litigation than any other educational legislation in the history of American public schools. Moreover, the IDEA and its regulations created a web of legal obligations about which educators constantly need to be updated. Further, this revised second edition of *Special Education and the Law* now includes the final version of the regulations that were promulgated in August 2006 incident to the 2004 version of the IDEA. We hope that this up-to-date information will be of use to all readers.

Given the far-reaching scope of the IDEA and its regulations, this book examines how federal and state courts have interpreted the statute and its regulations, addressing the delivery of special education and related services to students with disabilities. The book is organized around the major procedural and substantive issues in special education law. Specifically, the book examines the substantive and procedural requirements that the IDEA, its regulations, and litigation have placed on school officials. Among the major topics that this book addresses are the rights of students with disabilities to a free appropriate public education, procedural due process, proper placement, the receipt of related services, discipline, and remedies if school officials fail to adhere to the IDEA. The book also traces the legal history of special education while briefly discussing other statutes that affect the delivery of special education services.

This book is not intended to replace the advice and counsel of a school board's attorney. Rather, it is designed to make school officials, especially at the building level, more aware of the various requirements of the laws governing special education, in the hope that understanding the laws will put them in a better position to implement the myriad legal requirements.

As such, readers are cautioned always to consult their school board's attorney when difficult situations arise.

Chapter 1 provides a historical perspective of the special education movement. It begins with an overview of the various sources of law in order to place the rest of the book in its proper legal context. The chapter then discusses the forces that led to the development of special education legislation in the United States and goes on to review the various laws that currently affect the delivery of special education services and the rights of children with disabilities.

Chapter 2 presents information relative to the specific rights of students to receive special education and related services. The chapter reviews information on who is eligible to receive services, along with the legal requirements for providing a free appropriate public education in the least restrictive environment. The chapter next discusses the components of an appropriate education and the factors that must be considered when making placement decisions. Also included here is material about when private day school and residential school programs must be provided and when extended school year programs are warranted.

Students with disabilities are entitled to receive related, or supportive, services to the extent that these services are necessary for them to benefit from their special education programs. Chapter 3 provides detailed information concerning the supportive services that qualify as related services and the circumstances under which they must be provided. The chapter also examines issues surrounding assistive technology and transition services.

One of the IDEA's unique features is its elaborate due process safeguards. These safeguards are designed to ensure that students with disabilities receive the free appropriate public education that they are guaranteed by the law. Chapter 4 outlines the specific procedural rights that students with disabilities and their parents have under the IDEA regarding children's identification, the assessment of children with disabilities, and the development of children's individualized education programs.

Unfortunately, since students with disabilities, like students without disabilities, sometimes commit acts of misconduct, they are not immune to being disciplined. Nonetheless, the disciplinary sanctions meted out must not deprive students with disabilities of the free appropriate public education they are guaranteed by the IDEA. Chapter 5 discusses the special procedures that school officials must adhere to when disciplining special education students.

When Congress enacted the IDEA, it envisioned a system whereby school officials and parents would work together to plan and develop a student's educational program. Congress was not naïve, however. It realized that disputes would arise and included in the IDEA procedures relating to dispute resolution. These procedures are reviewed in Chapter 6.

Parents have recourse when school board officials fail to provide the free appropriate public education that the IDEA requires. Since the enactment of the IDEA, the courts have provided parents with a number of compensatory remedies in addition to prospective relief. Chapter 7 outlines the remedies available to parents when a school board fails to live up to its responsibilities. This chapter includes information regarding awards of tuition reimbursement, compensatory educational services, and attorney fees, plus a general discussion of punitive damages.

A new Chapter 8 briefly reflects on the practical issues in dealing with the legal system. Most notably, this chapter reviews the emerging area of preventative law and dispute resolution. The chapter also provides insights for school officials about the value of having a good attorney who is knowledgeable about special education and how to locate such a professional.

The book includes a brief glossary of terms. The glossary does not cover terms that are defined and explained within the text. Rather, it is designed to define the legal and technical terms with which the reader may be unfamiliar. There are also Internet resources at the end of the book, including Web sites of state departments of education, special education services, and education law.

ACKNOWLEDGMENTS

We could not have written a book of this magnitude without the support, encouragement, and assistance of many friends, colleagues, and family members. Thus, while it may be almost impossible to acknowledge all who have in some way influenced us and so contributed to this book, we would at least like to extend our gratitude to those who have had the greatest impact in our lives. This group includes all who have contributed to our knowledge and understanding of the subject matter of this book, most notably our many friends and colleagues who are members of the Education Law Association. These professionals have not only consistently shared their knowledge with us but also, more importantly, provided constructive criticism and constantly challenged our thinking.

We are also most fortunate to work with a group of professionals who understand the importance of our work and provide us with the resources to continue our research. The contributions of many colleagues from the Quincy Public Schools and the University of Dayton can never be adequately acknowledged.

I (Allan Osborne) especially thank Richard DeCristofaro and Carmen Mariano, Superintendent and Assistant Superintendent, respectively, and the entire administrative team of the Quincy Public Schools for their continuing encouragement and support. I would also like to extend a very warm thank you to the faculty, parents, and students of the Snug Harbor

Community School in Quincy, Massachusetts, for more than two decades of inspiration. Special thanks are extended to Bob Limoncelli, Chris Karaska, and Amy Carey-Shinney, who provide a wonderful network of support on a daily basis. A school administrator is no better than his or her secretarial staff. I am fortunate to have the best. Much appreciation and love is extended to Angie Priscella and Mary Anne McLellan for putting up with me. Finally, I wish to thank two good friends and colleagues: Dennis Carini, for providing me with advice, motivation, and many light moments when they were most needed and Carol Shiffer, who, by example, has taught me much about perseverance.

I also wish to thank my friend and former doctoral mentor, Dr. Phil DiMattia of Boston College, for first encouraging me to investigate many of the issues contained in this book and for continuing to challenge my thinking.

At the University of Dayton, I (Charlie Russo) would like to express my thanks to Rev. Joseph D. Massucci, Chair of the Department of Educational Leadership; Thomas Lasley, Dean of the School of Education and Allied Professions at the University of Dayton; and my colleagues, Associate Dean Dr. Dan Raisch and Dr. Timothy Ilg, for all of their ongoing support and friendship. I also extend a special note of thanks to Elizabeth Pearn for her valuable assistance in helping to process the manuscript. Thanks, too, to Colleen Wildenhaus for her help proofreading the manuscript and to Marianne E. Graham, University of Dayton School of Law, class of 2007, for her assistance in preparing the resources at the end of the book that contain the various Web sites related to special education.

I would like to extend my thanks to two of my former professors and long-term friends from my student days at St. John's: many thanks to Dr. David B. Evans who, even while I was an undergraduate, taught me a great deal about the skills necessary to succeed in an academic career. I would also like to thank my doctoral mentor, Dr. Zarif Bacilous, for helping me to complete my studies and enter the academy.

We would both like to thank our acquisitions editor at Corwin, Lizzie Brenkus, and her predecessor, Robb Clouse, for their support as we conceptualized and wrote both editions of this book. It is a pleasure working with such outstanding professionals and their colleagues at Corwin. They certainly helped to make our jobs easier. Further, we would like to acknowledge the superb job of our copyeditor, Kristin Bergstad, in meticulously going over the manuscript and preparing it for publication.

On a more personal note, we both extend our appreciation to our parents, Helen J. Russo and the late James J. Russo and the late Allan G. Osborne and late Ruth L. Osborne. Our gratitude can never be adequately expressed. The influence of our parents over the course of our lifetimes has been profound.

I (Charles Russo) also extend a special note of thanks and appreciation to my two wonderful children, David Peter Russo and Emily Rebecca Russo. These two bright and inquisitive children have grown to be wonderful young adults who provide me with a constant source of inspiration and love.

Our wonderful wives, the two Debbies, have been the major influence in our lives and professional careers. Our best friends, they encourage us to write and have shown great patience as we ramble on endlessly about litigation in special education. We would not be able to do all that we do if it were not for their constant love and support. Thus, we dedicate this book to them with all of our love.

—A.G.O.
—C.J.R.

Corwin Press gratefully acknowledges the contributions of the following individuals:

Kathy Bradberry
Exceptional Needs Specialist
Hartsville High School
Darlington, SC

John Casper
Supervisor of Secondary Instruction
Nelson County Public Schools
Bardstown, KY

Susan M. Dannemiller
Director of SPED and Pupil Services
School District of Grafton
Grafton, WI

Randall L. De Pry
Associate Professor, SPED
College of Education
University of Colorado at Colorado Springs
Colorado Springs, CO

John Enloe
Director of Special Education
Sevier County School District
Sevierville, TN

Lisa Ward, NBCT
NTSD TSA Special Education Field Support
Oakland Unified School District
Oakland, CA

About the Authors

 **Allan G. Osborne, Jr.,** EdD, is the Principal of the Snug Harbor Community School in Quincy, Massachusetts, and a former visiting Associate Professor at Bridgewater State College. He received his doctorate in educational leadership from Boston College. He has authored or coauthored numerous articles, monographs, textbooks, and textbook chapters on special education law, along with textbooks on other aspects of special education. A past President of the Education Law Association (ELA), he has been a frequent presenter at ELA conferences and writes the "Students with Disabilities" chapter of the *Yearbook of Education Law,* which is published by ELA. Allan Osborne is on the Editorial Advisory Committee of *West's Education Law Reporter* and is coeditor of the "Education Law Into Practice" section of that journal. He also serves as an editorial consultant for many other publications in education law and special education.

 **Charles J. Russo,** JD, EdD, is the Joseph Panzer Chair in Education in the School of Education and Allied Professions and Adjunct Professor in the School of Law at the University of Dayton. The 1998–1999 President of the Education Law Association and 2002 winner of its McGhehey (Lifetime Achievement) Award, he is the author of more than 150 articles in peer-reviewed journals and the author, coauthor, editor, or coeditor of 24 books. He has been the editor of the *Yearbook of Education Law* for the Education Law Association since 1995 and has written or coauthored in excess of 600 publications. He speaks and teaches extensively on issues in education law in the United States and throughout the world. In recognition of his work in other countries, Charles Russo received an honorary PhD from Potchefstroom University, now the Potchefstroom Campus of North-West University, in Potchefstroom, South Africa, in May of 2004.

1

Special Education Law

An Introduction

One of the major challenges facing educators today is addressing the educational needs of students with disabilities. Amazingly, though, this was not always a concern for school officials.

In fact, unlike today, until well into the nineteenth century, most schools in the United States did virtually nothing to meet the educational needs of students with disabilities. Special schools and classes began to emerge for children who were visually and hearing impaired as well as for those with physical disabilities during the latter half of the 19th century; children who were retarded or had emotional problems or serious physical disabilities were still largely ignored at that time.

During the late nineteenth and early twentieth centuries, educational reformers developed classes for students who were mentally retarded. Even so, these programs were segregated, typically offered little for children with physical disabilities, and often were taught by personnel who were insufficiently prepared for their jobs. Moreover, much of the progress that occurred in the early part of the century came grinding to a halt with the onset of the Great Depression. Fortunately, during the latter half, or more precisely, the final third, of the twentieth century, American educational leaders, lawmakers, and others recognized the need to meet the educational concerns of students with disabilities.

In light of the framework of statutes, regulations, cases, and other sources of law that protect the rights of students with disabilities, the first of the three sections in this chapter presents a brief overview of the American legal system by discussing the sources of law. Even though some might perceive this material as overly legal, this section is designed to help readers who may be unfamiliar with the general principles of educational law so that they may better understand both the following chapters and the legal system within which they work. The second section briefly examines the history of the movement to obtain equal educational opportunity rights for students with disabilities, highlighting key cases that shaped legal developments in this area. The final section offers an overview of major federal legislation that safeguards the educational rights of children with disabilities; this part of the chapter also acknowledges that the states have adopted similar laws.

SOURCES OF LAW

Simply put, the U.S. Constitution is the law of the land. As the primary source of American law, the Constitution provides the framework within which the entire legal system operates. To this end, all actions taken by the federal and state governments, including state constitutions (which are supreme within their states as long as they do not contradict or limit rights protected under their federal counterpart), statutes, regulations, and common law, are subject to the Constitution as interpreted by the U.S. Supreme Court.

As important as education is, it is not mentioned in the Constitution. Under the Tenth Amendment, according to which "[t]he powers not delegated to the United States by the Constitution, nor prohibited by it to the States, are reserved to the States respectively, or to the people," education is primarily the concern of individual states. The federal government can intervene in disputes that arise under state law, as in *Brown v. Board of Education* (*Brown*, 1954), where state action deprived individuals of rights protected under the Constitution. More precisely, in *Brown*, the Supreme Court struck down state-sanctioned racial segregation because it violated the students' rights to equal protection under the Fourteenth Amendment by denying them equal educational opportunities. The Court was able to intervene in what was essentially a dispute under state law because once states create, and open, public schools, the Fourteenth Amendment dictates that they be made available to all children on an equal basis.

Along with delineating the rights and responsibilities of Americans, the Constitution establishes the three coequal branches of government that exist on both the federal and state levels. The legislative, executive, and judicial branches of government, in turn, give rise to the three other sources of law.

The legislative branch "makes the law." In other words, once a bill completes the legislative process, it is signed into law by a Chief Executive, who has the authority to enforce the new statute. Federal statutes are located in the United States Code (U.S.C.) or the United States Code Annotated (U.S.C.A.), a version that is particularly useful for attorneys and other individuals who work with the law because it provides brief summaries of cases that have interpreted these statutes. This book cites the U.S.C. rather than the unofficial U.S.C.A., since the U.S.C. is the official source of federal statutory laws. The statutes are identical in both locations. State laws are identified by a variety of titles.

Keeping in mind that a statute provides broad directives, the executive branch "enforces" the law by providing details in the form of regulations. For example, a typical compulsory attendance law requires that "[e]xcept as provided in this section, the parent of a child of compulsory school age shall cause such child to attend a school in the school district in which the child is entitled to attend school" (Ohio Revised Code, § 3321.03, 2001). Insofar as statutes are typically silent on such matters as curricular content and the length of the school day, these elements are addressed by regulations that are developed by personnel at administrative agencies who are well versed in their areas of expertise. Given the extensiveness of regulations, it is safe to say that the professional lives of educators, especially in public schools, are more directly influenced by regulations than by statutes. Federal regulations are located in the Code of Federal Regulations (C.F.R.). State regulations are identified by a variety of titles.

From time to time the U.S. Department of Education, and particularly its Office of Special Education Programs, issues policy letters, typically in response to inquiries from state or local educational officials, either to clarify a regulation or to interpret what is required by federal law (Zirkel, 2003). These letters are generally published in the *Federal Register* and are often reproduced by loose-leaf law-reporting services.

The fourth and final source of law is judge-made or common law. *Common law* refers to judicial interpretations of issues, as judges "interpret the law" by examining issues that may have been overlooked in the legislative or regulatory process or that may not have been anticipated when statutes were enacted. In the landmark case of *Marbury v. Madison* (1803), the Supreme Court asserted its authority to review the actions of other branches of American government. Although there is an occasional tension between the three branches of government, the legislative and executive branches generally defer to judicial interpretations of their actions.

Common law is rooted in the concept of precedent, the proposition that a majority ruling of the highest court in a given jurisdiction, or geographic area over which a court has authority, is binding on all lower courts within its jurisdiction. In other words, a ruling of the U.S. Supreme Court is binding throughout the nation, while a decision of a state supreme court is binding only in a given state. Persuasive precedent, a ruling from another jurisdiction, is actually not precedent at all. That is, as a court in Massachusetts seeks to resolve a novel legal issue, the judge would typically review precedent from other jurisdictions to determine whether it has been addressed elsewhere. However, since a court is not bound to follow precedent from a different jurisdiction, it remains only persuasive in nature.

The federal courts and most state judicial systems have three levels: trial courts, intermediate appellate courts, and courts of last resort. In federal court, trial courts are known as federal district courts; state trial courts employ a variety of names. Each state has at least one federal district court and some densely populated states, such as California and New York, have as many as four. Federal intermediate appellate courts are known as Circuit Courts of Appeal; as discussed below, there are 13 circuit courts; state intermediate appellate courts employ a variety of names. The highest court of the land is the U.S. Supreme Court; while most states refer to their high courts as supreme courts, here, too, a variety of titles is in use.

Trial courts typically involve one judge and a jury. The role of the judge, as trier of law, is to apply the law by resolving such issues as the admissibility of evidence and proper instructions for juries on how to apply the law in the disputes under consideration. Federal judges, at all levels, are appointed for life based on the advice and consent of the U.S. Senate. State courts vary, as judges are appointed in some jurisdictions and elected by popular vote in others. Juries function as triers of fact, meaning that they must weigh the evidence, decide what happened, and enter verdicts based on the evidence presented at trial. As the trier of fact in a special education suit, a jury (or, in a nonjury trial, the judge) reviews the record of administrative, or due process, hearings and additional evidence and hears the testimony of witnesses. In a distinction with a significant difference, parties who lose civil suits are liable while those who are found to be at fault in criminal trials, a matter well beyond the scope of this book, are guilty.

Other than a few select areas such as constitutional issues and special education, which is governed by the Individuals with Disabilities Education Act (IDEA), few school-related cases are directly under the jurisdiction of the federal courts. Before disputes can proceed to federal courts, they must generally satisfy one of two broad categories. First, cases must involve diversity of citizenship, namely that the plaintiff and defendant are from two different jurisdictions, and the amount in controversy must be at least $75,000; this latter requirement is imposed because of the high costs associated with operating the federal court system. Second, disputes must involve a federal question, meaning that they must be over the interpretation of the U.S. Constitution, a federal statute, federal regulation, or crime.

The party that is not satisfied with the decision of a trial court ordinarily has the right to seek discretionary review from an intermediate appellate court. Figure 1.1 illustrates the locations of the 13 federal judicial circuits in the United States. Under this arrangement, which is designed, in part, for administrative ease and convenience, each circuit is comprised of several states. By way of illustration, the Sixth Circuit consists of

Figure 1.1   Federal Circuit Courts of Appeal

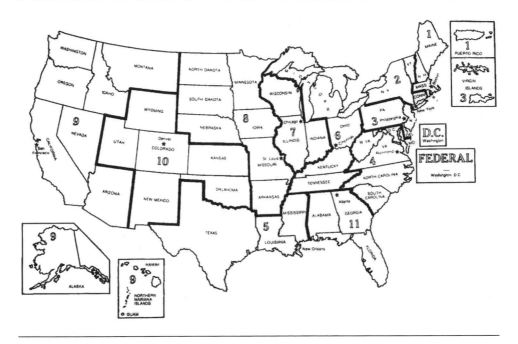

Michigan, Ohio, Kentucky, and Tennessee. State courts with three-tiered systems most often refer to this intermediate appellate level as a court of appeals. Intermediate appellate courts typically consist of three judges and ordinarily review cases for errors in the record of a trial court. This means that appellate panels usually inquire into such matters as whether a trial court judge properly admitted or excluded evidence from trial, not overturning earlier judgments unless they are clearly erroneous, rather than the facts.

A party not satisfied with the ruling of an intermediate appellate court may seek review from the high court in a jurisdiction. In order for a case to reach the Supreme Court, a party must file a petition seeking a writ of *certiorari* (literally, to be informed). In order to be granted a writ of *certiorari*, at least four of the Court's nine Justices must agree to hear an appeal. Insofar as the Court receives in excess of 7,000 petitions per year and takes, on average, fewer than 100 cases, it should be clear that few disputes will be heard by the Supreme Court. The denial of a writ of *certiorari* is of no precedential value and merely has the effect of leaving the lower court's decision unchanged. It is generally easier for discretionary appeals in state courts to reach the court of last resort, typically composed of five, seven, or nine members, especially where state law is at issue.

The opinions of the Justices in cases from the Supreme Court can be located in a variety of sources. The official version of Supreme Court cases can be found in the United States Reports. The same text, with additional research aids, is located in the Supreme Court Reporter (S. Ct.) and the Lawyer's Edition, now in its second series (L. Ed.2d). Federal appellate cases are found in the Federal Reporter, now in its third series (F.3d) while federal trial court rulings are in the Federal Supplement, now in its second series (F. Supp.2d). State cases are published in a variety of publications, most notably in West's National Reporter system, which breaks the country up into seven regions: Atlantic, North Eastern, North Western, Pacific, South Eastern, South Western, and Southern.

Prior to being published in bound volumes, most cases are available in so-called slip opinions, from a variety of loose-leaf services, and from electronic sources. Statutes and regulations are also available in similar readily accessible formats. Legal materials are available online from a variety of sources, most notably WestLaw. State laws and regulations are generally available online from each state (see the list of state Web sites in Resource B at the end of the book).

Legal citations are easy to read. The first number indicates the volume number where a case, statute, or regulation is located; the abbreviation refers to the book or series in which the material may be found; the second number indicates the page on which a case begins or the section number of a statute or regulation; the last part of a citation includes the name of the court, for lower court cases, and the year in which the dispute was resolved. For example, the citation for *Board of Education of the Hendrick Hudson Central School District v. Rowley*, 458 U.S. 176 (1982), the first Supreme Court case involving special education, reveals that it can be found on page 176 of volume 458 of the United States Reports. The earlier case between the parties, *Rowley v. Board of Education of the Hendrick Hudson Central School District*, 632 F.2d 945 (2d Cir. 1980), which was decided by the Second Circuit in 1980, begins on page 945 of volume 632 in the Federal Reporter, second series. Similarly, the Individuals with Disabilities Education Act (IDEA), 20 U.S.C. § 1400 *et seq.* (2005) can be found starting in section 1400 of Title 20 of the U.S. Code.

HISTORY OF THE EQUAL EDUCATIONAL OPPORTUNITY MOVEMENT

Prior to 1975, the federal government did not require states to provide comprehensive special education services for students with disabilities. Previously, some states enacted legislation offering special education services to students with disabilities, but these states were in the minority. Before the enactment of these laws, as discussed at the outset of this chapter, school boards routinely excluded students with disabilities. When such practices were challenged, the courts largely upheld the exclusionary practices. This changed in the early 1970s. Federal involvement in special education came after a long battle by advocates of the disabled to gain equal rights and was spurred on as a direct result of the civil rights movement.

The impetus for ensuring equal educational opportunities for all American children can be traced to *Brown v. Board of Education* (1954). Although the problem of equal access to education was resolved in the context of school desegregation, in *Brown* a unanimous Supreme Court set the tone for later developments, including those leading to protecting the rights of students with disabilities, in its assertion that "[e]ducation is perhaps the most important function of state and local governments" (p. 493). The Court added that "[i]n these days, it is doubtful that any child may reasonably be expected to succeed in life if he is denied the opportunity of an education. Such an opportunity, where the State has undertaken to provide it, is a right that must be made available to all on equal terms" (p. 493). These statements have often been either quoted directly or paraphrased by innumerable other courts in cases where parties sought equal educational opportunities for students with disabilities.

> Education is perhaps the most important function of state and local governments . . . in these days, it is doubtful that any child may reasonably be expected to succeed in life if he is denied the opportunity of an education. (*Brown v. Board of Education*, 1954, p. 493)

Unfortunately, immediately following *Brown* the rights of the disabled continued to be overlooked. Throughout the 1950s, more than half of the states had laws calling for the sterilization of individuals with disabilities, while other states limited these individuals' basic rights, such as voting, marrying, and obtaining a driver's license. By the 1960s, the percentage of children with disabilities who were served in public schools began to rise; while 12% of the students in public schools in 1948 were disabled, the number of disabled students had increased to 21% by 1963 and to 38% by 1968 (Zettel & Ballard, 1982). As of July 1, 1974, the federal Bureau for the Education of the Handicapped reported that about 78.5% of America's 8,150,000 children with disabilities received some form of public education. Of these students, 47.8% received special education and related services, 30.7% received no related services, and the remaining 21.5% received no educational services at all (House Report, 1975).

A major push for the development of special education came as a result of judicial actions that set the stage for statutory developments. Rather than trace the full history of this litigation, this brief review focuses on arguably the two most significant cases that contributed to developments aimed at protecting the rights of students with disabilities. These disputes, although decided in trial courts, are considered landmark cases insofar as they provided the impetus for Congress to pass sweeping legislation that safeguarded the rights of students with disabilities, regardless of the severity or nature of their conditions.

Pennsylvania Association for Retarded Children v. Pennsylvania (PARC) (1971, 1972) helped to establish the conceptual bases for what developed into the IDEA. In *PARC*, advocates filed suit in a federal trial court against the Commonwealth of Pennsylvania on behalf of all mentally retarded individuals between the ages of 6 and 21 who were excluded from the public schools. The commonwealth sought to justify the exclusions on the basis of four statutes that relieved local school boards of any obligation to educate children whom school psychologists certified as uneducable and untrainable, allowed officials to postpone the admission of children who had not attained a mental age of 5 years, excused children from compulsory attendance if they were found unable to profit from education, and defined compulsory school age as 8 to 17 (but used these limits to exclude mentally retarded children who were not between those ages). The plaintiffs challenged the constitutionality of the statutes and sought to enjoin their enforcement.

PARC was resolved via a consent decree, meaning that the parties essentially reached a settlement on their own that the court later approved. According to the decree, no mentally retarded children, or children who were thought to have been mentally retarded, could have been assigned to or excluded from special education programs without due process. This meant that placements in regular school classrooms were preferable to ones in more restrictive settings for children with disabilities and that they could neither be denied admission to public schools nor subjected to changes in educational placements unless they, through their parents, received procedural due process. The court added not only that all children can learn in school settings but also that Pennsylvania was obligated to provide each student who was mentally retarded with a free appropriate public education and a training program appropriate to his or her capacity.

Similarly, in *Mills v. Board of Education of the District of Columbia (Mills,* 1972), the parents of seven named exceptional children filed a class action suit in a federal trial court on behalf of perhaps as many as 18,000 students with disabilities who were not receiving programs of specialized education. Most of the children, who were minorities, were classified as having behavior problems or being mentally retarded, emotionally disturbed, and/or hyperactive. The plaintiffs sought a declaration of their rights and an order directing the school board to provide a publicly supported education to all students with disabilities. The court rejected the school board's claims that since it lacked the resources for all of its students, it could deny services to children with disabilities.

Unlike *PARC*, which was a consent decree, *Mills* was a decision on the record, meaning that the court reached its judgment after a trial on the merits of the dispute. The court found that the U.S. Constitution, coupled with the District of Columbia Code and its own regulations, required school officials to provide a publicly supported education to all children, including those with disabilities. The court ruled that the school board had to expend its funds equitably so that all students would receive an education consistent with their needs and abilities. If sufficient funds were not available, the court directed that existing resources would have to be distributed in such a manner that no child would be entirely excluded and the inadequacies would not be allowed to bear more heavily on one class of students. In addition, the court ordered the board to provide due process safeguards before any children were excluded from the public schools, were reassigned, or had their special education services terminated. At the same time, the court outlined elaborate due process procedures that helped to form the foundation for the due process safeguards that were included in the IDEA. Insofar as *Mills* originated in Washington, D.C., it was probably among the more significant influences moving federal lawmakers to act to ensure adequate protection for children with disabilities when they adopted Section 504 of the Rehabilitation Act of 1973 and the IDEA.

In light of legal developments following *PARC* and *Mills*, the remainder of this book reviews major developments designed to safeguard the educational rights of children with disabilities. In the wake of the literally thousands of suits that have been filed in federal and state courts, the chapters review selected cases under appropriate headings throughout the book rather than as separate entries.

LEGISLATIVE MANDATES

Special education in the United States is governed by four major federal statutes—the IDEA, Section 504 of the Rehabilitation Act, the Americans with Disabilities Act (ADA), the No Child Left Behind Act (NCLB)—and numerous state laws. After highlighting key features of the IDEA, this chapter provides an overview of Section 504 before taking a brief look at the ADA and NCLB. The remainder of the book focuses on the IDEA, paying particular attention to its application by school administrators.

Individuals With Disabilities Education Act

Insofar as the remainder of this book focuses on the IDEA, this section serves as a very brief overview of this comprehensive statute. In 1975 Congress enacted Public Law (P.L.) 94-142, the 142nd piece of legislation introduced during the 94th Congress; at that time it was known as the Education for All Handicapped Children Act. In 1990, Congress amended this landmark statute while renaming it the Individuals with Disabilities

Education Act (IDEA). The IDEA underwent additional major changes in 1997. Most recently, on December 3, 2004, President Bush signed the Individuals with Disabilities Education Improvement Act of 2004 into law; the new law became fully effective on July 1, 2005. For the sake of clarity, this book refers to the IDEA by this title throughout.

Unlike Section 504, which has fairly broad standards, in order to qualify for services under the IDEA, children with disabilities must meet four statutory requirements. First, children must be between the ages of 3 and 21 (20 U.S.C. § 1412(a)(1)(A)). Second, children must have specifically identified disabilities (20 U.S.C. § 1401(3)(A)(i)). Third, children must be in need of special education (20 U.S.C. § 1401(3)(A)(ii)), meaning that they must be in need of specially designed instruction to receive a free appropriate public education (FAPE) (20 U.S.C. § 1401(9)) in the least restrictive environment (LRE) (20 U.S.C. § 1412(5)) that conforms to an individualized education program (IEP) (20 U.S.C. §§ 1401(14), 1414(d)). Fourth, children with disabilities must be in need of related services (20 U.S.C. § 1401(3)(A)(ii)), such as transportation, psychological services, physical therapy, and occupational therapy, to assist them in benefiting from their IEPs.

The IDEA includes an elaborate system of procedural safeguards to protect the rights of children and their parents (20 U.S.C. § 1415). The IDEA requires school officials to provide written notice and obtain parental consent prior to evaluating children (20 U.S.C. § 1414(a)(1)(d)(i)(I)), making initial placements, or initiating changes in placements (20 U.S.C. § 1415(b)(3)(A)). Further, the parents of children with disabilities must be afforded the opportunity to participate in the development of the IEPs for and placement of their children (20 U.S.C. §§ 1414(d)(1)(B)(i), 1414(f)). Once placed, the situations of all children must be reviewed at least annually (20 U.S.C. § 1414(d)(4)) and reevaluated at least once every three years unless their parents and local school officials agree that reevaluations are unnecessary (20 U.S.C. § 1414(a)(2)(A), (B)(ii)). Further, the IDEA includes provisions, supplemented by the Family Educational Rights and Privacy Act (29 U.S.C. § 1232g) and its regulations (C.F.R. §§ 99.1 *et seq.*), as well as the IDEA's additional regulations (34 C.F.R. § 300.611 *et seq.*), preserving the confidentiality of all information used in the evaluation, placement, and education of students.

Section 504 of the Rehabilitation Act of 1973

The Rehabilitation Act of 1973, which traces its origins back to 1918, a time when the American government sought to provide rehabilitation services for military veterans of World War I, was the first federal civil rights law protecting the rights of the disabled. Pursuant to Section 504 of the Rehabilitation Act (Section 504), "[n]o otherwise qualified individual with a disability in the United States . . . shall, solely by reason of her or his disability, be excluded from the participation in, be denied the benefits of,

Table 1.1   Major Differences Between the IDEA and Section 504

Points of Consideration	IDEA	Section 504
Age limits	3–21	None: all are covered
Disabilities/ impairments	Covers only specified disabilities	Covers all who have, had, or are believed to have had impairments that affect major life activities
Limits/defenses	None: zero rejected	Cost; major change in program; health/safety
Funding	School boards receive additional federal aid	No extra funding for compliance
Dispute resolution	Must exhaust administrative remedies	Exhaustion not necessary; may file suit directly

or be subjected to discrimination under any program or activity receiving [f]ederal financial assistance . . ."(29 U.S.C. § 794(a)).

Section 504, which is predicated on an institution's receipt of "federal financial assistance," applies to virtually all schools because this term is interpreted so expansively (*Bob Jones University v. United States,* 1983) and offers broad-based protection to individuals under the more amorphous concept of impairment rather than disability. It is important to keep in mind that even though Section 504 covers children, employees, and others who may visit a school, this book focuses on the rights of students. Section 504 defines an individual with a disability as one "who (i) has a physical or mental impairment which substantially limits one or more of such person's major life activities, (ii) has a record of such an impairment, or (iii) is regarded as having such an impairment (29 U.S.C. § 706(7)(B))." The regulations define physical or mental impairments as including

(A) any physiological disorder or condition, cosmetic disfigurement, or anatomical loss affecting one or more of the following body systems: neurological; musculoskeletal; special sense organs; respiratory, including speech organs; cardiovascular; reproductive, digestive, genito-urinary; hemic and lymphatic; skin; and endocrine; or
(B) any mental or psychological disorder, such as mental retardation, organic brain syndrome, emotional or mental illness, and specific learning disorders. (45 C.F.R. § 84.3(j)(2)(i), 34 C.F.R. § 104.3(j)(2)(i))

A note accompanying this list indicates that it merely provides examples of the types of impairments that are covered; it is not meant to be exhaustive.

In order to have a record of impairment, individuals must have a history of, or been identified as having, a mental or physical impairment that substantially limits one or more major life activities. As defined in one of Section 504's regulations, individuals who are regarded as having impairment are those who have

> (A) a physical or mental impairment that does not substantially limit major life activities but that is treated by a recipient as constituting such a limitation; (B) a physical or mental impairment that substantially limits major life activities only as a result of the attitudes of others toward such impairment; or (C) none of the impairments . . . but is treated by a recipient as having such an impairment. (45 C.F.R. § 84.3(j)(2)(iv), 34 C.F.R. § 104.3(j)(2)(iv))

"'Major life activities' means functions such as caring for one's self, performing manual tasks, walking, seeing, hearing, speaking, breathing, learning, and working" (45 C.F.R. § 84.3(j)(2)(i)). Once students are identified as having impairments, the next step is to evaluate whether they are "otherwise qualified." In order to be "otherwise qualified" under Section 504, as the term is applied to students, children must be "(i) of an age during which nonhandicapped persons are provided such services, (ii) of any age during which it is mandatory under state law to provide such services to handicapped persons, or (iii) [a student] to whom a state is required to provide a free appropriate public education [under the IDEA] (45 C.F.R. § 84.3(k)(2)." Students who are "otherwise qualified," meaning that they are eligible to participate in programs or activities despite the existence of their impairments, must be permitted to take part as long as it is possible to do so by means of "reasonable accommodation[s]" (34 C.F.R. § 104.39).

Once identified, qualified students are entitled to an appropriate public education, regardless of the nature or severity of their impairments. In order to guarantee that an appropriate education is made available, Section 504's regulations include due process requirements for evaluation and placement similar to, but not nearly as detailed as, those under the IDEA (34 C.F.R. § 104.36).

In making modifications for students, educators must provide aid, benefits, and/or services that are comparable to those available to children who do not have impairments. Accordingly, qualified students must receive comparable materials, teacher quality, length of school term, and daily hours of instruction. Moreover, programs for qualified children should not be separate from those available to students who are not impaired unless such segregation is necessary for their educational programming to be effective. While schools are not prohibited from offering separate programs for students who have impairments, these children cannot be required to attend such classes unless they cannot be served adequately in such settings (34 C.F.R. § 104.4(b)(3)). If such programs are offered separately, facilities must, of course, be comparable (34 C.F.R. § 104.34(c)).

Reasonable accommodations may involve minor adjustments such as permitting a child to be accompanied by a service dog (*Sullivan v. Vallejo City Unified School District*, 1990), modifying a behavior policy to accommodate a student with an autoimmune disease who was disruptive (*Thomas v. Davidson Academy*, 1994), or providing a hearing interpreter for a student (*Barnes v. Converse College*, 1977). On the other hand, school officials do not have to grant all requests for accommodations. For example, in addition to the cases discussed below under the defenses to Section 504, a federal trial court in Missouri ruled that school officials did not have to maintain a "scent-free" environment for a child with severe asthma because she was not otherwise qualified to participate in its educational program (*Hunt v. St. Peter School*, 1997).

Examples of academic modifications include permitting children longer periods of time to complete examinations or assignments, using peer tutors, distributing outlines in advance, permitting children to obtain copies of notes from peers, employing specialized curricular materials, and/or permitting students to use laptop computers to record answers on examinations. In modifying facilities, school officials do not have to make every classroom and/or area of a building accessible; it may be enough to bring services to children, such as offering a keyboard for musical instruction in an accessible classroom rather than revamping an entire music room for a student who wishes to take piano classes.

In a related concern, Section 504's only regulation directly addressing private schools declares that officials in such schools may not exclude students on the basis of their conditions if they can, with minor adjustments, be provided with appropriate educations (34 C.F.R. § 104.39(a)). Further, this regulation stipulates that private schools "may not charge more for the provision of an appropriate education to handicapped persons than to nonhandicapped persons except to the extent that any additional charge is justified by a substantial increase in cost to the recipient" (34 C.F.R. § 104.39(b)). As such, private schools may be able to charge additional costs to parents of children with impairments.

Even if children appear to be "otherwise qualified," school officials can rely on one of three defenses to avoid being charged with noncompliance of Section 504. This represents a major difference between Section 504 and the IDEA, since no such defenses are applicable under the latter. Another major difference between the laws is that the federal government provides public schools with direct federal financial assistance to help fund programs under the IDEA but offers no financial incentives to aid institutions, public and nonpublic, as they seek to comply with the dictates of Section 504.

The first defense under Section 504 is that officials can be excused from making accommodations that result in "a fundamental alteration in the nature of [a] program" (*Southeastern Community College v. Davis*, 1979,

p. 410). The second defense permits school officials to avoid compliance if a modification imposes an "undue financial burden" (*Southeastern Community College v. Davis*, 1979, p. 412) on the institution or entity as a whole. The third defense is that an otherwise qualified student with a disability can be excluded from a program if his or her presence creates a substantial risk of injury to himself, herself, or others (*School Board of Nassau County v. Arline*, 1987). As such, a child with a severe visual impairment could be excluded from using a scalpel in a biology laboratory. However, in order to comply with Section 504, school officials would probably have to offer a reasonable accommodation, such as providing a computer-assisted program to achieve an instructional goal similar to the one that would have been achieved in a laboratory class.

Finally, Section 504, which is enforced by the Office of Civil Rights, requires recipients of federal financial aid to file an annual assurance of compliance; provide notice to students and their parents that their programs are nondiscriminatory; engage in remedial actions where violations are proven; take voluntary steps to overcome the effects of conditions that resulted in limiting the participation of students with disabilities in their programs; conduct self-evaluations; designate a staff member, typically at the central office level, as compliance coordinator; and adopt grievance procedures (34 C.F.R. § 104.5).

Admissions Evaluations

Some public (and many nonpublic) schools may require students with disabilities to take admissions examinations and/or be interviewed prior to acceptance or placement in order to evaluate whether these applicants are otherwise qualified; provisions in Section 504 address this situation. The regulations cover four areas: preplacement evaluation, evaluation, placement, and reevaluation (34 C.F.R. § 104.35).

As to preplacement evaluation, the regulations require school officials to evaluate all children who, because of their conditions, need or are believed to need special education or related services. Educators must complete these evaluations before taking any actions with respect to the initial placements of children in regular or special education as well as before any subsequent significant changes in placements.

The evaluation provisions in Section 504's regulations require school systems to follow procedures similar to those under the IDEA. More specifically, officials must validate tests and other evaluation materials for the specific purposes for which they are used, and the tests must be administered by trained personnel in conformance with the instructions provided by their producer. These materials must also be tailored to assess specific areas of educational need and cannot be designed to provide a single general intelligence quotient. Further, these materials must be selected and administered in a way that best ensures that when tests are administered to students with impaired sensory, manual, or speaking skills, the results accurately reflect their aptitude or achievement level or whatever other factor the test purports to measure, rather than reflecting their impaired sensory, manual, or speaking skills, except where those skills are the factors that the tests purport to measure.

When educators apply placement procedures to students under Section 504, their interpretations of data must consider information from a variety of sources, including aptitude and achievement tests, teacher recommendations, physical condition, social and cultural background, and adaptive behaviors that have been documented and carefully considered. In addition, not only must any such decision be made by a group of persons, including individuals who are knowledgeable, but each child must be periodically reevaluated in a manner consistent with the dictates of the IDEA.

Under Section 504, schools relying on examinations or interviews may be required to provide reasonable accommodations to applicants who are impaired. While school officials are not required to alter the content of examinations or interviews, they may have to make accommodations in how tests are administered or interviews are conducted. In other words, school officials would not be required to make an examination easier so that students who simply lacked the requisite knowledge could pass them, but they would have to alter the conditions under which examinations are administered, or interviews are conducted, so that students with impairments who have the requisite knowledge and skills to pass or express themselves fully could do so despite their conditions.

The accommodations that educators provide for examinations may be as simple as providing a quiet room without distractions, essentially a private room away from others, for students who suffer from attention deficit hyperactivity disorder or procuring the services of readers or Braille versions of examinations for applicants who are blind. Moreover, students with physical disabilities may require special seating arrangements, a scribe to record answers to questions, and/or to be permitted to use computers to record answers on examinations. Similarly, whether as part of examinations or admissions interviews, students who are hearing impaired might be entitled to the services of sign language interpreters to communicate directions that are normally given orally. At the same time, school officials may be required to provide students with learning disabilities with extra time in which to complete examinations, or they may make computers available to children who are more comfortable with computers than with traditional paper-and-pencil tests.

Prior to receiving an accommodation, students must prove that they have needs such as learning disabilities (*Argen v. New York State Board of Law Examiners*, 1994) that necessitate their taking additional time to complete examinations. The purpose of providing the extra time is to allow students who might have difficulty processing information sufficient opportunity to show that they are capable of answering the questions. Unlike the IDEA, which imposes an affirmative obligation on school officials to identify, assess, and serve children with disabilities, under Section 504, students, and/or their parents, are responsible for making school officials aware of the fact that they have impairments and are in need of accommodations for such activities as testing or interviewing. Accordingly, administrators can request proof that students have impairments in need of accommodations in order to demonstrate knowledge and skills on examinations. In such situations, students, through their parents, should also suggest which accommodations would be most appropriate. In considering whether students are entitled to accommodations, school officials must make individualized inquiries. School officials would violate Section 504 if they refused to make testing accommodations or made modifications only for students with certain specified disabilities.

Section 504 Service Plans

As noted, students who qualify under Section 504 are entitled to reasonable accommodations so that they may access the programs that schools offer. Making accommodations may involve alterations to physical plants, such as building wheelchair ramps or removing architectural barriers, so that students may physically enter and get around school buildings. School officials must also allow students to bring service dogs into the classroom (*Sullivan v. Vallejo City Unified School District*, 1990) but are not required to provide accommodations that go beyond what can be considered to be reasonable. To this end, accommodations that are excessively expensive, that expose a school's staff to excessive risk, or that require officials to make substantial modifications to the missions or purposes of their programs are not required.

In another departure from the IDEA, neither Section 504 nor its regulations mandate the creation of written agreements with regard to student accommodations or specify the content of such documents. Even so, school officials in many districts meet with parents to formalize the accommodations and services that they provide to eligible students. These written agreements are euphemistically referred to as Section 504 service plans. In practical terms, school officials should be sure to include the following components in each written Section 504 service plan:

- **Demographic Data**—student's name, date of birth, school identification number, grades, schools attended, teachers, parents' names, addresses, telephone numbers, and the like
- **Team Members**—a listing of all team members who contributed to the development of the service plans and their respective roles
- **Disability**—a description of the child's impairments and their severity along with explanations of how they impede the student's educational progress

- **Accommodations and Services**—a detailed description of the accommodations and services to be offered under the plan, including the frequency and location of services, where they are to be provided, and by whom they are to be provided

In addition, officials should attach the evaluative reports or assessments that helped to determine the nature of a student's impairment and the need for accommodations and services.

Americans With Disabilities Act

Patterned largely after Section 504 of the Rehabilitation Act, the Americans with Disabilities Act (42 U.S.C. §§ 12101 *et seq.*), enacted in 1990, protects the disabled by imposing far-reaching obligations on private sector employers, public services and accommodations, and transportation. As indicated in its preamble, the purpose of the Americans with Disabilities Act (ADA) is "to provide a clear and comprehensive national mandate for the elimination of discrimination against individuals with disabilities" (42 U.S.C. § 12101). This clarifies that the ADA intends to extend the protections afforded by Section 504 to private programs and activities that are not covered by Section 504 because they do not receive federal funds.

The ADA provides a comprehensive federal mandate to eliminate discrimination against people with disabilities and to provide "clear, strong, consistent and enforceable standards" (42 U.S.C. § 12101(b)(2)) to help accomplish this goal. The ADA's broad definition of a disability is comparable with the one in Section 504: "(a) a physical or mental impairment that substantially limits one or more of the major life activities; (b) a record of such an impairment; or (c) being regarded as having such an impairment" (§ 12102(2)). Further, like in Section 504, "major life activities" include caring for oneself, hearing, walking, speaking, seeing, breathing, and learning. The ADA, like Section 504, does not require that individuals have certificates from doctors or psychologists in order to be covered by its provisions.

The ADA specifically excludes a variety of individuals, of whom few are likely to be students but some may be school employees, most notably those who use illegal drugs (42 U.S.C. § 12210). The ADA also specifically excludes transvestites (42 U.S.C. § 12208); homosexuals and bisexuals (42 U.S.C. § 12211(a)); transsexuals, pedophiles, exhibitionists, voyeurs, and those with sexual behavior disorders (42 U.S.C. § 12211(b)); and those with conditions such as psychoactive substance use disorders stemming from current illegal use of drugs (42 U.S.C. § 12211(c)). Further, the ADA modifies Section 504 insofar as it covers individuals who are no longer engaged in illegal drug use, including those who have successfully completed drug treatment or have otherwise been rehabilitated and those who have been "erroneously" regarded as being drug users (42 U.S.C. § 12110). The ADA permits drug testing by employers to ensure that workers are in compliance with the Drug-Free Workplace Act of 1988 (41 U.S.C. § 701). Although it permits employers to prohibit the use of illegal drugs or alcohol in the workplace, the ADA is less clear over the status of alcoholics, as it appears that the protections afforded rehabilitated drug users extends to recovering alcoholics.

There are five major Titles in the ADA. Title I of the ADA addresses employment in the private sector and is directly applicable to private schools. Like Section 504, this requires school officials to make reasonable accommodations for otherwise qualified individuals once officials are aware of students' conditions; this means that in order to be covered by the ADA, students and staff need to inform school officials of their conditions along with specific suggestions on how their needs can be met. Title II of the ADA covers public services of state and local governments for both employers and providers of public services, including transportation, and most notably education, as part of the law applies to public schools. Insofar as the reasonable accommodations specifications in these provisions imply academic program accommodations, qualified students with disabilities can participate in school activities.

Title III of the ADA, which expands the scope of Section 504, deals with public accommodations, covering both the private and public sectors. This Title includes private businesses and a wide array of community services, including buildings, transportation systems, parks, recreational facilities, hotels, and theaters. Title IV of the ADA deals with telecommunications, specifically voice and nonvoice systems. In Title V, the ADA's miscellaneous provisions, the ADA stipulates not only that the law cannot be construed as applying a lesser standard than that under Section 504 and its regulations but also that qualified individuals are not required to accept services that do not meet their needs. In addition, the ADA employs defenses that parallel those in Section 504.

The ADA's impact on schools is most significant in the areas of reasonable accommodations for employees and academic program accommodations for students. Insofar as schools are subject to many ADA-like regulations through the rules enacted pursuant to Section 504, officials can avoid difficulties with the ADA by keeping proactive policies and procedures in place to ensure reasonable accommodations. School systems should designate ADA compliance officers who keep up to date on current ADA regulations and policies in the areas of employment and academic inclusion. In sum, if school systems have faithfully implemented Section 504 and its regulations, they should not have difficulties with the ADA.

No Child Left Behind Act

Perhaps the most controversial federal education law in recent memory is the No Child Left Behind Act (NCLB) that was enacted in 2002. The NCLB, which is actually an extension of the original Elementary and

Secondary Education Act of 1965, has the potential to have an impact on the delivery of special education services (Raisch & Russo, in press). The key elements in the NCLB are to improve the academic achievement of students who are economically disadvantaged; assist in preparing, training, and recruiting highly qualified teachers (and principals); provide improved language instruction for children of limited English proficiency; make school systems accountable for student achievement, particularly by imposing standards for annual yearly progress for students and districts; require school systems to rely on teaching methods that are research based and that have been proven effective; and afford parents better choices while creating innovative educational programs, especially where local school systems are unresponsive to parents' needs (Wenkart, 2003). As part of the process of complying with the revised IDEA and the NCLB, school officials must "take measurable steps to recruit, hire, train, and retain highly qualified school personnel to provide special education and related services" (20 U.S.C. § 1412 (a)(14)(D)) for students with disabilities.

The IDEA and NCLB are both similar and dissimilar. The laws are alike to the extent that they both address the needs of students with disabilities, albeit in varying degrees, through state agencies and local school systems; focus on student achievement and outcomes; emphasize parental participation; and require the regular evaluation or assessment of students and staffs. On the other hand, the laws also have some significant differences. The most important difference between the two statutes is that IDEA focuses on the performances of individual students in an array of areas, while the NCLB is more interested in systemwide outcomes.

One of the IDEA's most controversial additions, its definition of "highly qualified" teachers (20 U.S.C. §§ 1402(10), 1412 (a)(14)), which also applies to related services personnel and paraprofessionals (20 U.S.C. § 1412 (a)(14)(B)), parallels the language of the NCLB. In order to be classified as "highly qualified," a standard that is based on state rather than federal law, subject area teachers in public schools must not only be certified fully in special education or pass state-designed special education licensure examinations, but must also possess bachelor's degrees and demonstrate knowledge of each subject for which they are the primary instructors (20 U.S.C. § 1402(10)). According to these provisions, which apply the same deadlines as the NCLB, currently employed teachers must have met the standards by the end of the 2005–2006 academic year even if they teach multiple subjects. New special education teachers have up to two years after they are hired to become approved as "highly qualified" in different subjects as long as they are fully certificated in at least one. The IDEA adds that while teachers who satisfy its requirements as highly qualified also qualify for this title under the NCLB (20 U.S.C. § 1402 (10)(F)), the law does not create a private right of action that can be judicially enforced to ensure that children are taught by such teachers (20 U.S.C. § 1412(a)(14)(E)). In other words, parents cannot file a suit to ensure that their children are taught by teachers who meet the standards under the IDEA and the NCLB. The IDEA's regulations specify that the requirements concerning how to be categorized as highly qualified do not apply to teachers in private schools (300 C.F.R.§ 300.18(g)).

State Statutes

Insofar as education is a state function, special education is governed by state statutes as well as the federal laws discussed above. While each state's special education laws must be consistent with the federal laws, differences do exist. Most states have laws that are similar in scope, and even language, to the IDEA. Several states, however, have provisions in their legislation that go beyond the IDEA's substantive and procedural requirements, in that they have set higher standards of what constitutes an appropriate education for a student with disabilities. Further, most states have established procedures for implementing programs associated with special education that either are not explicitly covered by federal law or have been left to their own determination, such as the qualifications and preparation of hearing officers. If a conflict develops between provisions of the federal law and a state law, federal law is supreme.

A comprehensive discussion of the laws of each of the 50 states, the District of Columbia, and U.S. possessions and territories is beyond the scope of this book. Indeed, an entire book could be written on the special education laws of each state. The purpose of this book is to provide information on the federal mandate, the law that encompasses the entire nation. Thus, educators are cautioned that they cannot have a complete understanding of special education law if they are not familiar with state law and thus should seek out a source of information on pertinent state law to supplement this book.

RECOMMENDATIONS

Even though educators wisely rely largely on their attorneys when dealing with technical aspects of disputes involving special education, they should acquaint themselves with both federal and state legal systems. By familiarizing themselves with the legal system(s), educators can assist their attorneys and school systems because such a working knowledge can help to cut right to the heart of issues and help to avoid unnecessary delays. Even so, school officials need to do the following:

- Provide regular professional development sessions for all professional staff, and board members, to help them to have a better understanding of how their legal systems operate and, more specifically, to

Figure 1.2   Frequently Asked Questions

Q: Why was the IDEA passed in the first place?

A: When the IDEA was initially passed in 1975, many states did not have laws addressing the educational rights of students with disabilities. Congress found that many students with disabilities were excluded from the public schools and that those who attended public schools did not always receive an appropriate education. Prior to the passage of the IDEA, advocates for students with disabilities had won some significant judicial victories against states and school boards. The IDEA was passed, in part, in response to those cases but mostly to provide students with disabilities with equal educational opportunities.

Q: What is the difference between federal and state laws governing special education?

A: State laws must, of course, be consistent with federal laws but can provide students with disabilities with additional rights and protections. If there is a conflict between state and federal laws, the latter govern under the supremacy clause of the U.S. Constitution. As such, it is important for school officials to be familiar with both federal and state laws that protect the educational rights of students with disabilities.

Q: Why are some students with disabilities covered only by Section 504 and not the IDEA?

A: According to the IDEA, in order to be eligible, students with disabilities must need special education and related services as a result of their disabilities. Thus, if students have disabilities that require no special education, they are not entitled to the rights and protections of the IDEA. However, these students may qualify for protections against discrimination under Section 504 if their impairments impact their ability to receive an education.

Q: What is the purpose of the IDEA's implementing regulations?

A: The IDEA provides general guidelines explaining the services that state and local school boards must provide. The regulations, written by the U.S. Department of Education, are more specific. The regulations reflect the statute and in many cases are identical to it in actual wording. Even so, the regulations provide more detailed step-by-step guidance on how the IDEA (or any law) is to be implemented.

Q: Why is it important to be familiar with the outcome of court decisions?

A: Although the IDEA and its regulations are comprehensive, their authors could not possibly have anticipated every possible situation that could arise. Thus, many of the IDEA's provisions are open to interpretation when applied to specific sets of circumstances. Courts provide interpretations of how the law is to be applied in many unique situations. Studying judicial opinions will give school officials and attorneys a better understanding of how the courts have interpreted the law and make them better prepared to implement the IDEA's mandates in specific situations.

recognize the significant differences and interplay between and among Section 504, the IDEA, and other federal and state disability-related laws so as to better serve the needs of children with disabilities and their parents.

- Offer similar informational sessions for parents and qualified students to help ensure that they are aware of their rights.
- Develop appropriate handout materials explaining in writing how various federal and state disability laws operate, including detailed information on eligibility criteria under such key statutes as the IDEA and Section 504.
- Make sure that all board policies and procedures relating to the delivery of special education and related services are up to date. Among the policies that school systems should have in place are those dealing with what materials parents should receive on a regular basis, such as progress reports and report cards for students, notice provisions, and ones calling for parental involvement.
- Prepare checklists to help ensure that staff members are responding to parental requests in a timely and appropriate manner.
- Determine whether students with disabilities who do not qualify for services under the IDEA require reasonable accommodations under Section 504 and/or the ADA.
- Take steps to ensure that students with disabilities are not subjected to differential treatment because of their disabilities or because of their need for accommodations.
- Ensure that compliance officers regularly monitor or audit educational programming to make sure that it complies with the dictates of the IDEA, Section 504, the ADA, NCLB, and other applicable federal and state laws.
- Recognize that in light of the complexity of disability law, it is important to rely on the advice of an attorney who specializes in education law, especially one who focuses on special education. If school officials are unable to find such attorneys on their own, they should contact their state school boards associations, bar associations, or professional groups such as the Education Law Association or National School Boards Association.

REFERENCES

Americans with Disabilities Act, 42 U.S.C. § 12101 *et seq.* (1990).

Argen v. New York State Board of Law Examiners, 860 F. Supp. 84 (W.D.N.Y. 1994).

Assistance to the States for the Education of Children with Disabilities, 34 C.F.R. §§ 300.1–300.818 (2006).

Barnes v. Converse College, 436 F. Supp. (D.S.C. 1977).

Board of Education of the Hendrick Hudson Central School District v. Rowley 458 U.S. 176 (1982).

Bob Jones University v. United States, 461 U.S. 574 (1983).

Brown v. Board of Education, Topeka, 347 U.S. 483 (1954).

Code of Federal Regulations (C.F.R.), as cited.

House Report No. 332, 94th Congress (1975).

Hunt v. St. Peter School, 963 F. Supp. 843 (W.D. Mo. 1997).

Individuals with Disabilities Education Act, 20 U.S.C. § 1400 *et seq.* (2005).

Marbury v. Madison, 5 U.S. 137 (1803).

Mills v. Board of Education of the District of Columbia, 348 F. Supp. 866 (D.D.C. 1972).

No Child Left Behind Act, 20 U.S.C. § 6301 *et seq.* (2002).

Ohio Revised Code, § 3321.03 (2001).

Pennsylvania Association for Retarded Children v. Pennsylvania, 334 F. Supp. 1257 (E.D. Pa. 1971), 343 F. Supp. 279 (E.D. Pa. 1972).

Raisch, C. D., & Russo, C. J. (in press). The No Child Left Behind Act: Federal over-reaching or necessary educational reform? *Education Law Journal.*

Rehabilitation Act, Section 504, 29 U.S.C. § 794 (1973).

Rowley v. Board of Education of the Hendrick Hudson Central School District, 632 F.2d 945 (2d Cir. 1980), *reversed and remanded sub nom. Board of Education of the Hendrick Hudson Central School District v. Rowley* 458 U.S. 176 (1982).

School Board of Nassau County v. Arline, 480 U.S. 273 (1987).

Southeastern Community College v. Davis, 442 U.S. 397 (1979).

Sullivan v. Vallejo City Unified School District, 731 F. Supp. 947 (E.D. Cal. 1990).

Thomas v. Davidson Academy, 846 F. Supp. 611 (M.D. Tenn. 1994).

Wenkart, R. D. (2003). The No Child Left Behind Act and Congress' power to regulate under the Spending Clause. *Education Law Reporter, 174,* 589–597.

Zettel, J. J., & Ballard, J. (1982). Introduction: Bridging the gap. In J. Ballard, B. A. Ramirez, & F. J. Weintraub (Eds.), *Special education in America: Its legal and governmental foundations* (pp. 1–9). Reston, VA: The Council for Exceptional Children.

Zirkel, P. A. (2003). Do OSEP policy letters have legal weight? *Education Law Reporter, 171,* 391–396.

2

Rights to a Free Appropriate Public Education

INTRODUCTION

The Individuals with Disabilities Education Act (IDEA), which provides students with disabilities with unprecedented access to public education, directs all school systems in the United States to provide each child with special needs with a free appropriate public education (FAPE). The IDEA requires teams to describe what must be provided as part of a FAPE in the Individualized Education Programs (IEPs) that they prepare for students with disabilities, consisting of the needed special education and related services in the least restrictive environment possible. Even though the IDEA (2005) now provides a definition of a FAPE (20 U.S.C. § 1401(9)), it has still to establish substantive standards by which to judge the adequacy of special education services.

In *Board of Education of the Hendrick Hudson Central School District v. Rowley* (1982), its first case interpreting the IDEA, the Supreme Court held that a child with hearing impairments was entitled to personalized instruction and support services sufficient to permit her to benefit from the instruction that she received. At the same time, in denying the service of a sign language interpreter, as requested by the parents, the Court cautioned lower courts not to impose their views of preferable educational methods on school officials. Not surprisingly, courts are frequently called on to consider the level of services required to meet the IDEA's minimum standards.

This chapter reviews who is eligible to receive special education and related services, an important matter since questions of eligibility often arise insofar as students must meet one of the IDEA's disability categories in order to be eligible for services. This chapter also delineates the specific rights of children to access services and programs regardless of whether they attend public or nonpublic schools.

FREE APPROPRIATE PUBLIC EDUCATION

According to the IDEA, each child with a disability is entitled to a FAPE. The statute states that

(9) The term "free appropriate public education" means special education and related services that—
  (A) have been provided at public expense, under public supervision and direction, and without charge;
  (B) meet the standards of the State educational agency;
  (C) include an appropriate preschool, elementary school, or secondary school education in the State involved; and
  (D) are provided in conformity with the individualized education program required under [this law]. (20 U.S.C. § 1401(9))

In order to qualify under the IDEA, children with disabilities must meet three statutory requirements. First, children must be between the ages of 3 and 21 (20 U.S.C. § 1412(a)(1)(A)); under this provision, children remain 21 until the day before they turn 22 unless state law extends this limitation. Second, children must have specifically identifiable disabilities. The IDEA defines children with disabilities as having

mental retardation, hearing impairments (including deafness), speech or language impairments, visual impairments (including blindness), serious emotional disturbance (referred to in this chapter as "emotional disturbance"), orthopedic impairments, autism, traumatic brain injury, other health impairments, or specific learning disabilities. (20 U.S.C. § 1401(3)(A)(i))

The 2004 version of the IDEA made a significant change with regard to the last of these categories, students with learning disabilities. The IDEA changed the evaluation procedures for children with disabilities by no longer requiring educators to consider whether these students have severe discrepancies between achievement and intellectual ability in oral expression, listening comprehension, written expression, basic reading skill, reading comprehension, mathematical calculation, or mathematical reasoning (20 U.S.C. § 1401(30)). Instead, officials may use processes that consider whether children respond to scientific, research-based interventions as part of evaluation procedures (20 U.S.C. § 1401(c)(5)(F)). Students who fail to respond to the interventions called for in the IDEA may be considered eligible for special education services.

The latest version of the IDEA also added language addressing the needs of children aged 3 through 9:

> The term "child with a disability" for a child aged 3 through 9 (or any subset of that age range, including ages 3 through 5), may, at the discretion of the State and the local educational agency, include a child—
>
> (i) experiencing developmental delays, as defined by the State and as measured by appropriate diagnostic instruments and procedures, in 1 or more of the following areas: physical development; cognitive development; communication development; social or emotional development; or adaptive development. (20 U.S.C. § 1401(3)(B)(i))

The third requirement under the IDEA is that qualified children, "by reason thereof, need [. . .] special education and related services" (20 U.S.C. §§ 1401(3)(A)(ii), (B)(ii)). This means that children must receive a FAPE in the least restrictive environment that is directed by the contents of IEPs. Pursuant to the IDEA,

> The term "free appropriate public education" means special education and related services that—
>
> (A) have been provided at public expense, under public supervision and direction, and without charge;
>
> (B) meet the standards of the State educational agency;
>
> (C) include an appropriate preschool, elementary school, or secondary school education in the State involved; and
>
> (D) are provided in conformity with the individualized education program required under section 1414(d) of this title. (20 U.S.C. § 1401(9))

The IDEA defines an IEP as "a written statement for each child with a disability that is developed, reviewed, and revised in accordance with section 1414(d) of this title" (20 U.S.C. § 1401(14)). In addition, an IEP must outline students' current levels of performance, annual goals, and short-term objectives, as well as the specific educational services that children are to receive (20 U.S.C. § 1414(d)(1)(A)(i)).

The IDEA and its regulations require school board officials to provide a continuum of alternative placements for all students with disabilities. In practice, the range of options for students with disabilities moves from full inclusion in a regular education classroom to inclusion with supplementary assistance (such as an aide) to partial inclusion (meaning that a child splits time between a regular classroom and a resource room placement)

Figure 2.1   Components of a Free Appropriate Public Education

- *Specifically designed instruction:* personalized instruction designed to meet the unique needs of students with disabilities
- *Appropriate peer group:* students should be educated, whenever possible, with peer groups including children of approximately the same age and developmental level
- *Least restrictive environment:* to the maximum extent feasible, students must be educated with peers who are not disabled
- *Educational benefit:* special education and related services should be such that students make meaningful progress toward the goals and objectives of their IEPs
- *Procedural requirement:* IEPs must be developed in accordance with all of the requirements of the IDEA and state law
- *Related services:* supportive services must be provided if they are necessary for students to benefit from their educational programs
- *Public expense:* programs and all of their components must be provided at no cost to students or their parents

(*A.B. ex rel. D.B. v. Lawson*, 2004) to a self-contained or individualized placement (*Lt. T.B. ex rel. N.B. v. Warwick School Committee*, 2004); the IDEA expects that all four of these options should be provided in the local neighborhood schools that children would otherwise have attended. The more restrictive settings on the continuum range from special day schools to hospital or homebound instruction (which should not be confused with home schooling) to residential placements (34 C.F.R. § 300.115(b)(1)).

While the first four options are, as noted, supposed to be offered in the local neighborhood schools that children with disabilities would attend, the IDEA offers little guidance in defining what may be considered appropriate. The IDEA's regulations indicate that an appropriate education consists of special education and related services that are provided in conformance with IEPs (34 C.F.R. § 300.17). Inasmuch as neither the IDEA nor its regulations include a precise definition of the term *appropriate*, it is necessary to turn to judicial interpretations for further guidance on the meaning of FAPE.

The *Rowley* Standard

In *Board of Education of the Hendrick Hudson Central School District v. Rowley* (*Rowley*, 1982), the Supreme Court offered what amounts to a minimal definition of a FAPE. *Rowley* involved parents who challenged school officials after they refused to provide their hearing-impaired kindergarten-aged daughter with a sign language interpreter. A hearing officer and lower courts ordered the school board to provide an interpreter for the child on the basis that an appropriate education was one that would have afforded her the opportunity to achieve at a level commensurate with that of her peers who were not disabled. The Supreme Court, in pointing out that the child was achieving passing marks and advancing from grade to grade without the sign language interpreter, reversed in favor of the board. In deciding that the child was not entitled to an interpreter, the Court ruled that an appropriate education was one that is formulated pursuant to all of the IDEA's procedures and is "sufficient to confer some educational benefit" (*Rowley*, 1982, p. 200) on children with disabilities, a standard that courts continue to apply (*A.B. ex rel. D.B. v. Lawson*, 2004). To the extent that the child in *Rowley* received "some educational benefit" without the sign language interpreter, the Court reasoned that educators were not required to provide her with one even though she might have achieved at a higher level had she received this additional assistance.

> An appropriate education is one that is formulated in accordance with all of the IDEA's procedures and is "sufficient to confer some educational benefit" on children with disabilities.

As noted, *Rowley* established a minimum standard for what constitutes a FAPE under federal law. In fact, one state, West Virginia, has gone so far as to enact a statute specifying that no "state rule, policy, or standard . . . nor any county board rule, policy, or standard governing special education may exceed the requirements of federal law or regulation" (W.Va. Code Ann., 2004). Even so, North Carolina (*Burke County Board of Education v. Denton*, 1990), New Jersey (*Geis v. Board of Education of Parsippany-Troy Hills*, 1985), Michigan (*Barwacz v. Michigan Department of Education*, 1988), and California (*Pink v. Mt. Diablo Unified School District*, 1990) have higher standards of appropriateness. Further, in the cases from New Jersey, the Third Circuit court declared that the higher state standards replaced the federal requirements because one of the essential elements of the IDEA is that special education programs must "meet the standards of the state educational agency" (*Geis v. Board of Education of Parsippany-Troy Hills*, 1985, at p. 581, citing then 20 U.S.C. § 1401(18)(B), currently codified at 20 U.S.C. § 1401(9)(B)).

Shortly after *Rowley*, lower courts began to expand their interpretations of the "some educational benefit" criterion, asserting that an appropriate education for students with disabilities requires more than just minimal or trivial benefits (Osborne, 1992; *M.C. v. Central Regional School District*, 1996). While the initial cases reflected the judicial position that minimal benefits met this standard, later disputes explained that the IDEA required more. For example, the Fourth Circuit affirmed that *Rowley* permits courts to make case-by-case evaluations of the substantive standards needed to meet the criterion that IEPs must be reasonably calculated to enable students to receive educational benefits (*Hall v. Vance County Board of*

Education, 1985). The student in this case made only minimal progress, a situation that the court thought was insufficient in view of the child's intellectual potential. The court stated that Congress certainly did not intend for school board officials to provide a program for the child that produced only trivial academic advancement. In another case, the same court found that since a goal of four months' progress during an academic year was unlikely to allow the student to advance from one grade to the next with passing marks, it was insufficient to provide her with an appropriate education (*Carter v. Florence County School District Four*, 1991, 1993).

The Third Circuit wrote that in order to comply with *Rowley's* mandate, an IEP must confer an educational benefit that is appropriate, meaning that it is likely to produce progress, not trivial educational advancement (*Board of Education of East Windsor Regional School District v. Diamond*, 1986). The same court later reiterated that since the IDEA calls for more than just trivial educational benefit, Congress intended to provide students with disabilities with educational services that would have resulted in meaningful benefits (*Polk v. Central Susquehanna Intermediate Unit 16*, 1988). Another court added that the educational benefit must be appreciable (*Chris C. v. Gwinnett County School District*, 1991).

Similar cases expanded on what the courts meant in declaring that students must make more than trivial academic gains; the Second Circuit was of the view that because a school board is not required to maximize the potential of a student with disabilities, officials were only required to meet the "some educational benefit" criterion (*Walczak v. Florida Union Free School District*, 1998). Along these same lines, the Eleventh Circuit determined that an appropriate education may be defined as one wherein a student makes measurable and adequate gains in the classroom (*J.S.K. v. Hendry County School Board*, 1991). The same court later reasoned that a child's having demonstrated serious behavioral problems at home did not render his special education program inappropriate (*Devine v. Indian River County School Board*, 2001). In this latter case, the court rejected the parental argument that the child's placement was inadequate because the student could not generalize learned skills across settings. The court was convinced that generalization across settings is not required to show educational benefit. The court also discounted a parental argument that the IEP was insufficient on the ground that it failed to provide respite care for the family, given that the parents were unable to demonstrate how this would have provided a benefit for their child. Further, the Fifth Circuit upheld a board's proposed IEP in concluding that a student received significant benefit from his special education program because he not only achieved passing grades but also demonstrated an increased ability to focus on tasks (*Teague Independent School District v. Todd D.*, 1993). In like manner, the Eighth Circuit observed that where a student achieved passing grades and improved his reading skills, his IEP was appropriate (*Fort Zumwalt School District v. Clynes*, 1997, 1998).

Indicators of Educational Benefit

In *Rowley*, the Supreme Court held that the program provided to a student in a special education placement who attends school in a regular classroom setting should enable the child to achieve passing marks and advance from one grade to the next (Osborne, 1992). Other courts, however, responded that promotion to the next grade by itself is not proof that students received an education that was appropriate. For instance, the Fourth Circuit ruled that promotion alone, especially in conjunction with test scores revealing minimal progress, did not satisfy *Rowley's* standard of "some educational benefit" (*Hall v. Vance County Board of Education*, 1985). In a later case, the same court found that passing marks and annual grade promotions were important considerations under the IDEA but that achieving each did not automatically mean that a student received an appropriate education (*In re Conklin*, 1991). Further, the high court of Massachusetts remarked that a student's having graduated and received a high school diploma did not mean that that he received an appropriate education. The court thus rescinded the diploma that was awarded to an 18-year-old student who was unable to adapt to life in a sheltered workshop or to live independently after graduation (*Stock v. Massachusetts Hospital School*, 1984). The court was of the opinion that awarding a diploma to the student, who was unable to earn one under normal requirements even by the age of 22, was substantively inappropriate.

In considering whether a proposed IEP is appropriate, evidence of a student's academic progress is relevant in evaluating whether a child received a FAPE (*CJN v. Minneapolis Public Schools*, 2003a, 2003b). Other courts ruled that past progress in the same or similar programs, along with evidence that the progress should continue, was an indicator that the programs would confer educational benefit (*Bonnie Ann F. v. Calallen Independent School District*, 1993, 1994), even if it is incremental in nature (*Adam J. v. Keller Independent School District*, 2003). Likewise, courts have agreed that the continuation of IEPs that had not resulted in educational benefit in the past would have been inappropriate (*Ojai Unified School District v. Jackson*, 1993; *Nein v. Greater Clark County School Corporation*, 2000). Conversely, a federal trial court in Texas was satisfied that a student who stayed within two grade levels of her peers was making meaningful academic progress (*Socorro Independent School District v. Angelic Y.*, 2000). Similarly, an appellate court in Virginia affirmed that although a child did not advance at the same rate as his peers, there was no reason to change his placement because his progress was real and measurable (*White v. School Board of Henrico County*, 2001).

On the related topic of regression, courts tend to interpret declines in student performances after services or programs are discontinued as indicators that the education that was provided following the cessation of services was not meaningful (*Johnson v. Lancaster-Lebanon Intermediate Unit 13, Lancaster City School District*, 1991). Generally speaking, a special education student's progress should be comparable with the progress made by other similarly situated children (*School Board of Campbell County v. Beasley*, 1989). To this end, at least one court noted that progress should be measured in terms of a student's abilities as a child with disabilities (*Mavis v. Sobol*, 1994). Yet, lack of progress does not necessarily mean that a student's program is inappropriate. The courts recognize that some students are not motivated and that other factors, such as poor conduct, failure to complete homework, and absenteeism, may contribute to a student's lack of success (*Hampton School District v. Dobrowolski*, 1992). In order to evaluate whether meaningful or significant progress has occurred, the courts may rely on objective data, including test scores and the opinions of experts in the field, such as psychologists and educational diagnosticians.

Even though IEPs are prospective, courts or hearing officers can examine them retrospectively. Insofar as due process appeals and judicial actions generally occur after IEPs were to have been implemented, those reviewing IEPs have the benefit of history in evaluating their appropriateness. How much weight subsequent history should be given was the subject of a great deal of debate in a case from the Third Circuit (*Fuhrmann v. East Hanover Board of Education*, 1993). Affirming that the school board's actions could not have been judged exclusively in hindsight, a divided court explained that such a determination had to have been based on whether the child's IEP was appropriate when it was developed, not on whether he actually received benefit as a result of a placement. The court also decreed that a student's gains could be attributed to other factors besides the educational program. The dissenting judge argued that evidence of what actually happened was material even though it might not have impacted the final outcome.

LEAST RESTRICTIVE ENVIRONMENT

The IDEA requires that all students with disabilities be educated in the least restrictive environment (LRE) (20 U.S.C. § 1412(a)(5)(A)). This provision applies across the continuum of placement alternatives discussed earlier. Specifically, the IDEA requires states to establish procedures assuring that students with disabilities are educated, to the maximum extent appropriate, with children who do not have disabilities. Further, children can be placed in special classes, separate facilities, or otherwise be removed from the general education environment only when the nature or severity of their disabilities is such that instruction in general education classes cannot be achieved satisfactorily, even with supplementary aids and services (Osborne & DiMattia, 1994).

These provisions apply to students who attend private schools, institutions, or other care facilities at public expense as well as to children who attend public schools. This means that local educational agencies are required to spend only a proportionate amount of federal funds on students who attend private schools at parental expense, which may limit the degree to which such children can be educated in inclusionary settings at their private schools (20 U.S.C. § 1412(a)(10)(A)(i)). The IDEA's LRE provisions are frequently cited in cases addressing the provision of a FAPE for students with disabilities.

In two important cases, federal appellate courts directed school boards to place students with disabilities in regular settings as opposed to segregated special education classrooms. The courts in both disputes agreed that educators must consider a variety of factors when formulating the LRE for children with disabilities. In *Oberti v. Board of Education of the Borough of Clementon School District* (1993), a case from New Jersey, the Third Circuit adopted a two-part test, originally proposed by the Fifth Circuit (*Daniel R.R. v. State Board of Education*, 1989), for assessing compliance with the LRE mandate. The first element of the test is whether children with disabilities can be educated satisfactorily in regular classrooms with the use of supplementary aids and services. The second part of the test adds that if placements outside of regular classrooms are necessary, educators must consider whether children were mainstreamed to the maximum extent appropriate.

As summarized by the Ninth Circuit in *Sacramento City Unified School District Board of Education v. Rachel H.* (1994), educators must consider four

Figure 2.2   Determining the Need for a More Restrictive Placement

Students may require a more restrictive placement when

- They have not progressed in their then-current placements, even with the use of supplemental aids and services.
- The cost of maintaining students in the less restrictive environment is unreasonable.
- They require specialized environments to receive a FAPE.
- They need specialized techniques or resources that are unavailable in regular public school programs.
- They have low-incidence–type disabilities requiring contact with peers who have similar disabilities.
- They need 24-hour programs of instruction and care.
- They require consistency of approach between their home and school environments.
- They need total immersion in programs in order to make progress.
- Their presence in the less restrictive environment is disruptive to the educational process of peers.
- They are dangerous.

factors in making placements: the educational benefits of placing children with disabilities in regular classrooms, the nonacademic benefits of such placements, the effect that the presence of students with disabilities would have on teachers and other children in a class, and the costs of inclusionary placements. Educators must take all of these factors into account in placing students with disabilities.

Inherent in both of these tests is the principle that educators must make reasonable efforts to place students with disabilities in fully inclusive settings by providing them with supplementary aids and services to ensure their success. Even with the focus on inclusion, not all students with disabilities must be placed in regular education classes. Courts have approved segregated settings over parental objections (see, e.g., *Beth B. v. Van Clay*, 2002) where IEP teams demonstrated that students with disabilities could not have functioned in regular classrooms or would not have benefited in such settings, even with supplementary aids and services (*Clyde K. v. Puyallup School District No. 3*, 1994; *Capistrano Unified School District v. Wartenberg*, 1995). In another case, the federal trial court in New Hampshire acknowledged that an IEP calling for inclusion in some, but not all, of the subjects, was inappropriate for a 15-year-old student who was reading on a first-grade level after having received special education since he entered school (*Manchester School District v. Christopher B.*, 1992). The bottom line is that an inclusionary placement should be the setting of choice, and a segregated setting should be contemplated only if a fully inclusive placement has failed despite the best efforts of educators or there is overwhelming evidence that it is not reasonable.

ENTITLEMENT TO SERVICES

The IDEA makes it clear that all eligible children are entitled to receive a FAPE regardless of the severity of their disabilities. In the case of a child with severe disabilities, the First Circuit decided that the IDEA's language is unequivocal and does not include an exception for students with severe disabilities, nor does it require a child to demonstrate an ability to benefit from services in order to be eligible (*Timothy W. v. Rochester, New Hampshire School District*, 1989). The court also defined education in a broad sense, encompassing training in basic life skills. The Supreme Court, in *Honig v. Doe* (1988), ruled that even students with disabilities who are dangerous cannot be denied the IDEA's educational benefits. As noted earlier, however, not all students with disabilities need be educated within public school settings. While the IDEA and its regulations allow residential or private placements of students, at no cost to them or their parents (34 C.F.R. §§ 300.104, 300.115(b)(1)), the law probably does not cover children who have problems with drug addiction or sexual aggression (Wenkart, 2000).

> The IDEA makes it clear that all eligible children are entitled to receive a FAPE regardless of the severity of their disabilities.

The IDEA requires states to provide special education services to students between the ages of 18 and 21 if they offer educational services to individuals of the same age who are not disabled (20 U.S.C. § 1412(a)(1)(B)). Even so, students may not continue to receive services until the age of 21 if services are no longer necessary or they have completed their formal educations. For example, a federal trial court in Michigan upheld a school board's permitting a student with disabilities to graduate and terminate his eligibility for special education services where the school board pointed out that he had received a FAPE and adequate transition services (*Chuhran v. Walled Lake Consolidated School,* 1993). The court was of the opinion that since the student completed all of his graduation requirements and had shown exceptional performance in mainstream classes, he was no longer eligible to receive special education services.

As straightforward as the IDEA and its regulations seem to be, controversy continues over who is eligible for special education and related services. A great deal of the debate evolved over the specified disability categories that are defined in the IDEA and its regulations. As reflected in the following sections, the most controversial eligibility suits examined the delivery of special education and/or related services to students attending private schools at the options of their parents.

Eligibility

Students who may be classified under any of the categories of disabilities listed in the IDEA are eligible for services as long as their educational performances are adversely affected by their disabilities. Individual states may specify disability categories in addition to those listed in IDEA or may provide special education services on a noncategorical basis. In *Rowley,* the Supreme Court, while reasoning that only the level of services that the IDEA required was to confer "some educational benefit" on students, suggested that children who achieved passing grades as they advanced from one grade to the next received educational benefit.

One of the more controversial disability categories listed in the IDEA addresses students with emotional disturbances (20 U.S.C. § 1401(3)(A)). In order to be classified as having emotional disturbances, students' educational performances must be adversely affected by their conditions. The definition in the Code of Federal Regulations (C.F.R.) lists characteristics of serious emotional disturbance as an inability to learn that cannot be explained by other factors, an inability to build and maintain interpersonal relationships, inappropriate behavior or feelings under normal circumstances, a general pervasive mood of unhappiness or depression, or a tendency to develop physical symptoms or fears (34 C.F.R. § 300.8(c)(4)). This definition includes schizophrenia but specifically excludes "children who are socially maladjusted, unless it is determined that they are seriously emotionally disturbed" (34 C.F.R. § 300.8(c)(4)(ii)).

Courts have reached mixed results when evaluating whether students qualify for services under the category of seriously emotionally disturbed. In an illustrative case, the Fourth Circuit affirmed that a student from Virginia was not seriously emotionally disturbed (*Springer v. Fairfax County School Board*, 1998). The court relied on the testimony of three psychologists who examined the student, accepting their testimony that he was not seriously emotionally disturbed. The court pointed out that a drop in the student's grades was directly attributable to his truancy, drug and alcohol use, and delinquent behavior rather than any emotional disturbance. Similarly, the Eighth Circuit commented that the factor that controls eligibility under the IDEA is not whether a student's problem is educational or noneducational. Rather, the court contended that the issue was whether the student's behavior needed to be addressed in order for her to learn (*Independent School District No. 284 v. A.C.*, 2001). The court thus concluded that because the student had social and emotional problems that prevented her from receiving educational benefit, she was entitled to receive special education services in a residential setting.

In another case, the Second Circuit ruled that a student whose inability to learn could not have been explained solely by intellectual, sensory, or health factors, and whose emotional difficulties adversely affected her educational development, was entitled to special education (*Muller v. Committee on Special Education of the East Islip Union Free School District*, 1998). The record reflected that the student exhibited a pervasive mood of unhappiness, depression, and despondency, as evidenced by a suicide attempt. The court was convinced that under normal circumstances the child exhibited inappropriate behavior, such as lying, cutting classes, failing to complete assignments, stealing, and being defiant. In addition, the Sixth Circuit was of the view that a student who had average intelligence, but demonstrated a long history of academic failure, difficulty making and maintaining friendships, and the inability to create normal social bonds, was seriously emotionally disturbed and entitled to services under the IDEA (*Babb v. Knox County School System*, 1992). In this case, the court determined that school officials did not conduct a proper evaluation of the student's disability insofar as they did not fully examine his academic, emotional, and psychological profile.

A growing area of concern involves children who are diagnosed as having attention deficit disorder (ADD) or attention deficit hyperactivity disorder (ADHD), conditions that are identified in the IDEA's regulations under "other heath impairment." In order to be covered by the IDEA, such students must demonstrate limited strength, vitality, or alertness, including a heightened alertness to environmental stimuli, that results in limited alertness with respect to the educational environment, that—

(i) Is due to chronic or acute health problems such as asthma, attention deficit or attention deficit hyperactivity disorder, diabetes, epilepsy, a heart condition, hemophilia, lead poisoning, leukemia, nephritis, rheumatic fever, sickle cell anemia, and Tourette syndrome; and

(ii) Adversely affects a child's educational performance. (34 C.F.R. § 300.8(c)(9))

In one case, the federal trial court in the District of Columbia upheld the school board's judgment that a student with ADHD was ineligible for special education services (*Lyons v. Smith*, 1993). The court agreed that the evidence supported the board's contention that ADHD did not adversely affect the child's academic performance in view of the fact that he did superior schoolwork. More recently, the Eighth Circuit, in two separate cases, agreed that school officials did not violate the rights of students with disabilities who were diagnosed as having ADHD by refusing to administer Ritalin to them in dosages that exceeded the amount called for in the *Physicians' Desk Reference,* a book that doctors commonly rely on in prescribing medication (*DeBord v. Board of Education of the Ferguson-Florissant School District*, 1997; *Davis v. Francis Howell School District*, 1998).

In a matter related to other health impairment, it is well settled that students with AIDS are entitled to a FAPE under the IDEA or Section 504 of the Rehabilitation Act (1998) and that their parents are not required to disclose the illness to school officials as a precondition for admission or continued enrollment (Gordon, Russo, Miles, & Leas, 1992). In addition, it is worth noting that children with AIDS cannot be classified as other health impaired unless their diseases have progressed and had an effect on their ability to perform in school. A state court in New York declared that an unidentified child was not disabled merely because he or she had AIDS, but such a child could become eligible for services under the IDEA as the disease progressed (*District 27 Community School Board v. Board of Education of the City of New York*, 1986). The court observed that in order to qualify as having a disability under the IDEA, a child's educational performance had to have been adversely affected as a result of limited strength, vitality, or alertness due to having AIDS. Similarly, a federal trial court in Illinois declared that the IDEA applied to students with AIDS only if their physical conditions adversely affected their ability to learn and to complete required classroom work (*Doe v. Belleville Public School District No. 118*, 1987). In both of these cases, as well as in other litigation involving students with AIDS, the courts made it clear that federal law protects the rights of children who are in need of special education services.

It is well settled that students with AIDS are entitled to a FAPE under the IDEA or Section 504.

More recently, in a case involving afterschool activities rather than a regular in-school class, the Fourth Circuit affirmed that a child in Virginia who suffered from AIDS did not have a right to participate in a private karate school due to his illness (*Montalvo v. Radcliffe*, 1999). When the school's proprietor discovered that the child had AIDS, a condition that his parents did not disclose on his application, he offered the child one-on-one instruction. When the boy's parents rejected this offer, they filed suit. Even though the case was resolved under the Americans with Disabilities Act (ADA), it is worth noting because that law applies essentially the same definition as under Section 504 of the Rehabilitation Act. The court ruled that since the child's condition posed a direct threat to the health and safety of others, he was beyond the coverage of the ADA. The court added that since neither "softening" the teaching styles of karate nor enhancing safety precautions that the parents sought were reasonable modifications that might have been suggested under the ADA, the owner was not required to take such steps.

In a related vein, students with disabilities cannot be excluded from public schools due to their health problems, even when they are afflicted with contagious diseases, if the risk of transmission of the illnesses is low. Exclusions on the basis of health problems would violate Section 504, the ADA, and/or the IDEA. In such a dispute, the Second Circuit affirmed that students who were carriers of the hepatitis B virus could not be excluded from their public schools or segregated within those schools because of their medical condition (*New York State Association for Retarded Children v. Carey*, 1979). In like fashion, a state court in Illinois posited that a student with hepatitis B was entitled to be educated in a regular setting (*Community High School District 155 v. Denz*, 1984). In both cases, the courts were satisfied that the risk of transmission was low and could be reduced further through the use of proper prophylactic procedures.

The analyses in the cases involving hepatitis can also be applied to litigation focusing on children with AIDS. To this end, the Eleventh Circuit held that before a student can be excluded from school, a court must evaluate whether reasonable accommodations can reduce the risk of transmission (*Martinez v. School Board of Hillsborough County, Florida*, 1989). The student in the case was classified as mentally retarded and excluded from the public schools in part because she was incontinent and drooled. On remand, the trial court decided that since the risk of transmission from the student's bodily secretions was remote, she was to be admitted to a special education classroom.

Extracurricular Activities

Students with disabilities are entitled to participate in nonacademic and extracurricular services such as counseling, athletics, transportation, health services, recreational activities, special interest groups, and clubs on an equal basis with their peers who are not disabled (34 C.F.R. § 300.107). While courts have refused to permit students with disabilities to participate in activities from which they cannot benefit unless unreasonable modifications are made (*Rettig v. Kent School District*, 1986), the courts have allowed children to take part if the required modifications are reasonable (*Crocker v. Tennessee Secondary School Athletic Association*, 1990).

Another difficulty for children with disabilities often occurs because, insofar as they repeat grades, they are older than other students at the same grade level. While most courts have upheld age requirements (*Pottgen v. Missouri State High School Athletic Association*, 1994; *McPherson v. Michigan High School Athletic Association*, 1997), others have granted waivers for athletic participation (*Bingham v. Oregon School Activities Association*, 1999; *Washington v. Indiana High School Athletic Association*, 1999). A question that remains is whether students with disabilities who fail courses can retain their eligibility to participate under "no pass, no play" rules. The answer is likely to depend on the individual circumstances of a given situation. If students fail as a direct result of their disabilities or due to inappropriate IEPs, courts may well agree that enforcement of such rules is discriminatory (Osborne & Battaglino, 1996).

Nontraditional Program Schedules and Extended School Year Programs

In most states, students typically attend school 6 hours a day, 180 days a year, for 12 years. Even so, courts agree that students with disabilities are entitled to programming arrangements and schedules that deviate from this pattern if this is necessary for them to receive a FAPE. Insofar as the IDEA requires IEPs to be tailored to meet the needs of individual students (20 U.S.C. §§ 1401(14), 1414(d)), this provision sometimes requires nontraditional schedules for the delivery of services.

> Courts agree that students with disabilities are entitled to educational programming that extends beyond the parameters of the traditional school year if the combination of regression during a vacation period and recoupment time prevents meaningful progress.

Students with disabilities sometimes repeat grades. Consequently, some students with disabilities may require more than 12 years to complete their general programs of study. In one such case, the Tenth Circuit wrote that students with disabilities are entitled to more than the standard 12 years of schooling if necessary (*Helms v. Independent School District*, 1984). School officials terminated educational services for the student in this case after she completed 12 years of school, when she reached her twenty-first birthday even though she was classified as a tenth grader. The court ordered the school board to provide the student with two more years of schooling.

As discussed below, courts agree that students with disabilities are entitled to educational programming that extends beyond the parameters of the traditional school year if the combination of regression during a vacation period and recoupment time prevents meaningful progress. Further, the IDEA's regulations stipulate that extended school year services must be provided only if IEP teams are convinced that the services are necessary for the provision of a FAPE (34 C.F.R. § 300.106(a)(2)). It should be noted that an extended school year program is required only to prevent regression, not to advance skills in IEPs that students have not yet mastered (*McQueen v. Colorado Springs School District No. 11*, 2006). Further, if students with disabilities require educational programs that extend beyond the regular school year, they must be provided at public expense (34 C.F.R. § 300.106(b)(1)(iii)).

Extended school year programs are generally necessary when students regress and the time necessary to recoup lost skills interferes with their overall progress toward attaining their IEP goals and objectives (*Battle v. Pennsylvania*, 1990). In a recent case, the Sixth Circuit held that a child with cerebral palsy who also had delayed cognitive and communication development was not entitled to an extended school year placement because his parents were unable to demonstrate that such a program was required to avoid more than adequately recoupable regression (*Kenton County School District v. Hunt*, 2004). The court decided that although the parents may have wished for a more extensive placement for their son than the IDEA required, he was not entitled to such a placement because school officials developed an appropriate IEP that placed him in an inclusive setting with special education support and assistive technology adaptations.

In order for students to qualify for extended school year placements, the regression that they experience must be greater than that which normally occurs during school vacations. In a leading case from Texas, the Fifth Circuit (*Alamo Heights Independent School District v. State Board of Education*, 1986) affirmed that a child was not entitled to an extended school year placement unless a regression was severe or substantial. More recently, federal trial courts in New Hampshire (*J.W. v. Contoocook Valley School District*, 2001) and California (*Moser v. Bret Harte Union High School District*, 2005) reiterated essentially the same position in holding that students' being academically behind was not a valid reason to require their school boards to provide them with extended school year placements.

Conversely, due to the nature of their disabilities, students who may be unable to tolerate long periods of instruction may require shortened school days. In apparently the only reported case dealing with the issue, the Fifth Circuit affirmed that a school board was not required to provide a full day of educational programming for a student with multiple disabilities whose educational programming consisted of basic sensory stimulation since it was not in his best interest (*Christopher M. v. Corpus Christi Independent School District*, 1991). Due to the child's inability to sustain prolonged stimulation, the court agreed with special educators in his district that there was no reason to provide him with a full school day since it was inappropriate to do so.

Private and Residential School Placements

The courts continue to recognize that the IDEA's preference for full inclusion is not feasible for all students with disabilities (*Poolaw v. Bishop*, 1995; *Hartmann v. Loudon County Board of Education*, 1997; Osborne, 1998). Consequently, the IDEA and its regulations require school officials to offer a continuum of placement alternatives to meet the educational needs of children with disabilities (34 C.F.R. § 300.115(a)). In this regard, public school officials may be required to place children in nonpublic schools when boards lack appropriate placements (IDEA, 20 U.S.C. § 1412(a)(10)(B); 34 C.F.R. § 300.325; *Board of Education v. Illinois State Board of Education*, 1991, 1992; *Cleveland Heights-University Heights City School District v. Boss*, 1998) such as when a student has a low-incidence disability and there are not enough children with the same type of disability within a system to warrant the development of a program (*Colin K. v. Schmidt*, 1983). These courts acknowledged that inasmuch as school boards in smaller districts probably cannot afford to develop specialized programs, they must look elsewhere for placements.

If private day or residential school placements are necessary for educational reasons, they must be made at no cost to students or their parents. States or local school boards may share the cost of placements with other agencies but may not assign any financial responsibility to parents. It is well settled that policies requiring parents to pay a portion of the costs of residential placements are unacceptable (*Parks v. Pavkovic*, 1985).

States have adopted different regulations regarding residential placements. To the extent that a number of states provide some, if not all, of the funding for residential placements, state agencies sometimes become involved in these placement decisions. Once placed, students with disabilities do not necessarily need to remain in private day or residential programs indefinitely. In view of the fact that one of the IDEA's major goals is to have students with disabilities educated in fully inclusive settings, children should be returned to such placements as soon as it is feasible to do so.

Courts may order residential placements for students with severe, profound, or multiple disabilities (*Gladys J. v. Pearland Independent School District*, 1981) if children need 24-hour-per-day programming or consistency between their school and home environments. Residential placements may also be necessary for students who have significant behavioral disorders (*Brown v. Wilson County School Board*, 1990), are emotionally disturbed (*Chris D. v. Montgomery County Board of Education*, 1990), or require total immersion in educational environments in order to progress (*Abrahamson v. Hershman*, 1983). For example, the Sixth Circuit ruled in favor of parents who unilaterally placed their child, who had behavioral disabilities, in a private residential facility (*Knable v. Bexley City School District*, 2001). The court approved of the placement since the child's behavior and grades improved in the school. Further, it is conceivable that children who are dangerous to themselves and/or others may be sent to residential facilities. For instance, the First Circuit recently decided that a student's need for constant supervision and an in-school psychologist necessitated a private school placement (*Zayas v. Commonwealth of Puerto Rico*, 2005).

If residential placements are required for purely educational reasons, school boards must bear their entire cost and cannot require parents to contribute toward payment (*Parks v. Pavkovic*, 1985). On the other hand, if placements are made for other than educational reasons, such as for medical or social purposes, or are essentially custodial in nature (*Dale M. ex rel. Alice M. v. Board of Education of Bradley-Bourbonnais High School District No. 307*, 2001), then school systems may be required to pay only for the educational components of the residential settings (*McKenzie v. Jefferson*, 1983) and may enter into cost-share agreements with other agencies.

Disputes often arise concerning whether residential placements are being made for medical, rather than educational, reasons. These disputes occur most often in the context of placements in psychiatric facilities. Under the IDEA, school boards are not required to pay medical expenses for students other than those for diagnostic or evaluative purposes (20 U.S.C. § 1401(a)(26)). Along the same line, psychiatric facilities often are characterized as hospitals since psychiatrists are medical doctors. Moreover, students with physical disabilities are frequently placed in facilities that offer a number of services of a medical nature. As some of the cases cited herein demonstrate, it is often impossible to separate out the various services provided by rehabilitation facilities and assign the costs accordingly. Whether programs taken as a whole are considered to be medical or educational depends on the extent and purpose of the provided medical services.

As Chapter 7 explains in greater detail, parents may be entitled to tuition reimbursement for unilaterally made private school placements if they can prove that their school boards failed to provide their children with appropriate placements in the first place. Yet even under these circumstances equitable considerations may limit reimbursement awards. In the first of two cases that are illustrative of these issues, the Seventh Circuit affirmed that a mother in Illinois, who due to her failure to cooperate by refusing to give school officials a reasonable opportunity to evaluate her son, forfeited any claim to tuition reimbursement for unilaterally placing him in a private school (*Patricia P. v. Board of Education of Oak Park and River Forest High School District No. 200*, 2000). The court rejected the mother's request because she enrolled her son in a private residential facility when he was not permitted to return to a religiously affiliated school, without first affording public school personnel the opportunity to evaluate his condition. Conversely, a federal trial court in Indiana awarded partial reimbursement where the private school that parents selected for their son provided him with an appropriate education but failed to notify the school board in writing of their intent to place him there at public expense (*Nein v. Greater Clark County School Corporation*, 2000). The court added that the parental move was acceptable because the board failed to provide the student with an appropriate educational program.

CHILD FIND

The IDEA and its regulations require states, through local educational agencies or school boards, to identify, locate, and evaluate all children with disabilities (34 C.F.R. § 300.111), regardless of the severity of their disabilities. As discussed below in more detail, this includes children whose parents have placed them in private schools, including religious elementary and secondary schools (34 C.F.R. § 131(a)).

The task of identifying children in need of services is generally delegated to individual school boards. In order to locate children who may have disabilities, school board officials typically disseminate information about the services available to students with disabilities via newspaper articles, radio announcements, and advertisements on cable television. In addition, many school officials may leave information pamphlets in locations frequented by parents of young children, such as pediatricians' offices, day care centers, and shopping malls.

Insofar as early identification and assessment of children with disabilities is identified as a related service in the IDEA (20 U.S.C. § 1401(26)), many school boards offer annual screenings for preschool and kindergarten-aged children. While the kindergarten screening process is generally conducted as part of normal registration activities, educators usually set up special dates to screen preschool-aged children. Parents who suspect that their children may be disabled can ask for screenings by appointment at any time during school years.

The courts have reached mixed results in disputes where school officials failed to identify children with disabilities due to concerns over increasing the cost of special education. In one such case, the Third Circuit, in a case from Pennsylvania, agreed that a mother was entitled to a damages award where educators failed to identify and evaluate her son in a manner consistent with the IDEA's child find provisions (*W.B. v. Matula*, 1995). Conversely, a federal trial court in Georgia refused to grant such an award where a mother charged that educational officials failed to evaluate her son's condition appropriately. The court observed that the mother withdrew the child from the public school that he attended, which deprived school officials of the opportunity to evaluate him (*Clay T. v. Walton School District*, 1997).

STUDENTS IN PRIVATE SCHOOLS

Students with disabilities who attend religiously affiliated private schools may be entitled to services under the IDEA and/or Section 504 (Russo, Massucci, Osborne, & Cattaro, 2002). Accordingly, this section primarily reviews issues that may come into play when educators in public schools seek to provide special education services to children who attend religiously affiliated private schools.

Issues surrounding the delivery of special education services to children who attend religiously affiliated private schools often involve the Establishment Clause to the First Amendment of the U.S. Constitution, which reads, "Congress shall make no law respecting an establishment of religion, or prohibiting the free exercise thereof. . . ." Even so, this section does not engage in a full discussion of the lengthy and complex history of litigation involving the limits of aid to religious schools under the Establishment Clause. Rather, it is sufficient to acknowledge that since the Supreme Court first enunciated the Child Benefit test, which permits a variety of forms of aid to children in nonpublic schools (*Everson v. Board of Education*, 1947) on the basis that the aid is directed at children (and their families), not their schools, it has had a checkered history. Put another way, depending on the composition of the Court, some Justices have been more supportive of the child benefit theory than others. Further, virtually all litigation involving the Establishment Clause has been examined in light of the tripartite test enunciated by the Supreme Court in *Lemon v. Kurtzman (Lemon)* (1971). Under this seemingly ubiquitous test,

> Every analysis in this area must begin with consideration of the cumulative criteria developed by the Court over many years. Three such tests may be gleaned from our cases. First, the statute must have a secular legislative purpose; second, its principal or primary effect must be one that neither advances nor inhibits religion; finally, the statute must not foster "an excessive government entanglement with religion. . . ." (*Lemon*, 1971, at pp. 612–613; internal citations omitted)

The low point of the Child Benefit test occurred in 1985 when, in *Aguilar v. Felton,* the Supreme Court banned the on-site delivery of remedial Title I services in religiously affiliated nonpublic schools in New York City. The Court struck down the program even in the absence of any allegation of misconduct or misappropriation of public funds based on the fear that having public school educators provide services in religious schools might have created "excessive entanglement" between the government and religion. Consequently, since school boards still had to provide services at public schools or neutral sites, many students who attended religiously affiliated nonpublic schools were denied equal educational opportunities under Title I.

The landscape with regard to state aid to K–12 education began to evolve in 1993 when the Supreme Court revitalized the Child Benefit test in *Zobrest v. Catalina Foothills School District (Zobrest).* In *Zobrest* the Court ruled that the Establishment Clause did not bar a public school board in Arizona from providing the on-site delivery of the services of a sign language interpreter for a student who attended a Roman Catholic high school. The Court reasoned that since the interpreter was essentially a conduit through whom information passed, the on-site delivery of such assistance did not violate the Establishment Clause (Osborne, 1994). Four years later, in *Agostini v. Felton* (1997), following up on *Aguilar,* the Court essentially lifted the ban against the on-site delivery of services to students who attended religiously affiliated nonpublic schools in New York City since appropriate safeguards were in place (Osborne & Russo, 1997).

> Regulatory modifications that were adopted in 1999, and which changed little in the 2004 amendments, created a dilemma. The regulations, and earlier case law, made it clear that children in religious schools are entitled to receive some special education services, but the laws set funding restrictions in place that limited the amount of services that these children can receive on-site in their religious schools.

Most recently, in *Mitchell v. Helms* (2000), the Court, in a plurality judgment, meaning that it lacked the necessary five Justice majority needed to make it binding precedent, upheld the constitutionality of Chapter 2, now Title VI, of Title I of the Elementary and Secondary Education Act, a far-reaching federal statute that permits the loan of state-owned instructional materials such as computers, slide projectors, television sets, tape recorders, maps, and globes to nonpublic schools. In the part of the case most relevant to special education, but which was not appealed to the Supreme Court, the Fifth Circuit (*Helms v. Picard,* 1998) upheld state laws that permitted the on-site delivery of special education services to children who attended Catholic schools and that granted them free transportation to and from school.

A major statutory change occurred in 1997 when congressional reauthorization of the IDEA included provisions clarifying the obligations of public school systems to provide special education and related services to students in nonpublic schools. Unfortunately, neither Congress nor the courts conclusively answered questions about the delivery of special education for children in religiously affiliated nonpublic schools. Regulatory modifications that were adopted in 1999, and that changed little in the 2004 amendments, created a dilemma. The regulations, and earlier case law, made it clear that children in religious schools were entitled to receive some special education services, but the laws set funding restrictions in place that limited the amount of services that these children can receive on-site in their religious schools. The net result is that these students are likely to receive fewer services if public school officials follow the letter of the law and do not make additional services available to qualified students in religious schools.

The IDEA (20 U.S.C. § 1412(a)(10)) and its regulations (34 C.F.R. § 300.132) make it clear that children whose parents voluntarily enroll them in private schools are entitled to some level of special education services. Further, the IDEA permits the on-site delivery of special education for students with disabilities whose parents have placed them in "private" schools, including religious, elementary, and secondary schools (20 U.S.C. § 1412(a)(10)(A)(i)(III)), as long as safeguards are in place to avoid "excessive entanglement" between public school systems and religious institutions. Such an approach is consistent with settled law that public school personnel can conduct diagnostic tests on-site in religiously affiliated nonpublic schools to evaluate whether children are eligible for services in programs that are supported by public funds (*Meek v. Pittenger*, 1975; *Wolman v. Walter*, 1977).

The regulations incorporate statutory changes and provide guidance on meeting the IDEA's requirements while borrowing from preexisting Education Department General Administrative Regulations (EDGAR regulations) (34 C.F.R. § 76.1 *et seq.*). The EDGAR regulations require school boards to provide students in nonpublic schools with opportunities for equitable participation in federal programs (34 C.F.R. § 76.651(a)(1)). This means that students in nonpublic schools are entitled to opportunities to participate in federal programs that are comparable in quality to those available to children in public schools (34 C.F.R. § 76.654(a)). In developing programs, public school personnel must consult with representatives of the nonpublic schools to consider which students will be served, how their needs will be identified, what benefits they will receive, how the benefits will be delivered, and how the programs will be evaluated (34 C.F.R. § 76.652(a)(1)-(5)).

Private School Students Defined

Public school officials must locate, identify, and evaluate all students with disabilities who attend "private schools" within their jurisdictions, including children whose parents place them in private schools (34 C.F.R. § 300.131(a)). This means that boards must develop plans to permit these students to participate in programs carried out pursuant to the IDEA (34 C.F.R. § 300.132). The regulations define students in nonpublic schools as those whose parents have voluntarily enrolled them in such schools or facilities (34 C.F.R. § 300.130). This definition does not include students whose school boards have placed them in private facilities at public expense in order to provide each of them with a FAPE.

Spending Restrictions

The IDEA and its regulations limit the amount of money that a school board must spend in providing services to pupils in nonpublic schools (34 C.F.R. § 300.133). The total is limited to a proportionate amount of the federal funds received based on the number of students in nonpublic schools in relation to the overall number of pupils in the district (20 U.S.C. § 1412(a)(10)(A)(i)(I), (II)). School boards are not prohibited from using state funds to offer more than the IDEA calls for given that the regulation establishes only a minimum amount that they must spend on qualified children (34 C.F.R. § 300.133(d)).

Under the regulations, IDEA funds cannot be used to benefit private schools (34 C.F.R. § 300.141). In other words, public funds cannot be used to offer impermissible aid to religious institutions by financing existing instructional programs, otherwise providing them with direct financial benefits such as money, or organizing classes based on students' religions or schools they attend (34 C.F.R. § 300.143). Even so, the regulations allow boards to employ public school personnel in these nonpublic schools as long as they are not supplanting services that are normally provided by those institutions (34 C.F.R. § 300.142(a)). The regulations further permit boards to hire personnel from nonpublic schools to provide services outside of their regular hours of work as long as they are under the supervision and control of officials from the public schools (34 C.F.R. § 300.142(b)). Finally, any property, equipment, or supplies purchased with IDEA funds can be used only on-site in nonpublic schools for the benefit of students with disabilities (34 C.F.R. § 300.144(c)).

Comparable Services

The regulations point out that students who attend private schools do not have an individual right to receive some or all of the special education and related services that they might have received in public schools (34 C.F.R. § 300.137(a)). This does not mean that children in private schools are denied all services under the IDEA. Rather, the regulations give public school officials the authority to develop service plans and to decide which students from private schools will be served (34 C.F.R. § 300.137(b)(2)). The regulations also require public school officials to ensure that representatives of private or religious schools have the opportunity to attend such meetings or participate by other means, such as individual or conference calls (34 C.F.R. § 300.137(c)(2)).

Students in private schools are entitled to receive services from personnel who meet the same standards as educators in public schools (34 C.F.R. § 300.138(a)(1)), even if they receive a different amount of services than their peers in public schools (34 C.F.R. § 300.138(a)(2)). Inasmuch as students with disabilities who attend private schools are not entitled to the same amount of services as similarly situated students who attend public schools, the regulations do not require the development of an IEP. Instead, the regulations require school officials to develop service plans describing the aid that they will provide to a student (34 C.F.R. § 300.138(b)(1)). Even so, service plans must not only meet the same content requirements as IEPs but must also be developed, reviewed, and revised in a manner consistent with the IEP process (34 C.F.R. § 300.138(b)(2)).

Delivery of Services

The regulations reiterate that services may be offered on-site in religiously affiliated nonpublic schools (34 C.F.R. § 300.139(a)). In order to differentiate between public and private schools, the regulations specifically use the phrase "including religious schools" to reflect the fact that religiously affiliated nonpublic schools are included within the IDEA's framework (34 C.F.R. § 300.139(a)).

If it is necessary for children to receive benefit from services that are not offered on-site and students must be transported to alternate locations to receive them, school boards must provide transportation between their schools or homes to sites where they receive services (34 C.F.R. § 300.139 (b)(1)(i)(A)) and from the service sites to their private schools or homes, depending on the time of day (34 C.F.R. § 300.139(b)(1)(i)(B)). At the same time, school boards are not required to transport private school students from their homes to their private schools (34 C.F.R. § 300.139(b)(1)(ii)). In addition, it is important to recognize that the cost of transportation may be included in calculating the minimum amount of federal funds that school boards must spend on students in nonpublic schools (34 C.F.R. § 300. 139(b)(2)).

Dispute Resolution

The IDEA's procedural safeguards generally do not apply to complaints that school boards failed to deliver services to students in nonpublic schools (34 C.F.R. § 300.140(a)). The due process provisions do apply to complaints that boards failed to comply with the child find requirements applicable to students in nonpublic schools (34 C.F.R. § 300.140(b)) and to complaints pursuant to allegations arising in connection with state administration of special education (34 C.F.R. § 300.140(c)).

Child Find in Private Schools

The 2004 modification of the IDEA and its regulations require officials in public schools to identify children with disabilities whose parents enrolled them in private schools (including religious, elementary, and secondary schools) in their districts rather than simply those who live within school districts (20 U.S.C. § 1412 (a)(10)(A)(I); 34 C.F.R. § 300.131(a)). Under these provisions, public school officials must provide accurate counts to state education agencies of the number of children from private schools who are evaluated, determined to have disabilities, and served (34 C.F.R. § 300.131(b)(2)).

These changes also require school boards to employ child find activities for students in private schools that are similar to those used to identify children who attend public schools (34 C.F.R. § 300.131(c)). Further, the cost of such activities does not count in calculating whether school systems exceeded the amount that they spent in serving students who attend private schools (34 C.F.R. § 300.131(d)).

RECOMMENDATIONS

Before turning to specific recommendations, it almost goes without saying that school officials should be honest, good listeners who provide support for parents. Yet, even in offering hope to parents, school officials should be realistic about the status of children and keep parents up to date at all times. Moreover, to the extent that all children with disabilities are entitled to IEPs to direct their schooling, educators would need to do the following:

- Work to provide all students (including, with limits, children whose parents place them in private and religiously affiliated nonpublic schools) with a free appropriate public education in the least restrictive environment. Thus, in seeking to become knowledgeable about all aspects of the IDEA, educational leaders must seek regular professional development opportunities for themselves and their staffs.
- Address the educational needs of all students on their individual merits since all children have unique talents, abilities, and needs. Even in recognizing that a continuum of placements is available, educators must make genuine efforts to serve the needs of all children, meaning that students should be provided with all the necessary related and support services.

Figure 2.3   Frequently Asked Questions

Q: Are school boards required to provide students with disabilities the best possible education regardless of cost?

A: No, the IDEA does not require school boards to provide students with disabilities with the best education possible regardless of cost unless state law dictates that they do so. Under the IDEA, school boards are required to provide an educational program that confers some educational benefit on students; benefits cannot be minimal or trivial.

Q: Are school boards required to educate all students with disabilities in an inclusionary setting?

A: No, the requirement is that students be educated in the least restrictive environment. For some students the least restrictive environment may be substantially separate programs. Even so, school boards may educate students with disabilities in more restrictive settings only when placements of this type are necessary to provide children with a FAPE. School boards must also provide reasonable supplementary aids and services that allow students to be educated in the less restrictive environment.

Q: When are school boards required to pay for residential placements?

A: School boards are required to pay for residential placements when they are necessary for educational reasons. Boards are not required to pay the room and board portion of such placements when they are made for noneducational reasons. Often, school boards can share the costs of residential placements with other agencies.

Q: When are school boards required to provide educational services beyond the traditional school year?

A: Students with disabilities are entitled to programming beyond the traditional school year if they suffer regression during school breaks that, combined with the time required to recoup lost skills, substantially interferes with the attainment of educational goals. When the cumulative effects of regression and recoupment time result in little or no educational gain over a period of time, students may be entitled to extended school year placements.

Q: What responsibility do school boards have for students who attend private schools at their parents' expense?

A: School boards are required to spend a proportionate share of the federal money they receive on students with disabilities who attend private schools, including those in religiously affiliated schools. School board representatives must consult with officials from private schools to decide how these funds will be spent. Insofar as students in private schools do not have an individual right to receive special education and related services at public expense, they lack the right to receive the same level of services that they would have received in public schools.

- Keep in mind that state standards, only a few of which provide greater protection than the IDEA, must be taken into consideration when determining whether a placement is appropriate. If higher state standards are in place, they must be satisfied.
- Avoid segregating special education students by placing them in the least restrictive environment.
- Balance an appropriate level of specialized services and full inclusion.
- Take nonacademic benefits into consideration when justifying inclusive settings, even if students' academic progress does not come as quickly as it would in a segregated setting.
- Be careful to avoid using private day or residential schools in lieu of inclusive placements for children with low-incidence–type disabilities.
- Recall that, if they are needed, placements in residential facilities, or year-round placements, should be made at no cost to parents. Even so, educators would be wise to consider ways of sharing the cost of such placements with other agencies, particularly when residential placements are required for reasons that are not strictly educational.
- Recall that since students with disabilities who attend religiously affiliated nonpublic schools may be entitled to some services under the IDEA and/or Section 504, liaisons should be appointed to work with staff in such schools.
- Take steps to ensure the early identification of all children with special needs, regardless of where they attend school.

REFERENCES

A.B. ex rel. D.B. v. Lawson, 354 F.3d 315 (4th Cir. 2004).

Abrahamson v. Hershman, 701 F.2d 223 (1st Cir. 1983).

Adam J. v. Keller Independent School District, 328 F.3d 804 (5th Cir. 2003).

Agostini v. Felton, 521 U.S. 203 (1997).

Aguilar v. Felton, 473 U.S. 402 (1985).

Alamo Heights Independent School District v. State Board of Education, 790 F.2d 1153 (5th Cir. 1986).

Babb v. Knox County School System, 965 F.2d 104 (6th Cir. 1992).

Barwacz v. Michigan Department of Education, 681 F. Supp. 427 (W.D. Mich. 1988).

Battle v. Pennsylvania, 629 F.3d 269 (3d Cir. 1990).

Beth B. v. Van Clay, 282 F.3d 493 (7th Cir. 2002).

Bingham v. Oregon School Activities Association, 37 F. Supp. 2d 1189 (D. Or. 1999).

Board of Education of East Windsor Regional School District v. Diamond, 808 F.2d 987 (3d Cir. 1986).

Board of Education of the Hendrick Hudson Central School District v. Rowley, 458 U.S. 176 (1982).

Board of Education v. Illinois State Board of Education, 938 F.3d 712 (7th Cir. 1991), *cert. denied* 502 U.S. 1066 (1992).

Bonnie Ann F. v. Calallen Independent School District, 835 F. Supp. 340 (S.D. Tex. 1993), *affirmed* 40 F.3d 386 (5th Cir. 1994) (mem).

Brown v. Wilson County School Board, 747 F. Supp. 436 (M.D. Tenn. 1990).

Burke County Board of Education v. Denton, 895 F.2d 973 (4th Cir. 1990).

Capistrano Unified School District v. Wartenberg, 59 F.3d 884 (9th Cir. 1995).

Carter v. Florence County School District Four, 950 F.2d 156 (4th Cir. 1991), *affirmed on other grounds sub nom. Florence County School District Four v. Carter*, 510 U.S. 126 (1993).

Chris C. v. Gwinnett County School District, 780 F. Supp. 804 (N.D. Ga. 1991).

Chris D. v. Montgomery County Board of Education, 743 F. Supp. 1524 (M.D. Ala. 1990).

Christopher M. v. Corpus Christi Independent School District, 933 F.2d 1285 (5th Cir. 1991).

Chuhran v. Walled Lake Consolidated School, 839 F. Supp. 465 (E.D. Mich. 1993).

CJN v. Minneapolis Public Schools, 323 F.3d 630 (8th Cir. 2003a), *cert. denied sub nom Nygren v. Minneapolis Public Schools, Special School Dist. No. 1*, 540 U.S. 984 (2003b).

Clay T. v. Walton School District, 952 F. Supp. 817 (M.D. Ga. 1997).

Cleveland Heights-University Heights City School District v. Boss, 144 F.3d 391 (6th Cir. 1998).

Clyde K. v. Puyallup School District No. 3, 35 F.3d 1396 (9th Cir. 1994).

Code of Federal Regulations, as cited.

Colin K. v. Schmidt, 715 F.2d 1 (1st Cir. 1983).

Community High School District 155 v. Denz, 463 N.E.2d 998 (Ill. App. Ct. 1984).

Conklin, In re, 946 F.2d 306 (4th Cir. 1991).

Crocker v. Tennessee Secondary School Athletic Association, 735 F. Supp. 753 (M.D. Tenn. 1990), *affirmed without published opinion sub nom. Metropolitan Government of Nashville and Davidson County v. Crocker*, 908 F.2d 973 (6th Cir. 1990).

Dale M. ex rel. Alice M. v. Board of Education of Bradley-Bourbonnais High School District No. 307, 237 F.3d 813 (7th Cir. 2001).

Daniel R.R. v. State Board of Education, 874 F.2d 1036 (5th Cir. 1989).

Davis v. Francis Howell School District, 138 F.3d 754 (8th Cir. 1998).

DeBord v. Board of Education of the Ferguson-Florissant School District, 126 F.3d 1102 (8th Cir. 1997).

Devine v. Indian River County School Board, 249 F.3d 1289 (11th Cir. 2001).

District 27 Community School Board v. Board of Education of the City of N.Y., 502 N.Y.S.2d 325 (N.Y. Sup. Ct. 1986).

Doe v. Belleville Public School District No. 118, 672 F. Supp. 342 (S.D. Ill. 1987).

Education Department General Administrative Regulations, 34 C.F.R. § 76.1 *et seq.*

Everson v. Board of Education, 330 U.S. 1 (1947).

Fort Zumwalt School District v. Clynes, 119 F.3d 607 (8th 1997), *cert. denied sub nom Clynes v. Fort Zumwalt School District*, 523 U.S. 1137 (1998).

Fuhrmann v. East Hanover Board of Education, 993 F.2d 1031 (3d Cir. 1993).

Geis v. Board of Education of Parsippany-Troy Hills, 774 F.2d 575 (3d Cir. 1985).

Gladys J. v. Pearland Independent School District, 520 F. Supp. 869 (S.D. Tex. 1981).

Gordon, W. M., Russo, C. J., Miles, A. S., & Leas, T. (1992). HIV infection: Legal implications for educators. *Record in Educational Administration and Supervision*, 13(1), 102–107.

Hall v. Vance County Board of Education, 774 F.2d 629 (4th Cir. 1985).

Hampton School District v. Dobrowolski, 976 F.2d 48 (1st Cir. 1992).

Hartmann v. Loudon County Board of Education, 118 F.3d 996 (4th Cir. 1997).

Helms v. Independent School District, 750 F.2d 820 (10th Cir. 1984).

Helms v. Picard, 151 F.3d 347 (5th Cir. 1998).

Honig v. Doe, 484 U.S. 305 (1988).

Independent School District No. 284 v. A.C., 258 F.3d 769 (8th Cir. 2001).

Individuals with Disabilities Education Act, 20 U.S.C. § 1400 *et seq.* (2005).

Johnson v. Lancaster-Lebanon Intermediate Unit 13, Lancaster City School District, 757 F. Supp. 606 (E.D. Pa. 1991).

J.S.K. v. Hendry County School Board, 941 F.2d 1563 (11th Cir. 1991).

J.W. v. Contoocook Valley School District, 154 F. Supp.2d 217 (D.N.H. 2001).

Kenton County School District v. Hunt, 384 F.3d. 269 (6th Cir. 2004).

Knable v. Bexley City School District, 238 F.3d 755 (6th Cir. 2001).

Lemon v. Kurtzman, 403 U.S. 602 (1971).

Lt. T.B. ex rel. N.B. v. Warwick School Committee, 361 F.3d 80 (1st Cir. 2004).

Lyons v. Smith, 829 F. Supp. 414 (D.D.C. 1993).

Manchester School District v. Christopher B., 807 F. Supp. 860, (D.N.H. 1992).

Martinez v. School Board of Hillsborough County, Fla., 861 F.2d 1502 (11th Cir. 1988), *on remand* 711 F. Supp. 1066 (M.D. Fla. 1989).

Mavis v. Sobol, 839 F. Supp. 968 (N.D.N.Y. 1994).

M.C. v. Central Regional School Dist., 81 F.3d 389 (3d Cir. 1996), *cert. denied*, 519 U.S. 806 (1996).

McKenzie v. Jefferson, EHLR 554:338 (D.D.C. 1983).

McPherson v. Michigan High School Athletic Association, 119 F.3d 453 (6th Cir. 1997).

McQueen v. Colorado Springs School District No. 11, 419 F. Supp.2d 1303 (D. Colo. 2006).

Meek v. Pittenger, 421 U.S. 349 (1975).

Mitchell v. Helms, 530 U.S. 793 (2000), *on remand*, 229 F.3d 467 (5th Cir. 2000).

Montalvo v. Radcliffe, 167 F.3d 873 (4th Cir. 1999).

Moser v. Bret Harte Union High School District, 366 F.Supp.2d 944 (E.D. Cal. 2005).

Muller v. Committee on Special Education of the East Islip Union Free School District, 145 F.3d 95 (2d Cir. 1998).

Nein v. Greater Clark County School Corporation, 95 F. Supp.2d 961 (S.D. Ind. 2000).

New York State Association for Retarded Children v. Carey, 612 F.2d 644 (2d Cir. 1979).

Oberti v. Board of Education of the Borough of Clementon School District, 995 F.2d 1204 (3d Cir. 1993).

Ojai Unified School District v. Jackson, 4 F.3d 1467 (9th Cir. 1993).

Osborne, A. G. (1992). Legal standards for an appropriate education in the post-*Rowley* era. *Exceptional Children, 58*, 488–494.

Osborne, A. G. (1994). Providing special education and related services to parochial school students in the wake of *Zobrest*. *Education Law Reporter, 87*, 329–339.

Osborne, A. G. (1998). *Hartmann v. Loudoun County:* Another round in the inclusion controversy. *Education Law Reporter, 125*, 289–302.

Osborne, A. G., & Battaglino, L. (1996). Eligibility of students with disabilities for sports: Implications for policy. *Education Law Reporter, 105*, 379–388.

Osborne, A. G., & DiMattia, P. (1994). The IDEA's least restrictive environment mandate: Legal implications. *Exceptional Children, 61*, 6–14.

Osborne, A. G., & Russo, C. (1997). The ghoul is dead, long live the ghoul: *Agostini v. Felton* and the delivery of Title I services in nonpublic schools. *Education Law Reporter, 119,* 781–797.

Parks v. Pavkovic, 753 F.2d 1397 (7th Cir. 1985).

Patricia P. v. Board of Education of Oak Park and River Forest High School District No. 200, 203 F.3d 462 (7th Cir. 2000).

Pink v. Mt. Diablo Unified School District, 738 F. Supp. 345 (N.D. Cal. 1990).

Polk v. Central Susquehanna Intermediate Unit 16, 853 F.2d 171 (3d Cir. 1988).

Poolaw v. Bishop, 67 F.3d 830 (9th Cir. 1995).

Pottgen v. Missouri State High School Athletic Association, 40 F.3d 926 (8th Cir. 1994).

Rehabilitation Act, Section 504, 29 U.S.C. § 794 (1998).

Rettig v. Kent School District, 788 F.2d 326 (6th Cir. 1986), *cert. denied,* 478 U.S. 1005 (1986).

Russo, C. J., Massucci, J. D., Osborne, A. G., & Cattaro, G. M. (2002). *Catholic schools and the law of special education: A reference guide.* Washington, DC: NCEA.

Sacramento City Unified School District Board of Education v. Rachel H., 14 F.3d 1398 (9th Cir. 1994), *cert. denied,* 512 U.S. 1207 (1994).

School Board of Campbell County v. Beasley, 380 S.E.2d 884 (Va. 1989).

Socorro Independent School District v. Angelic Y., 107 F. Supp. 2d 761 (W.D. Tex 2000).

Springer v. Fairfax County School Board, 134 F.3d 659 (4th Cir. 1998).

Stock v. Massachusetts Hospital School, 467 N.E.2d 448 (Mass. 1984).

Teague Independent School District v. Todd D., 999 F.2d 127 (5th Cir. 1993).

Timothy W. v. Rochester, N.H. School District, 875 F.2d 954 (1st Cir. 1989), *cert. denied,* 493 U.S. 983 (1989).

Walczak v. Florida Union Free School District, 142 F.3d 119 (2d Cir. 1998).

Washington v. Indiana High School Athletic Association, 181 F.3d 849 (7th Cir. 1999), *cert denied,* 528 U.S. 1046 (1999).

W.B. v. Matula, 67 F.3d 484 (3d Cir. 1995).

Wenkart, R. D. (2000). Juvenile offenders: Residential placement and special education. *Education Law Reporter, 144,* 1–13.

West Virginia Code Ann. §18-20-5 (3) (West 2004).

White v. School Board of Henrico County, 549 S.E.2d 16 (Va. Ct. App. 2001).

Wolman v. Walter, 433 U.S. 229 (1977).

Zayas v. Commonwealth of Puerto Rico, 378 F. Supp.2d 13 (D.P.R. 2005), *affirmed* 163 Fed. Appx. 4 (1st Cir. 2005).

Zobrest v. Catalina Foothills School District, 509 U.S. 1 (1993).

3

Related Services,
Assistive Technology,
and Transition Services

INTRODUCTION

The Individuals with Disabilities Education Act (IDEA) (2005) requires school boards to provide related, or supportive, services to students with disabilities who need such services to assist them in benefiting from their special education programs (20 U.S.C. §§ 1400(c)(5)(D), (d)(1)(A), 1401(3)(A)(i)). The IDEA defines related services as transportation and such developmental, corrective, and supportive services as speech-language pathology and audiology services, interpreting services, psychological services, physical and occupational therapy, recreation (including therapeutic recreation), social work services, school nurse services, counseling services (including rehabilitation counseling), orientation and mobility services, and medical services for diagnostic and evaluation purposes (20 U.S.C. § 1401(26)(A)).

The only limit on what could be a related service is that medical services are exempted unless they are specifically for diagnostic or evaluative purposes. The 2004 IDEA amendments made it clear that the term *related services* does not include medical devices that are surgically implanted or their replacements (20 U.S.C. § 1401(20)(B)). Further, the regulations specify that optimization of the functioning, maintenance, or replacement of

54

such devices is beyond the scope of a school board's responsibilities (34 C.F.R. § 300.34(b)). This does not mean, however, that school personnel lack all responsibility for monitoring such devices or making sure that they function properly (34 C.F.R. § 300.34(b)(2)). While these provisions were included to address a school board's responsibilities regarding cochlear implants, they apply to other surgically implanted devices as well (Russo, Osborne, & Borreca, 2006).

> Supportive services may be deemed related services if they assist students with disabilities to benefit from special education. Related services may be provided by persons of differing professional backgrounds with a variety of occupational titles.

The IDEA's regulations define each of the identified related services in detail (34 C.F.R. § 300.34). Insofar as this list is not exhaustive, other services may be deemed related services if they assist students with disabilities to benefit from special education. For example, services such as artistic and cultural programs or art, music, and dance therapy could be related services under the appropriate circumstances. These related services may be provided by persons of differing professional backgrounds with a variety of occupational titles.

The 1990 IDEA amendments added definitions of assistive technology devices and services. The 1997 and 2004 versions of the IDEA clarified and expanded these definitions. Assistive technology devices are any items, pieces of equipment, or product systems that are used to increase, maintain, or improve the functional capabilities of individuals with disabilities. These devices may include commercially available, modified, or customized equipment (20 U.S.C. § 1401(1)(A)) but, as with related services, do not include a surgically implanted medical device (20 U.S.C. § 1401 (1)(B)). Assistive technology services are designed to help individuals in the selection, acquisition, or use of assistive technology devices. Further, assistive technology services include evaluations of the needs of children, provision of assistive technology devices, training in their use, coordination of other services with assistive technology, and maintenance and repair of devices (20 U.S.C. § 1401(2)).

Interestingly, assistive technology is not specifically included in the definition of either special education or related services, but does fit within the definition of special education, as specially designed instruction, and within the definition of related services, as a developmental, corrective, or supportive service. Yet, rather than include assistive technology within either of these two definitions, Congress chose to create it as a category separate from both special education and related services. Accordingly, assistive technology can be a special education service, a related service, or simply a supplementary aid or service (34 C.F.R. § 300.105(a)). School boards are required to provide supplementary aids and services to students with disabilities to allow them to be educated in the least restrictive environment (LRE) (20 U.S.C. §§ 1401(33), 1412(a)(5)).

At the same time, the IDEA requires school boards to provide transition services to students with disabilities to promote movement from school to postschool activities such as employment, vocational training, and independent living. Transition services include related services, instruction, community experiences, and the acquisition of daily living skills (20 U.S.C. § 1401(34)). School officials must include statements in the individualized education plans (IEPs) of students identifying needed transition services beginning before they turn 16 years of age (20 U.S.C.A § 1414 (d)(1)(A)(i)(VIII)).

There has been much litigation, including two cases that reached the United States Supreme Court, over the related services provisions of the IDEA. The first part of this chapter reviews and analyzes that litigation. The next two sections outline the requirements for providing assistive technology and transition services. The final portion of the chapter offers guidelines for school personnel on situations where school boards must provide related services or assistive technology.

RELATED SERVICES

Transportation

It almost goes without saying that students cannot benefit from their IEPs if they cannot get to school. For this reason, transportation is probably the most common related service that school boards offer to students with disabilities. Transportation is typically provided in district-owned and -operated vehicles, in vehicles owned and operated by private service providers, and/or via public transportation; in rare cases, boards may

---

Figure 3.1   When Are Related Services Required?

Related services are required for students with disabilities when

- Such services are necessary for students to gain access to special education programs or the services outlined in their IEPs
- Such services are necessary for students to remain physically in educational programs
- Students cannot make meaningful progress toward the goals and objectives of their IEPs without such services
- Students' various needs are so intertwined that they need integrated programs of special education and related services
- Students' progress toward the goals and objectives of their IEPs depends on the resolution of other needs

enter into contracts with parents to transport their children to school. School officials need to make special transportation arrangements when students are unable to access their usual modes of transportation. The term *transportation,* as used in the IDEA and its regulations, embodies travel to and from school, between schools, and around school buildings. Specialized equipment, such as adapted busses, lifts, and ramps, are required when needed to provide the transportation (34 C.F.R. § 300.34 (c)(16)(iii)).

An early case from Rhode Island demonstrates that the term *transportation* includes transit from a house to a vehicle. After school officials refused to provide assistance for a child who, because he was physically challenged, was unable to get from his home to a school bus without help, his father drove him to school for a period of time. When the child's father could no longer take him to school, he stopped attending classes. The situation was finally rectified, but the court, holding that transportation clearly was the responsibility of the school board, awarded the parents compensation for their efforts in taking their son to school (*Hurry v. Jones,* 1983). As important as this related service is, though, door-to-door transportation is required only when a student is unable to get to school without such assistance (*Malehorn v. Hill City School District,* 1997).

If IEP teams place students in private schools, then these children are entitled to transportation (*Union School District v. Smith,* 1994). Moreover, if students attend residential private schools, they must be transported between their homes and schools for usual vacation periods. Regardless, one court affirmed that a student was not entitled to additional trips home for therapeutic purposes even though improved family relations was a goal of his IEP (*Cohen v. School Board of Dade County,* 1984). The court explained that a hearing officer did not abuse his discretion in deciding that parents were not entitled to reimbursement for more than three annual round trips from their home in Florida to a treatment facility in Georgia because the school board had met its obligation to provide transportation for the child.

Under the IDEA, an alteration in the delivery of related services can be a change in placement. Even so, the Third Circuit pointed out that a minor adjustment to a child's transportation plan did not constitute a change in placement (*DeLeon v. Susquehanna Community School District,* 1984). Recognizing that transportation could have an effect on a student's learning, the court found that an adjustment that added 10 minutes to the child's trip home from school did not impact his learning. At the same time, transportation arrangements cannot be unreasonable. For instance, a federal trial court in Virginia ordered school board officials to make better arrangements for a student whose ride took more than 30 minutes even though she lived only six miles from her school (*Pinkerton v. Moye,* 1981).

School boards may not be required to provide transportation when parents elect to send their children to schools other than the ones recommended by school personnel. In such a case, a state court in Florida held that a school board was not required to transport a student to a geographically distant facility after she was enrolled there at her parents' request. The court observed that transportation was unnecessary since the student could have received an appropriate education at a closer facility (*School Board of Pinellas County v. Smith*, 1989).

In today's world, many students do not return home after school; instead, they go to afterschool caretakers. According to the Fifth Circuit, students with disabilities are entitled to be transported to caretakers even when those caretakers live out of a district's attendance boundaries (*Alamo Heights Independent School District v. State Board of Education*, 1986). The court pointed out that the parents' request for the student's transportation to the caretaker was reasonable and would place no burden on the school board.

On the other hand, the Eighth Circuit reasoned that a special education student was not entitled to be dropped off at a daycare center that was outside of a school's attendance area. Here the school board's policy for all students dictated that children could be dropped off only within their school's attendance boundary. The court, noting that the board's policy was facially neutral and that the parent's request was based on her personal convenience and not the student's educational needs, determined that the board did not violate the IDEA by refusing to transport the child to his daycare center (*Fick ex rel. Fick v. Sioux Falls School District*, 2003). More recently, the federal trial court in Maine reached the same outcome. The court agreed that a hearing officer and a federal magistrate properly denied the request of the mother that her son, who had a severe learning disability, be allowed to ride a public school bus home and to be met by another adult since she could not be there to meet him when he returned from school (*Ms. S. ex rel. L.S. v. Scarborough School Committee*, 2005). In justifying its position, the court specified that the mother was not entitled to have her request granted because it was motivated by her childcare arrangements with her ex-husband, with whom she shared joint custody, rather than her son's educational needs.

As reflected in the previous paragraph, divorced parents reach a variety of shared custody agreements. In some cases, children reside with each parent on a rotating basis under joint custody arrangements. In a case illustrating an arrangement of this type, where a father lived outside of a district's boundaries, a court in Pennsylvania decided that a school board was required to provide transportation on the weeks when the child lived with his mother but not on the weeks when he lived with his father (*North Allegheny School District v. Gregory P.*, 1996). The court stated that the additional requested transportation did not address the boy's special needs, but rather served only to accommodate the parents' particular domestic situation.

Along with specialized equipment that may be needed to transport students safely, a case from Michigan demonstrates that school boards may have to provide aides on vehicles. A federal trial court ordered a school board to provide a trained aide to attend to a medically fragile student during transit (*Macomb County Intermediate School District v. Joshua S.*, 1989). The court asserted that under the IDEA, students with disabilities were entitled to transportation.

Counseling, Psychological, and Social Work Services

The IDEA's regulations define counseling as a service that is provided by a qualified social worker, psychologist, guidance counselor, or other qualified person (34 C.F.R. § 300.34(c)(2)). The definition of psychological services includes psychological counseling (34 C.F.R. § 300.34(c)(10)(v)), while the definition of social work services includes group and individual counseling (34 C.F.R. § 300.34(c)(14)(ii)). On the other hand, the regulations neither use nor define the term *psychotherapy*.

> Counseling, psychological, and social work services clearly are required related services only when needed by a student with a disability to benefit from special education. These may be required as related services for students with emotional difficulties who may not be able to benefit from their special education programs until their emotional problems are addressed.

One of the controversies that developed over the medical exclusion clause of the related services mandate concerns the provision of psychotherapy. Counseling, psychological, and social work services clearly are required related services only when students with disabilities need them to benefit from special education. While psychotherapy can be classified as a psychological service, in some situations it falls within the medical exclusion. Whether psychotherapy is a psychological or medical service depends on individual state laws governing psychotherapy. Put another way, some state laws stipulate that only psychiatrists can provide psychotherapy, while other states allow clinical psychologists to provide psychotherapy. Insofar as psychiatrists are licensed physicians, psychotherapy is an exempted medical service in states that restrict its provision to psychiatrists.

The distinguishing criterion regarding whether psychotherapy is a related service or an exempted medical service is how it is defined in a state law, not by whom it is actually provided. In Illinois, where state law allows nonpsychiatric professionals to provide psychotherapy, a federal trial court decided that a school board was responsible for the costs of psychotherapy even though the psychotherapy was actually provided by a psychiatrist (*Max M. v. Thompson*, 1984). The court ascertained that the criterion that services that must be performed by a physician were exempted did not mean that services that could be provided by a nonphysician, but were in actuality provided by a physician, were excluded. The court, however, indicated that the board was required to pay for the services only to the extent of the costs of their being performed by a nonphysician.

Counseling, psychotherapy, or social work services may be required as related services for students with emotional difficulties who may not be able to benefit from their special education programs until their emotional problems are addressed. The Supreme Court of Montana, turning to the dictionary for a definition of the term *psychotherapy,* found that according to *Webster's* "psychotherapy" is a psychological service. Thus, the court treated psychotherapy as a related service (*In re A Family,* 1979). The federal trial court in New Jersey also categorized psychotherapy as a counseling or psychological service, pointing out that it was a required related service (*T.G. and P.G. v. Board of Education of Piscataway,* 1983).

Federal trial courts in Illinois, Massachusetts, and New Jersey agreed that psychotherapy is a required related service because it assists some children in benefiting from their educational programs (*Gary B. v. Cronin,* 1980; *T.G. and P.G. v. Board of Education of Piscataway,* 1983; *Doe v. Anrig,* 1987). Further, a federal trial court in Illinois determined that although psychotherapy is related to mental health, it may be required before a child can derive any benefit from education. Similarly, the court in New Jersey was persuaded that psychotherapy was an essential service that allowed an emotionally disturbed student to benefit from his educational program.

Insofar as counseling is generally not considered to be a medical service, it may not be an exempted service. For example, the federal trial court in Connecticut was of the opinion that psychological and counseling services that a student with disabilities needed to benefit from his special education program were not embraced within the exempted medical services clause (*Papacoda v. State of Connecticut,* 1981). The court added that because the therapy services offered as part of a residential placement were essential to render the child educable, they were required related services.

An important element in the requirement to provide related services is that they must be necessary for students to benefit from special education services. In such a case, the Fourth Circuit remarked that counseling services were not required for a student who made great improvement under an IEP that did not include counseling (*Tice v. Botetourt County School Board,* 1990).

If a therapeutic service can be classified as psychiatric, courts are likely to declare that it falls within the medical exception. The federal trial court for the District of Columbia decreed that the school board was not required to pay for the residential component costs of a placement in a psychiatric hospital and school because the primary reasons for the child's placement were medical, not educational (*McKenzie v. Jefferson,* 1983). In like fashion, a federal trial court in Illinois concluded that psychiatric services are exempted medical services because psychiatrists are licensed physicians (*Darlene L. v. Illinois Board of Education,* 1983). At least four other courts agreed that since psychiatric facilities are medical facilities, school boards are not required to pay for the services that they offer (*Doe v. Anrig*, 1987; *Metropolitan Government of Nashville and Davidson County v. Tennessee Department of Education*, 1989; *Clovis Unified School District v. California Office of Administrative Hearings*, 1990; *Tice v. Botetourt County School Board*, 1990).

Psychiatric services are required as related services when they are for diagnostic or evaluative purposes. In the first of two cases from Tennessee, a federal trial court held that an evaluation by a neurologist was a related service (*Seals v. Loftis*, 1985). Five years later, another court in Tennessee acknowledged that the limited medical services a student received in a residential rehabilitation facility could not have been used to characterize her entire program as medical (*Brown v. Wilson County School Board*, 1990). The court contended that because medical services were provided to monitor and adjust the child's medication, they were for diagnostic and evaluative purposes. Similarly, the federal trial court in Connecticut, recognizing that a student had not made academic progress, ordered a school board to conduct a psychiatric evaluation to evaluate his need for counseling (*J.B. v. Killingly Board of Education*, 1997). Further, the federal trial court in Hawaii was of the view that hospitalization costs were a significant part of a student's diagnosis and evaluation as having a disability. Even though the student was hospitalized in response to a medical crisis, the court directed state officials to pay for the hospitalization because it was an integral part of her overall evaluation (*Department of Education, State of Hawaii v. Cari Rae S.*, 2001).

Whether placement in a facility that provides psychiatric services is primarily for medical or educational reasons may affect the costs that school boards are required to assume. Two cases that the Ninth Circuit resolved only months apart illustrate this point. In the first, *Clovis Unified School District v. California Office of Administrative Hearings* (1990), where a student was admitted to an acute care psychiatric hospital when the residential school she attended could no longer control her behavior, her parents unsuccessfully asked their school board to pay for this placement. In comparing the placement to one for a student suffering from a physical illness and declaring that it had been made for medical reasons, the court reasoned that room and board costs were medically related, not educationally related, because the hospital did not provide educational services. In the second, *Taylor v. Honig* (1990), after a student was placed in a residential school and psychiatric hospital for assaulting a family member, the court declared that the residential facility was a boarding school that had the capacity to offer necessary medical services. The court remarked that seeing as the placement was made for primarily educational reasons, it was appropriate under the IDEA.

Physical, Occupational, and Speech Therapy

Occupational therapy refers to services that improve, develop, or restore functions impaired or lost through illness, injury, or deprivation or that improve the ability to perform tasks for independent functioning (34 C.F.R. § 300.34(c)(6)). This also includes services to prevent the impairment or loss of function through early intervention. The IDEA's regulations define physical therapy simply as the services provided by a qualified physical therapist (34 C.F.R. § 300.34(c)(9)). Speech-language pathology includes the identification, diagnosis, and appraisal of speech or language impairments and the provision of appropriate services for the habilitation or prevention of communication impairments (34 C.F.R. § 300.34(c)(15)).

A federal trial court in New York ordered a school board to provide occupational therapy over the summer months when it realized that a student would have regressed in the areas of upper body strength and ambulation skills (*Holmes v. Sobol*, 1988). The court added that the child's ability to perform classroom work and to function in the classroom would have been adversely affected without the summer therapy. Conversely, the federal trial court for the District of Columbia believed that a proposed placement for a student with multiple disabilities was inappropriate since it did not provide for an integrated occupational therapy program as called for in her IEP (*Kattan v. District of Columbia*, 1988). The court maintained that the child did not need the program because she would not have benefited from her special education program even with this service. Even so, the amount of occupational therapy that students receive must be sufficient to confer educational benefit. In such a case, a federal trial court in California ordered a school board to provide additional therapy to a student who had delays in all areas of development (*Glendale Unified School District v. Almasi*, 2000).

Many school boards use the services of occupational therapy assistants to provide services. A federal trial court in Tennessee upheld this practice on the basis that the assistants were well trained and helped the child to make progress (*Metropolitan Nashville and Davidson County School System v. Guest*, 1995). In addition, the court suggested that school boards are not required to maximize a student's gains.

The Third Circuit remarked that physical therapy is an important facilitator of classroom learning for some children (*Polk v. Central Susquehanna Intermediate Unit 16*, 1988). Noting that the IDEA calls for an education that provides meaningful benefit, the court observed that physical therapy is an essential prerequisite for learning for some students with severe disabilities.

Insofar as the inability to communicate can effectively interfere with learning, speech and language therapy, when needed, are considered a related service. Although there has been no major litigation involving the need for speech or language therapy, it is safe to say that courts would require its delivery. Most school boards provide extensive speech and language therapy services; in some states it is considered to be a special education service rather than a related service.

Recreation and Enrichment Programs

The IDEA specifically identifies recreation and therapeutic recreation as related services (20 U.S.C. § 1401(26)(A)). The definition of recreation in the IDEA's regulations includes assessment of leisure function, recreation programs in schools and community agencies, and leisure education, along with therapeutic recreation (34 C.F.R. § 300.34(c)(11)). Moreover, the IDEA's regulations specify that school boards must provide nonacademic and extracurricular services and activities to the extent necessary to afford students with disabilities equal opportunities for participation (34 C.F.R. § 300.107). Nonacademic and extracurricular services and activities may include lunch, recess, athletics, recreational activities, special interest groups or clubs, employment, and many of the items listed as related services. These activities must be provided in inclusive settings to the maximum extent appropriate (34 C.F.R. § 300.117).

If students with disabilities are unable to participate in general extracurricular programs, school officials may need to develop special extracurricular programs for them. Further, students who meet the eligibility requirements for participation in general extracurricular programs cannot be denied access to them under Section 504 of the Rehabilitation Act (1998). This means that school officials may need to provide reasonable accommodations to allow students with disabilities to participate in general extracurricular programs. For example, courts may waive eligibility rules that might prevent students with disabilities from participating due to their disabilities (Osborne & Battaglino, 1996).

> School officials may need to provide reasonable accommodations to allow students with disabilities to participate in general extracurricular programs. If students with disabilities are unable to participate in general extracurricular programs, school officials may need to develop special extracurricular programs for them.

A state court in Michigan affirmed that a school board had to provide a summer enrichment program to a student with autism where testimony revealed that he needed a program that included outdoor activities (*Birmingham and Lamphere School Districts v. Superintendent of Public Instruction*, 1982). The court directed the board to act because it judged that the requested program fell within the parameters of special education and related services insofar as physical education was included in the definition of special education and recreation was a related service.

In like fashion, a federal trial court in Ohio issued a preliminary injunction ordering a school board to include participation in interscholastic athletics in a student's IEP. The court was swayed by evidence that the student's participation in sports resulted in academic, physical, and

Figure 3.2   Difference Between Medical and Health Services

Medical services are those that can legally be provided only by licensed physicians. Under the IDEA, school boards are not responsible for providing medical services except that they are required for diagnostic or evaluative purposes as part of the multidisciplinary evaluations that students undergo in determining whether they are eligible for special education and related services.

Health services are those that can be performed by school nurses, trained health aides, or other trained laypersons. Typically, students receive these services as part of a district's school nursing services. Other health procedures are included as long as they do not, by law, have to be provided by licensed physicians.

---

personal progress (*Kling v. Mentor Public School District*, 2001). On the other hand, a state court in New York did not think that a board was required to provide an afterschool program when such participation was unnecessary for the student to receive a free appropriate public education (FAPE) (*Roslyn Union Free School District v. University of the State of New York, State Education Department*, 2000).

School Nurse Services

According to the IDEA's regulations, school nurse services are those that are performed by qualified school nurses that are designed to enable students with disabilities to receive a FAPE (34 C.F.R. § 300.34(c)(13)). There has been controversy over the provision of health-related services in the schools because of the medical exclusion clause. To the extent that a number of medical procedures can be performed by registered nurses, questions have arisen as to whether certain nursing services fall within the definition of school health services or are exempted medical services.

> In the absence of a disability that requires special education, the need for related services does not create an obligation under the IDEA. School officials must provide only those services that are necessary to aid students in benefiting from special education.

The United States Supreme Court, in *Irving Independent School District v. Tatro* (1984), held that catheterization was a required related service for a student who could not voluntarily empty her bladder due to spina bifida. In conceding that the student had to be catheterized every three to four hours, the Court pointed out that services that allow a child to remain in class during the school day, such as catheterization, are no less related to the effort to educate than those that allowed her to reach, enter, or exit the school. The Court was satisfied that because the catheterization procedure could have been performed by a school nurse or trained health aide, Congress did not intend to exclude it as a medical service, thereby clarifying when related services must be provided to students with disabilities. The Court stated that in the absence of a disability that required special education, the need for related services did not create an obligation under the IDEA and that school officials must provide only those services that are necessary to aid students in benefiting from special education. The Court emphasized that a life support service would not be a related service if it did not need to be provided during school hours.

The federal trial court in Hawaii asserted that a school board was required to provide a student with cystic fibrosis with health services attendant to a tracheotomy tube even though the tube became dislodged occasionally and needed to be reinserted and mucus had to be suctioned from her lungs periodically (*Department of Education, State of Hawaii v. Katherine D.*, 1982). Again, where these procedures could have been performed by a school nurse or trained layperson, the court treated them as required related services.

According to a federal trial court in Illinois, school boards must also provide nursing services during transportation (*Skelly v. Brookfield LaGrange Park School District 95*, 1997). Previously, a federal trial court in Michigan was of the opinion that a school board was required to provide an aide on a school bus to attend to a medically fragile student (*Macomb County Intermediate School District v. Joshua S.*, 1989). The court observed that the provision of an aide or other health professional did not constitute an exempted medical service.

It is well settled that services that can be provided by school nurses, health aides, or even trained laypersons fall within the IDEA's mandated related services clause. Many students who attend school have fragile medical conditions that require the constant presence of nurses. The question arose as to whether school boards are required to pay for the services of full-time nurses for single students. Courts disagreed over whether full-time nursing services were more akin to exempted medical services (Osborne, 1999). The United States Supreme Court settled the controversy in 1999 in *Cedar Rapids Community School District v. Garret F. (Garret F.)*. In affirming that a school board was required to provide full-time nursing services for a student who was quadriplegic, the Court ruled that although continuous services may be more costly and may require additional school personnel, this did not render them more medical. Recognizing that cost was not a factor in the definition of related services, the Court concluded that even costly related services must be provided to help guarantee that students with significant medical needs are integrated into the public schools. *Garret F.* clearly has the potential to have a major impact on school board budgets in light of the costs associated with the delivery of nursing services, whether for one child or groups of students (Russo, 1999).

Diagnostic and Evaluative Services

The proper diagnosis and evaluation of students suspected of having disabilities is an important component of the special education process. Medical evaluations can be part of that process. The IDEA makes it clear that medical services can be related services when used for that purpose (34 C.F.R. § 300.34(c)(5)).

In a case from Tennessee, a federal trial court found that a school board was required to pay for the neurological and psychological evaluation that a pediatrician ordered (*Seals v. Loftis*, 1985). School personnel had requested that the pediatrician evaluate the child, who had a seizure disorder, visual difficulties, and learning disabilities, after his behavior and school performance deteriorated. The pediatrician referred the child to a neurologist who subsequently referred him to a psychologist. When a dispute arose over who was responsible for paying for the neurological and psychological evaluations, the court wrote that since the child's needs were intertwined, these evaluations were necessary for him to benefit from his special education. In language that should be of interest to school officials elsewhere, the court commented that the parents could have been required to use their health insurance to pay for the evaluations as long as they did not incur any costs in doing so. Insofar as the parents' policy placed a lifetime cap on psychological services that would have been reduced by the amount of the evaluation bill, the court decided that the board was responsible for payment. While no such cap existed for neurological services, the court indicated that the parents were required to use their insurance for that evaluation.

The term *diagnostic and evaluative services* does not refer only to assessments that may be conducted as part of initial evaluations. According to a federal trial court in Tennessee, the ongoing monitoring of a student's condition could fall within the realm of diagnostic and evaluative services (*Brown v. Wilson County School Board*, 1990). The court held that since the medical services at issue, which were designed to monitor and adjust the student's medication, were for diagnostic and evaluation purposes, the school board was responsible for their payment.

As indicated earlier, the federal trial court in Hawaii ordered the state to pay for hospitalization costs that were a significant part of a student's diagnosis and evaluation as disabled (*Department of Education, State of Hawaii v. Cari Rae S.*, 2001). The dispute arose after the child's stay in the hospital triggered, and was an integral part of, her diagnosis and evaluation. The court ascertained that preplacement medical costs limited to diagnosis and evaluation are recoverable where a student is subsequently found to have qualified for special education services.

Substance Abuse Prevention and Treatment

Acknowledging that Congress did not intend to create a federal claim for every activity or type of conduct that could impede an individual's ability to take advantage of educational opportunities, a federal trial court in California refused to interpret drug prevention treatment as a related service under the IDEA (*Armstrong by Steffensen v. Alicante School,* 1999). The case arose after a student who attended a private school ingested an illegal substance and his parents unsuccessfully alleged that school officials tolerated the use of illegal drugs on campus.

School boards are not required to provide substance abuse programs under the related services mandate if these intervention programs follow a medical model (Wenkart, 2000). The federal trial court in New Jersey held that a substance abuse program does not fall within the domain of related services that must be provided under the IDEA, even though it would benefit learning (*Field v. Haddonfield Board of Education,* 1991). In this case, when a special education student who attended a private school was expelled for possession of drugs, his parents were informed that he could return if he attended a substance abuse program. After the school board refused to pay for the program, the parents filed suit. The court indicated that the student was not entitled to public payment for the program because it was medical to the extent that it consisted of psychiatric counseling, physical examinations, and administration of medication.

A substance abuse program that is not primarily medical could be a required related service. The IDEA's regulations make it clear that since counseling, psychological, and social work services are required related services, a substance abuse program that primarily utilized one of those services could be a required related service.

Habilitation Services

The Fourth Circuit affirmed that in-home habilitation services do not fall within the definitions of special education and related services (*Burke County Board of Education v. Denton,* 1990). Parents had requested the services, which were primarily designed to help control their son's behavior at home, when he returned to the family home after attending a residential program. The court noted that the child had made educational progress without the requested services. On the other hand, a federal trial court in Georgia decided that vision therapy is a required related service because the student's vision problems impacted his future ability to benefit from special education (*DeKalb County School District v. M.T.V. ex rel. C.E.V.,* 2005).

Physical Plant Alterations

School boards may be required to alter the physical plants of schools in order to allow students with disabilities to participate fully in and benefit from their educational programs. Most of these alterations allow access to school buildings. A case from Texas reflects the notion that modifications may be required to allow students to remain in classrooms. Here a federal trial court ordered a school board to provide an air-conditioned classroom for a student who, due to brain injuries that he suffered in an accident, could not regulate his body temperature and thus required a temperature-controlled environment at all times (*Espino v. Besteiro*, 1981). While the board provided the student with an air-conditioned Plexiglas cubicle, and he achieved satisfactory academic progress, he had a limited ability to socialize and participate in group activities. The court pointed out that the use of the cubicle violated the LRE mandate because it caused the student to miss out on the class participation and group interactions that were important to his education.

Boards are not required to make alterations to all school buildings within districts in order to make them accessible to students with disabilities. In an illustrative case, the Eighth Circuit affirmed that a board complied with the IDEA by offering parents a placement for their daughter in an accessible school that was reasonably close to the family home (*Schuldt v. Mankato Independent School District No. 77*, 1991). The parents filed suit on behalf of their daughter, who used a wheelchair, seeking to require the board to modify her neighborhood school to make it accessible. The record revealed that three other schools in the district were wheelchair accessible and that the board offered the parents a placement for their daughter in one that was four miles from her home. The court upheld that arrangement, recognizing that by bussing the student to a nearby school, board officials provided her with a fully integrated education and that nothing in the IDEA required that they place her in the school closest to her home.

Parent Training and Counseling

As defined in the IDEA's regulations, parent training and counseling means assisting parents to understand the special needs of their children and provide them with information about child development (34 C.F.R. § 300.34(c)(8)). Courts sometimes order residential placements for students who require consistency and support that is not available in the home environment. Less restrictive placements can be appropriate if parents are trained to deal with their children appropriately in their homes, using techniques similar to those that are used at school. Yet, avoidance of a residential placement is not the sole criterion for providing parent training and counseling.

A federal trial court in Texas contended that an appropriate placement could be provided within a public school setting for a student with severe disabilities if her parents were given training and counseling, thereby averting the need for a residential placement (*Stacey G. v. Pasadena Independent School District*, 1982). The court observed that the child required a highly structured educational program that needed to be maintained year-round. In order to preserve that structure after school hours, the court ordered the school board to provide her parents with training in behavioral techniques. In addition, the court directed school officials to offer counseling to help relieve the stress of the burdensome demands that the child's disability placed on her parents. Similarly, a federal trial court in Alabama ordered a school board to provide training and counseling to the parents of a student who exhibited academic and behavioral problems (*Chris D. v. Montgomery County Board of Education*, 1990). In stating that the student's overall IEP was not appropriate, the court noted that educators ignored a crucial component of a behavioral control program by failing to counsel and instruct the parents in how to reinforce the training the child received at school in their home.

Residential Placements and Lodging

Many students with disabilities require placements in residential schools or facilities in order to receive an appropriate education. In some cases, residential placements are called for because children need instructional services on a round-the-clock basis in order to receive an appropriate education. In other situations, students who do not necessarily require 24-hour-per-day instruction must remain at such schools on a residential basis since they are the only facilities that can provide an appropriate education and are not within commuting distance. Under these circumstances, school boards must still pay for the room-and-board portion of residential placements, as such arrangements are considered to be a related service.

According to the IDEA's regulations, if a residential program "is necessary to provide special education and related services to a child with a disability, the program, including nonmedical care and room and board, must be at no cost to the parents of the child" (34 C.F.R. § 300.104). This regulation applies whether the residential portion of the placement is needed for educational reasons or access reasons.

Boards may be required to provide off-campus lodging to students with disabilities if appropriate arrangements cannot be made for them to live at their schools and they are located too far from home to commute (*Ojai Unified School District v. Jackson*, 1993; *Union School District v. Smith*, 1994). This can occur when the schools that students attend either do not offer residential components or do not have any room for children in their residential programs but have openings in their day programs.

Residential placements are not considered to be related services if their sole purpose is to provide confinement. Explaining that it stretches the IDEA too far to classify confinement as a related service, the Seventh Circuit asserted that a student whose problems were not primarily educational did not require a residential placement at public expense (*Dale M. v. Board of Education of Bradley-Bourbonnais High School District No. 307*, 2001).

Teacher Training

Realizing that that the IDEA's list of related services is not all-inclusive, the Supreme Court of South Dakota refused to order a school board to include specific teacher training in a student's IEP (*Sioux Falls School District v. Koupal*, 1994). In so doing, the court rejected the request of the parent of an autistic student who wanted a clause included in her son's IEP calling for his teachers to be trained in a particular instructional methodology. The court specified that insofar as teacher competency is in the control of school administrators, a parent cannot dictate how teachers are to be trained or how their competency is to be measured.

ASSISTIVE TECHNOLOGY

Assistive technology may be provided as a special education service, as a related service, or as a supplementary aid and service. Assistive technology is required when it is necessary for students to receive an appropriate education under the standard established by the Supreme Court in *Board of Education of the Hendrick Hudson School District v. Rowley* (1982). Further, because assistive technology may allow many students with disabilities to benefit from education in less restrictive settings, it may be required under the IDEA's least restrictive environment provision.

> Assistive technology may allow many students with disabilities to benefit from education in less restrictive settings.

IEP teams must consider whether children require assistive technology devices and services in order to receive an appropriate education (34 C.F.R. § 300.324(a)(2)(v)). If teams determine that students need assistive technology, then they must write this into their IEPs. Even so, the IDEA does not require teams to document that they considered providing students with assistive technology devices and services but found that they were not needed.

The IDEA specifically requires school boards to ensure that assistive technology devices and services are made available to students if either or both are required as part of the child's special education, related services, or supplementary aids and services (34 C.F.R. § 300.105(a)). The IDEA calls for the use of school-provided assistive technology devices in the homes of students if their IEP teams determine that they need access to assistive technology in order to receive a FAPE (34 C.F.R. § 300.105(b)).

In explanatory material accompanying the 1999 IDEA regulations, the Department of Education made it clear that school boards are not required to provide personal devices, such as eyeglasses, hearing aids, and braces, that students would require regardless of whether they attended school

(Assistance to the States for the Education of Children with Disabilities: Appendix B, as cited in the *Federal Register,* 1999, p. 12540). Of course, nothing prohibits school systems from providing students with these items. In addition, the Department of Education stipulated that students with disabilities are entitled to have access to any general technology that is available to peers who are not disabled. When students with disabilities require accommodations in order to use general technology, educators must make sure to provide these modifications (Assistance to the States, 1999, p. 12540).

In an illustrative case, a federal trial court in Pennsylvania held that a school board's provision of assistive technology to a student with multiple disabilities was inadequate (*East Penn School District v. Scott B.,* 1999). The court was of the view that the student required a laptop computer with appropriate software but that school personnel wasted nearly a year before obtaining and setting up the device. Further, the court found fault with the school's chosen software program and keyboarding instruction. In Maryland, the federal trial court upheld a hearing officer's order for a school board to provide a student with appropriate software to use at home and school and to provide instruction in how to use the software (*Board of Education of Harford County v. Bauer,* 2000).

A case from New York highlights the point that an assistive technology device should aid students in receiving a FAPE by mitigating the effects of their disabilities but should not circumvent the learning process. Here, although a student with learning disabilities that affected his ability in mathematics was allowed to use a calculator, educators denied his request to use a more advanced calculator on the ground that doing so would have circumvented the learning process. The Second Circuit affirmed a hearing officer's adjudication that school officials provided the student with appropriate assistive technology and that the more advanced calculator was not needed (*Sherman v. Mamaroneck Union Free School District,* 2003).

TRANSITION SERVICES

Pursuant to the IDEA, school boards must provide transition services to students with disabilities in order to facilitate their passages from school to postschool activities. Transition services not only involve instruction and training but may also encompass related services.

The federal trial court in Connecticut ruled that a 20-year-old student was entitled to instruction in community and daily living skills because they fell within the ambit of transition services (*J.B. v. Killingly Board of Education,* 1997). In Pennsylvania, a federal trial court, observing that transition services should be designed to prepare a student for life outside the school system, posited that providing him with only vocational evaluations and training was insufficient as they did not meet all of his needs (*East Penn School District v. Scott B.,* 1999).

The federal trial court in Hawaii approved a coordinated set of activities that was clearly designed to promote a student's movement from school to postschool activities. These activities, which were written into the student's IEP, were aimed at assisting him in completing high school, becoming part of his community, exploring careers and colleges, and meeting with vocational counselors (*Browell v. LeMahieu,* 2000). Similarly, a federal trial court in Louisiana found that transition plans that detailed desired adult outcomes, including school action steps and family action steps, were appropriate (*Pace v. Bogulusa City School Board,* 2001).

RECOMMENDATIONS

In addition to special education, school boards must provide students with disabilities with related services when they are necessary for students to benefit from their special education programs. The only limitation that has been placed on what may be considered related services is that medical services are exempted unless they are for diagnostic or evaluative purposes. Not surprisingly, the large amount of litigation that ensued in disputes over the IDEA's related services provisions offers school officials considerable guidance. The following recommendations have been developed from that litigation.

When dealing with students with disabilities, school officials should

- Provide related services to students who are receiving special education if they are necessary for children to receive educational benefits.
- Consider whether students who are not receiving special education may be entitled to related services under Section 504.
- Provide students with disabilities with services of a life-support nature if necessary during the school day.
- Provide students with medical services if they are needed for diagnostic or evaluative purposes.
- Provide students with all necessary school health services that can be performed by school nurses, health aides, or other trained laypersons.
- Provide full-time nurses to help guarantee that students with significant medical needs are integrated into the public schools.
- Check to see whether students who require extensive health-related services are eligible for Medicaid benefits that could offset the costs of many expensive health-related services.
- Investigate the option of using parents' health insurance, particularly for diagnostic and evaluative services; at the same time, recall that parents cannot be required to use their health insurance if doing so incurs a cost to them in the form of a reduction in benefits, a cap on benefits, or increased premiums.

Figure 3.3   Frequently Asked Questions

Q: Medical services are exempted from the related services provision of the IDEA, but when do health-related services become medical services?

A: Medical services, by definition, are those that, by law, can only be provided by licensed physicians. State law is important in this regard since it typically dictates the requirements for persons who provide certain services. For example, in some states only psychiatrists can provide psychotherapy while in others clinical psychologists or licensed clinical social workers can provide psychotherapy.

Q: Are school boards required to provide substance abuse programs to students with disabilities who have drug or alcohol problems?

A: Insofar as school boards are required to provide counseling and social work services, substance abuse programs utilizing counseling or social work models could be required as a related service. However, school boards are not responsible for any such programs that follow a medical model.

Q: When are school boards obligated to provide special transportation for students with disabilities?

A: School boards must provide special transportation arrangements when the disabilities of students call for such services. If students are able to access regular transportation, special transportation is not required. For example, students with hearing impairments, under most circumstances, should be able to ride regular school buses. On the other hand, students in wheelchairs may need vehicles equipped to accommodate their wheelchairs.

Q: Are school boards required to provide transportation to daycare centers or other afterschool caretakers?

A: School boards are required to provide transportation to daycare centers or other afterschool caretakers for students with disabilities to the same extent that they provide such transportation to students who are not disabled. School boards should develop policies regarding transportation to locations other than the homes of students. School officials must apply these policies equally to all students, regardless of their disability status.

Q: Why are school boards required to provide health services?

A: Health services may be equated to modifications to physical plants that allow students with disabilities to access educational programs. Many students cannot be physically present in classrooms without such services. For instance, students who require catheterization every three to four hours may not be able to attend school for a typical six-hour day unless school officials provide catheterization.

Q: Are school boards required to provide students with special extracurricular services?

A: Under Section 504, students with disabilities are entitled to access regular extracurricular activities as long as they are otherwise qualified to participate in them with reasonable accommodations. If participation in extracurricular activities assists students in benefiting from their special education programs, they can be a required related service. School officials may need to provide special programs if students are unable to participate in regular extracurricular offerings.

- Provide psychotherapy, social work services, or counseling when the resolution of emotional concerns is a prerequisite to helping students make successful progress toward their IEP goals.
- Be diligent in ascertaining exactly what the primary reason for residential placements is since placements that are noneducational in nature may not be the responsibility of school boards.
- Provide special transportation when students are unable to access standard modes of transportation.
- Avoid excessively long bus or van rides to schools since these can be considered unreasonable in light of the fact that transportation arrangements must be reasonable.
- Make provisions for children whose disabilities prevent them from getting to and from their transportation vehicles.
- Provide students with transportation to and from their residential facilities.
- Establish neutral policies regarding transportation of all students to day care centers or afterschool caretakers.
- Ensure that students with disabilities are given the same considerations as peers who are not disabled regarding transportation outside of a school's attendance boundaries.
- Provide an aide on transportation vehicles, if necessary, to ensure safe passage for students who are medically fragile.
- Make alterations to physical plants to allow students with disabilities to participate fully in and benefit from their educational program; keep in mind that another option may be to transport students to nearby schools that are accessible if the required alterations would be excessively costly.
- Provide parents with training so that there is consistency between the techniques used in school and at home; this option may be a viable alternative to residential placements.
- Pay room and board expenses for students if the only facilities that can provide a FAPE are not within commuting distance from their homes.
- Provide full access to sports or other extracurricular activities whenever students qualify for participation.
- Include participation in sports or other extracurricular activities in IEPs if these activities may assist students in benefiting from their educational programs.
- Provide assistive technology to students with disabilities when needed, recalling that school boards are not required to provide personal devices that children would require regardless of whether they attended school.
- Consider instruction in daily living skills when developing transition services for students who are close to exiting educational systems.

REFERENCES

A Family, In re, 602 P.2d 157 (Mont. 1979).

Alamo Heights Independent School District v. State Board of Education, 790 F.2d 1153 (5th Cir. 1986).

Armstrong by Steffensen v. Alicante School, 44 F. Supp.2d 1087 (E.D. Cal. 1999).

Assistance to the States for the Education of Children with Disabilities: Appendix B. (1999). *Federal Register, 64*(48), 12481–12672.

Birmingham and Lamphere School Districts v. Superintendent of Public Instruction, 328 N.W.2d 59 (Mich. Ct. App. 1982).

Board of Education of Harford County v. Bauer, 2000 WL 1481464 (D. Md. 2000).

Board of Education of the Hendrick Hudson Central School District v. Rowley, 458 U.S. 176 (1982).

Browell v. LeMahieu, 127 F. Supp.2d 1117 (D. Haw. 2000).

Brown v. Wilson County School Board, 747 F. Supp. 436 (M.D. Tenn. 1990).

Burke County Board of Education v. Denton, 895 F.2d 973 (4th Cir. 1990).

Cedar Rapids Community School District v. Garret F. 119 S. Ct. 992 (1999).

Chris D. v. Montgomery County Board of Education, 753 F. Supp. 922 (M.D. Ala. 1990).

Clovis Unified School District v. California Office of Administrative Hearings, 903 F.2d 635 (9th Cir. 1990).

Code of Federal Regulations (C.F.R.), as cited.

Cohen v. School Board of Dade County, 450 So. 2d 1238 (Fla. Dist. Ct. App. 1984).

Dale M. v. Board of Education of Bradley-Bourbonnais High School District No. 307, 237 F.3d 813 (7th Cir. 2001).

Darlene L. v. Illinois Board of Education, 568 F. Supp. 1340 (N.D. Ill. 1983).

DeKalb County School District v. M.T.V. ex rel. C.E.V., 413 F. Supp.2d 1322 (N.D. Ga. 2005).

DeLeon v. Susquehanna Community School District, 747 F.2d 149 (3d Cir. 1984).

Department of Education, State of Hawaii v. Cari Rae S., 158 F. Supp.2d 1190 (D. Haw. 2001).

Department of Education, State of Hawaii v. Katherine D., 531 F. Supp. 517 (D. Haw. 1982), *affirmed* 727 F.2d 809 (9th Cir. 1983).

Doe v. Anrig, 651 F. Supp. 424 (D. Mass. 1987).

East Penn School District v. Scott B., 1999 WL 178363 (E.D. Pa. 1999).

Espino v. Besteiro, 520 F. Supp. 905 (S.D. Tex. 1981).

Fick ex rel. Fick v. Sioux Falls School District, 337 F.3d 968 (8th Cir. 2003).

Field v. Haddonfield Board of Education, 769 F. Supp. 1313 (D.N.J. 1991).

Gary B. v. Cronin, 542 F. Supp. 102 (N.D. Ill. 1980).

Glendale Unified School District v. Almasi, 122 F. Supp.2d 1093 (C.D. Cal. 2000).

Holmes v. Sobol, 690 F. Supp. 154 (W.D.N.Y. 1988).

Hurry v. Jones, 560 F. Supp. 500 (D.R.I. 1983), *affirmed in part, reversed in part* 734 F.2d 879 (1st Cir. 1984).

Individuals with Disabilities Education Act, 20 U.S.C. § 1400 *et seq.* (2005).

Irving Independent School District v. Tatro, 468 U.S. 883 (1984).

J.B. v. Killingly Board of Education, 990 F. Supp. 57 (D. Conn. 1997).

Kattan v. District of Columbia, 691 F. Supp. 1539 (D.D.C. 1988).

Kling v. Mentor Public School District, 136 F. Supp.2d 744 (N.D. Ohio, 2001).

Macomb County Intermediate School District v. Joshua S., 715 F. Supp. 824 (E.D. Mich. 1989).

Malehorn v. Hill City School District, 987 F. Supp. 772 (D.S.D. 1997).

Max M. v. Thompson, 566 F. Supp. 1330 (N.D. Ill. 1983), 585 F. Supp. 317 (N.D. Ill. 1984), 592 F. Supp. 1437 (N.D. Ill. 1984), 592 F. Supp. 1450 (N.D. Ill. 1984), 629 F. Supp. 1504 (N.D. Ill. 1986).

McKenzie v. Jefferson, EHLR 554:338 (D.D.C. 1983).

Metropolitan Government of Nashville and Davidson County v. Tennessee Department of Education, 771 S.W.2d 427 (Tenn. Ct. App. 1989).

Metropolitan Nashville and Davidson County School System v. Guest, 900 F. Supp. 905 (M.D. Tenn. 1995).

Ms. S. ex rel. L.S. v. Scarborough School Committee, 366 F. Supp.2d 98 (D. Me. 2005).

North Allegheny School District v. Gregory P., 687 A.2d 37 (Pa. Commw. Ct. 1996).

Ojai Unified School District v. Jackson, 4 F.3d 1467 (9th Cir. 1993).

Osborne, A. G. (1999). Supreme Court rules that schools must provide full-time nursing services for medically fragile students. *Education Law Reporter, 136,* 1–14.

Osborne, A. G., & Battaglino, L. (1996). Eligibility of students with disabilities for sports: Implications for policy. *Education Law Reporter, 105,* 379–388.

Pace v. Bogulusa City School Board, 137 F. Supp.2d 711, (E.D. La. 2001), *affirmed* 325 F.3d 609 (5th Cir. 2003).

Papacoda v. State of Connecticut, 528 F. Supp. 68 (D. Conn. 1981).

Pinkerton v. Moye, 509 F. Supp. 107 (W.D. Va. 1981).

Polk v. Central Susquehanna Intermediate Unit 16, 853 F.2d 171 (3d Cir. 1988).

Rehabilitation Act, Section 504, 29 U.S.C. § 794 (1998).

Roslyn Union Free School District v. University of the State of New York, State Education Department, 711 N.Y.S.2d 582 (N.Y. App. Div. 2000).

Russo, C. J. (1999). *Cedar Rapids Community School District v. Garret F.:* School districts must pay for nursing services under the IDEA. *School Business Affairs, 65*(6), 35–38.

Russo, C. J., Osborne, A. G., & Borreca, E. A. (2006). *What's Changed? A side-by-side analysis of the 2006 and 1999 Part B regulations.* Horsham, PA: LRP Publications.

School Board of Pinellas County v. Smith, 537 So. 2d 168 (Fla. Dist. Ct. App. 1989).

Schuldt v. Mankato Independent School District No. 77, 937 F.2d 1357 (8th Cir. 1991).

Seals v. Loftis, 614 F. Supp. 302 (E.D. Tenn. 1985).

Sherman v. Mamaroneck Union Free School District, 340 F.3d 87 (2d Cir. 2003).

Sioux Falls School District v. Koupal, 526 N.W.2d 248 (S.D. 1994).

Skelly v. Brookfield LaGrange Park School District 95, 968 F. Supp. 385 (N.D. Ill. 1997).

Stacey G. v. Pasadena Independent School District, 547 F. Supp. 61(S.D. Tex. 1982), *vacated and remanded on other grounds* 695 F.2d 949 (5th Cir. 1983).

Taylor v. Honig, 910 F.2d 627 (9th Cir. 1990).

T.G. and P.G. v. Board of Education of Piscataway, 576 F. Supp. 420 (D.N.J. 1983).

Tice v. Botetourt County School Board, 908 F.2d 1200 (4th Cir. 1990).

Union School District v. Smith, 15 F.3d 1519 (9th Cir. 1994).

Wenkart, R. D. (2000). Juvenile offenders: Residential placement and special education. *Education Law Reporter, 144,* 1–13.

4

Due Process Procedures for Evaluation, Development of IEPs, and Placement

INTRODUCTION

The Individuals with Disabilities Education Act (IDEA) (2005) is unique to the extent that it provides an elaborate system of due process safeguards to ensure that students with disabilities are properly identified, evaluated, and placed according to its dictates (20 U.S.C. § 1415). The IDEA's safeguards are designed to make parents equal partners (and/or guardians) with school officials in the education of their children. Never before has the law afforded parents such explicit rights to safeguard the education of their children.

The IDEA requires school officials to work with parents to develop individualized education programs (IEPs) for all children in need of special education and related services (20 U.S.C. § 1414(d)). In fact, the IDEA's regulations make it clear that states, through local school officials, must provide parents of students with disabilities with opportunities to participate in the development of IEPs for their children (300 C.F.R. §§ 345.320–328).

Prior to the passage of the IDEA, school personnel typically made placement decisions for students with disabilities without considering either their wishes or those of their parents. Unfortunately, allowing school personnel to unilaterally make all placement decisions for students with disabilities, especially those who were difficult to educate, led to these students being excluded from many school activities. The IDEA and its regulations ensure that school officials cannot act without parental knowledge or informed parental consent prior to conducting evaluations (20 U.S.C. § 1414(a)(1)(d)(i)(I)) or making initial placements (34 C.F.R. § 300.300(a)(1)). Moreover, the IDEA makes it clear that parental consent for initial evaluations cannot be treated as consent for placements and receipt of special education and related services (20 U.S.C. § 1414(a)(1)(d)(i)(II)). The IDEA also requires prior written notice whenever school officials propose to or refuse to initiate changes after making original placements (20 U.S.C. § 1415(b)(3)).

> The importance of procedural compliance cannot be overemphasized because the U.S. Supreme Court ruled that an educational program is not appropriate unless it is developed according to the IDEA's procedures.

This chapter outlines the IDEA's due process mechanisms as they relate to the identification, evaluation, and placement of students with disabilities. The importance of procedural compliance cannot be overemphasized because the U.S. Supreme Court ruled that an educational program is not appropriate unless it is developed according to the IDEA's procedures (*Board of Education of the Hendrick Hudson Central School District v. Rowley*, 1982).

EVALUATION PROCEDURES

The IDEA, in an approach that makes it different from just about all other education-related laws, places an affirmative obligation on states, through local school boards and their officials, to establish procedures to ensure that all children with disabilities are properly identified and evaluated to determine whether they are entitled to receive special education and related services (20 U.S.C. § 1212(a)(3)(A)). This means that school officials must conduct full initial evaluations before providing students with special education and related services (20 U.S.C. § 1414(a)(1)(A)). Once students are identified as being in need of special education and related services, their IEPs must be reviewed at least annually (20 U.S.C. § 1414(d)(4)) and reevaluated at least once every three years unless their parents and local school officials agree that reevaluations are unnecessary (20 U.S.C. § 1414(a)(2)).

In light of ongoing difficulties with regard to the overrepresentation of minority students (Russo & Talbert-Johnson, 1997), the most recent revision of the IDEA included a new provision addressing the status of children based on race and ethnicity that is worth reviewing before turning to the substance of the law's evaluation procedures. The IDEA now requires states and local school systems to develop policies and procedures to prevent the overidentification or disproportionate representation by race and ethnicity of children with disabilities (20 U.S.C. §§ 1412(a)(24), 1418(d)(1)(A)(B)). In addition, this provision requires educators to record the number of students from minority groups in special education classes and to provide early intervention services for children in groups deemed to be overrepresented. In a related provision, the IDEA directs educators to examine data, including information that is disaggregated by race and ethnicity, to consider whether there are significant discrepancies in the rate of long-term suspensions and expulsions of students with disabilities (20 U.S.C. §§ 1412(a)(22)(A), 1418(d)(1)(C)). The IDEA further mandates that officials review, and if appropriate, revise, policies, procedures, and practices related to the implementation of IEPs; the law additionally requires educators to use positive behavioral interventions and supports as well as procedural safeguards to ensure that they comply with the law (20 U.S.C. § 1412(a)(22)(B)) in avoiding this problem.

According to the IDEA, school officials must complete evaluations of students who may have disabilities within 60 days of when they receive informed parental consent or within the parameters of state guidelines if states establish their own rules (20 U.S.C. §§ 1414(a)(1)(C)(i)(I), 1414(a)(1)(D)(i)(I); 34 C.F.R. 300.301(c)(1)). Depending on how state laws are worded, school officials may be required to conduct evaluations over summer vacation periods if necessary to complete them within the prescribed time limits. For instance, a federal trial court in Maryland, where state law required evaluations to be completed within 45 calendar days of referrals, reasoned that a school board violated a student's rights by not conducting an evaluation within that time frame (*Gerstmyer v. Howard County Public Schools*, 1994). The record indicated that the child's mother requested an evaluation in May, but school officials informed her that they could not complete it over the summer months.

The IDEA's 60-day rule does not apply if "the parent of a child repeatedly fails or refuses to produce the child for the evaluation" (20 U.S.C. § 1414(a)(1)(C)(ii)(II)). Even if a parent refuses to respond to a request to provide consent for an initial evaluation or to services, educational officials may still continue with such an evaluation as long as they follow the procedures outlined in the IDEA (20 U.S.C. § 1414(a)(1)(D)(ii)(I), (II)). In another clarification, a new regulation specifies that generalized screenings that educators perform for instructional purposes, such as at the beginning of terms to evaluate the ability of students in classes, cannot be considered evaluations for special education and related services (34 C.F.R. § 300.303).

In conducting evaluations, school officials must "use a variety of assessment tools and strategies to gather relevant functional, developmental, and academic information, including information provided by the parent" (20 U.S.C. § 1414(b)(2)(A)), examining students "in all areas of suspected disability" (20 U.S.C. § 1414(b)(3)(B)) that may assist in determining whether they are eligible for IDEA services. Put another way, since the evaluation process needs to be individualized and multidisciplinary, no single procedure can be the sole criterion for determining eligibility or placement (34 C.F.R. § 300.304(b)(2)). More specifically, all testing and evaluation materials and procedures must be

> selected and administered so as not to be discriminatory on a racial or cultural basis; are provided and administered in the language and form most likely to yield accurate information on what the child knows and can do academically, developmentally, and functionally, unless it is not feasible to so provide or administer; are used for purposes for which the assessments or measures are valid and reliable; are administered by trained and knowledgeable personnel; and are administered in accordance with any instructions provided by the producer of such assessments. (20 U.S.C. § 1414(b)(3)(A)(i)-(v))

If parents are dissatisfied with the results of assessments, they have the right to obtain independent evaluations of their children (20 U.S.C. § 1415(b)(1); 34 C.F.R. §§ 300.502(b)(1), (2)). Parents do not need to notify school board officials that they are seeking independent evaluations (*Raymond S. v. Ramirez*, 1996; *Warren G. v. Cumberland County School District*, 1999). School board officials can challenge independent evaluations in attempts to show that their own evaluations were correct. If school boards succeed in proving that their evaluations were correct, then they do not have to pay for independent evaluations (*Evanston Community Consolidated School Dist. Number 65 v. Michael M.*, 2004; *Hudson v. Wilson*, 1987).

Independent evaluations are to be conducted at public expense if parents can demonstrate that the initial evaluations completed by their school boards were inappropriate. If due process hearing officers agree that evaluations were appropriate, parents retain the right to independent evaluations, but not at public expense (34 C.F.R. § 300.502(b)(3)). School officials may ask parents why they are seeking independent evaluations, but cannot require them to provide explanations; in addition, this section forbids officials unreasonably delaying either providing evaluations at public expense or filing requests for due process hearings to defend their public evaluations (34 C.F.R. § 300.502(b)(4)).

If parents seek independent evaluations, the onus is on school board officials to request hearings to demonstrate that the board's evaluations were appropriate or that the parents' independent evaluations were not appropriate in order to avoid paying for independent evaluations (*Evans v. District No. 17, Douglas County,* 1988). Ultimately, parents are entitled to public payment for only one independent evaluation (34 C.F.R. § 300.502(b)(5)); *Board of Education of Murphysboro Community Unit School District No. 186 v. Illinois State Board of Education,* 1994). In a variation of this issue, the federal trial court in Connecticut explained that parents were not entitled to reimbursement for an independent evaluation where they agreed that an initial review was comprehensive and sought a second assessment merely to have another source of information (*R.L. ex rel. Mr. L. v. Plainville Board of Education,* 2005).

When parents obtain independent evaluations at their own expense, school officials must take them into consideration as long as they meet district assessment criteria (34 C.F.R. § 300.502(b)(1)). Requiring school officials to consider the results of independent evaluations does not mean that they must adopt the recommendations of independent evaluators (34 C.F.R. § 300.502(c)(1)).

In a dispute over an independent evaluation, the First Circuit affirmed that the requirement that school officials consider the content of such assessments did not mean that an IEP team had to engage in a substantive discussion of its findings (*G.D. v. Westmoreland School District,* 1991). Similarly, the federal trial court in Connecticut indicated that the IDEA does not require school officials to accept the recommendations of independent evaluations or that these assessments be accorded any particular weight (*T.S. v. Ridgefield Board of Education,* 1992, 1993). The Second Circuit, in affirming that the plain meaning of the word *consider* is to reflect on or think about with care, did not require a board to comply with a hearing officer's recommendations. These cases reveal that school boards satisfy the IDEA's requirement that they consider independent evaluations as long as they review their results at IEP conferences. Once completed, either party may present the results of parentally initiated evaluations at due process hearings over the placement of children (34 C.F.R. § 300.502(c)(2)).

> IEPs can be invalidated if they are not based on proper evaluations of children. Assessments must address all areas of suspected disabilities.

The importance of the evaluation process is reflected in the fact that hearing officers and courts can invalidate IEPs if they are not based on proper evaluations. One federal trial court held that a proposed IEP for a child who was deaf was inappropriate because school board personnel failed to follow proper evaluation procedures (*Bonadonna v. Cooperman,* 1985). The court discovered that the school board's evaluation team based its conclusions regarding placement on simple observations. The court pointed out that school officials acted improperly since they did not use validated instruments to measure the child's aptitude and the procedures that they used tended to be biased against students with hearing impairments. The court also acknowledged that board officials did not include an expert on the education of students with hearing impairments on the evaluation team. Subsequently, the Ninth Circuit interpreted the IDEA as requiring evaluations to be completed by multidisciplinary teams including at least one person with knowledge in the suspected area of disability (*Seattle School District No. 1 v. B.S.*, 1996). In a dispute from Kansas, the Tenth Circuit affirmed that an evaluation by a multidisciplinary team that included assessments in all areas of suspected disability met the IDEA's requirements (*Logue v. Shawnee Mission Public School Unified School District No. 512*, 1997, 1998).

In a very early case involving the education of students with emotional problems causing acting out and aggressive behavior, a federal trial court found that their being placed in special education was improperly based on vague criteria that tended to discriminate against minorities (*Lora v. Board of Education of the City of New York*, 1978, 1980, 1984). The court observed that once the students were placed they were not reevaluated as mandated by state and federal law. In seeking to remedy the situation, the parties implemented a court-approved nondiscriminatory assessment procedure.

School personnel are not required to leave states in order to evaluate students whose parents unilaterally place their children in out-of-state facilities. Where parents enrolled their child in an out-of-state residential school without their school board's knowledge or consent, a federal trial court decided that the board had the right to evaluate the student whose parents requested that it pay tuition for the out-of-state residential school. At the same time, the court made it clear that officials were not required to leave the state to evaluate the child (*Lenhoff v. Farmington Public Schools*, 1988). More recently, the Seventh Circuit affirmed that school personnel were not required to leave a state to evaluate a student (*Patricia P. v. Board of Education of Oak Park and River Forest High School District No. 200*, 1998, 2000).

As noted, the IDEA requires that students be evaluated before they can be initially placed in special education (20 U.S.C. § 1414(d)(4)) and reevaluated at least once every three years unless their parents and local school officials agree that reevaluations are unnecessary (20 U.S.C. § 1414(a)(2)). When dealing with disputes of this nature, the Fifth and Seventh Circuits agreed that school board officials may insist on evaluating students using their own personnel rather than be forced to rely on outside evaluations (*Andress v. Cleveland Independent School District*, 1995; *Johnson v. Duneland School Corporation*, 1996; *Patricia P. v. Board of Education of Oak Park and River Forest High School District No. 200*, 1998, 2000). In *Andress*, the case from the Fifth Circuit, when the parents, acting on recommendations from the child's physician, refused to allow the school board to evaluate the student but provided several third-party evaluations, officials responded that the evaluations did not meet state criteria. Reversing an earlier judgment in favor of the parents, the court agreed with board officials that the evaluation was inappropriate.

Figure 4.1   Steps in the Evaluation and Placement Process

- Teachers, counselors, principals, parents, or other knowledgeable persons can refer students who are suspected of having disabilities and being in need of special education.
- School officials notify parents or guardians that their children have been referred; this notice must also include the reasons for the referral.
- School officials request consent to conduct evaluations.
- After obtaining consent, educators schedule and complete evaluations by multidisciplinary teams. Students must be assessed in all areas of suspected disabilities.
- School officials convene a meeting to discuss the results of the evaluation; make a determination as to whether students need special education and related services; and, if so, develop IEPs.
- IEP teams, including the parents or guardians of students with disabilities, should develop IEPs. The parents or guardians may accept or reject proposed IEPs, formulate alternative IEPs, or postpone decisions while seeking independent evaluations of their children.
- If parents or guardians accept IEPs, they must be implemented immediately.
- If parents or guardians reject IEPs, the IDEA's dispute resolution procedures become operative. IEPs are then implemented on resolution of the dispute(s).
- School officials must ensure that all IEPs are reviewed annually and students are reevaluated at least every three years.

Conversely, as reflected by a case from the nation's capitol, local board officials may not be able to insist on conducting their own assessments if they would duplicate tests that were administered by outside evaluators (*Holland v. District of Columbia*, 1995). This means that educators may rely on outside evaluations or tests conducted by personnel from other school districts as long as the information is still relevant (*Poolaw v. Bishop*, 1995; *Briley v. Board of Education of Baltimore County*, 1999; *Pitchford ex. rel M. v. Salem-Keizer School District No. 24J*, 2001).

DEVELOPMENT OF INDIVIDUALIZED EDUCATION PROGRAMS

The IDEA defines IEPs as written statements for each child with disabilities that are developed, reviewed, and revised in accordance with its dictates. IEPs must contain eight major elements. First, IEPs must include statements about students' current level of academic achievement and functional performance (20 U.S.C. § 1414(d)(1)(A)(i)(I)). Second, IEPs must contain measurable annual goals for children, including academic and functional goals (20 U.S.C. § 1414(d)(1)(A)(i)(II)). Third, IEPs must provide descriptions of how officials will measure the progress that children make toward meeting their annual goals and when such periodic reports are to be provided, as well as statements of special education and related services and supplementary aids and services, based on peer-reviewed research to the extent practicable (20 U.S.C. § 1414(d)(1)(A)(i)(III)).

Fourth, IEPs must include statements specifying what special education, related services, and supplementary aids and services children will receive (20 U.S.C. § 1414(d)(1)(A)(i)(IV)). Fifth, IEPs must contain explanations of the extent, if any, to which children will not participate in regular classes with peers who are not disabled (20 U.S.C. § 1414(d)(1) (A)(i)(V)). Sixth, IEPs must include information detailing individual appropriate accommodations that are necessary to measure the academic achievement and functional performance of students on state and district assessments (20 U.S.C. § 1414(d)(1)(A)(i)(VI)). Seventh, IEPs must identify the projected date of initiation and duration of special education services that children are to receive (20 U.S.C. § 1414(d)(1)(A)(i)(VII)). Eighth, IEPs, starting no later than the first IEPs that will be in effect for students who are 16 years old, must include a statement of appropriate measurable postsecondary education goals, to be updated annually, and transition services; this also requires that at least one year before children reach the age of majority they must be provided with notice of the rights that will transfer to them (such as rights associated with their educational records) on reaching the age of majority (20 U.S.C. § 1414(d)(1)(A)(i)(VIII)).

The 2005 IDEA includes two significant changes that have an impact on the formation of IEPs. First, the IDEA no longer specifies the need for benchmarks and short-term objectives for children with disabilities other than those who take alternate assessments aligned to alternate achievement standards (20 U.S.C. § 1414(d)(1)(A)(I)). Even so, educators should be aware that state law may still require benchmarks and short-term objectives. Second, the IDEA allows up to 15 states to pilot comprehensive multiyear IEPs that do not exceed three years and are designed to coincide with natural transition points in a child's education (20 U.S.C. § 1414(d) (5)(A)). For example, if children are scheduled to move to high schools for ninth grade, their IEP teams can develop three-year IEPs while they are in sixth grade. Of course, nothing in this new provision prevents parents or school officials from requesting shorter IEPs or earlier reviews if they think that doing so is in the best interests of children.

Two related changes accompany the proposed three-year IEP provision. The first addition seeks to help school officials to reduce the significant amount of paperwork associated with the delivery of special education services (20 U.S.C. §§ 1400(c)(5)(G), 1400(c)(9)). This change permits up to 15 states to pilot paperwork-reduction plans to reduce the burden on teachers, administrators, and related service providers (20 U.S.C. § 1414(d)(5)(B)(i)). The second enhancement complements the paperwork reduction provisions. This change directs the Secretary of Education to provide copies of model forms for filing due process complaints in accord with the IDEA's provisions (20 U.S.C. § 1417(e); 34 C.F.R. § 300.509(a)). Parents and school officials may use other forms as long as they meet the requirements of filing due process complaint outlined elsewhere in the regulations (34 C.F.R. § 300.509(b)).

It almost goes without saying that teams must develop IEPs before they can provide eligible children with special education and related services (34 C.F.R. § 300.323(a)). Once initial IEPs are developed, school personnel must implement them "as soon as possible" after the meetings at which they were developed are completed (34 C.F.R. § 300.323(c)(2)). All IEPs must be reviewed at least annually (20 U.S.C. § 1414(d)(4)(A)(i)), and children must be fully reevaluated at least every three years unless parents and local school officials agree that doing so is unnecessary (20 U.S.C. § 1414(a)(2)(B)(ii)).

IEPs must be developed at meetings that include a wide variety of people. IEP teams must include the parents of children with disabilities; at least one of a student's regular education teachers if the student is in, or will be participating in, regular education; at least one special education teacher or, if appropriate, one special education provider; a representative of the school system who is qualified to provide or supervise the delivery of special education and knowledgeable about general education, the school system's resources, and evaluation procedures (typically this is a director of special education or an assistant superintendent for students); an individual who can interpret the instructional implications of evaluation results; other individuals, at the discretion of parents or school officials, who are knowledgeable or have special expertise concerning the student(s) at issue; and, when appropriate, the children (34 C.F.R. § 300.321(a)).

Four recent cases reached differing results about the composition of IEP teams. The Ninth Circuit held that the failure of a school system in Washington to include a regular education teacher on a child's IEP team constituted a significant violation of the IDEA since the child was going to spend time in a regular education setting (*M.L. v. Federal Way School District*, 2005a, 2005b). In like manner, a federal trial court in New York was of the opinion that a school board failed to comply with the IDEA's procedural requirements when it did not include a representative, either by telephone or in person, from its recommended therapeutic placement for a child at the child's IEP meeting (*Werner v. Clarksville Central School District*, 2005).

On the other hand, the Fourth Circuit affirmed that it was unnecessary for a school board in North Carolina to have a regular education teacher at an IEP meeting since the student was not being considered for a placement in regular education (*Cone v. Randolph County Schools*, 2004, 2005). Similarly, the federal court in Kansas ruled that a school board did not violate the IDEA by excluding a regular education teacher from a child's IEP team because he was not going to spend any time in a regular education setting (*Johnson ex rel. Johnson v. Olathe District Schools Unified School District. No. 233, Special Services Division*, 2003).

IEP meetings must take place within 30 calendar days of findings that children require special education and related services (34 C.F.R. § 300.323(c)(1)). School boards are required to take steps to ensure the participation of at least one of a student's parents at IEP meetings (34 C.F.R. § 300.322(a)). If students attend private schools, then representatives of the private schools should be present at IEP conferences (34 C.F.R. § 300.325).

An overriding theme of the IDEA is that IEPs and educational programs for students with disabilities must be individualized. This means that IEPs should be designed according to the unique characteristics of individual children, taking into consideration their strengths and weaknesses. Programs must be developed to fit individual children. Courts agree that IEPs that are not individualized are inappropriate. For instance, a federal court ruled that an IEP that did not contain academic objectives and methods of evaluation addressing the student's unique needs and abilities was inappropriate (*Chris D. v. Montgomery County Board of Education*, 1990). Another court criticized an IEP that was not specific to the child since it was assembled using portions of IEPs that were developed for other students (*Gerstmyer v. Howard County Public Schools*, 1994).

> Parental input into the IEP process cannot be minimized. One of the IDEA's unique features is that it provides for parental participation. Parents cannot simply be given token opportunities for participation. Their input into the process has to be genuine.

Parental input into the IEP process cannot be minimized. One of the IDEA's unique features is that it provides for parental participation. Parents cannot simply be given token opportunities for participation since their input into the process has to be genuine. The Ninth Circuit affirmed that an IEP that was developed without input from a student's parents and his teacher at his private school was invalid (*W.G. and B.G. v. Board of Trustees of Target Range School District No. 23, Missoula, Montana*, 1991, 1992). The court explained that procedural violations that infringe on the parents' opportunity to participate in the formulation of IEPs result in the denial of a free appropriate public education (FAPE). Similarly, a federal trial court reasoned that the failure of public school officials to attend an IEP meeting that took place at a private school in which a student was enrolled rendered their proposed placement invalid (*Smith v. Henson*, 1992).

Informal contacts between parents and school officials do not fully meet the IDEA's parental participation requirements. A court in Pennsylvania wrote that impromptu meetings between a student's mother and school officials did not satisfy the IDEA's requirement of affording parents the opportunity to participate in the development of an IEP for their child (*Big Beaver Falls Area School District v. Jackson*, 1992). According to the Eighth Circuit, however, school officials cannot be faulted if the parents refuse to participate in discussions about placement options (*Blackmon v. Springfield R-XII School District*, 1999).

A trial court in Michigan explained that school districts are required to ensure, if possible, that a child's teachers participate in IEP meetings before drastic changes in placements occur (*Brimmer v. Traverse City Area Public Schools*, 1994). The court maintained that simply inviting teachers to attend IEP meetings did not fulfill that duty since they had to be active participants. Yet, a trial court in Tennessee asserted that the failure of a child's teacher to attend an IEP meeting was harmless in view of the fact that persons knowledgeable about the student were present (*Daugherty v. Hamilton County Schools*, 1998). In a similar case, the federal trial court in Maryland noted that a school board's failure to include representatives from the treatment center a student attended in an IEP conference was not a serious procedural violation because data that were obtained from the treatment center were used in developing the child's IEP (*Briley v. Board of Education of Baltimore County*, 1999). The Sixth Circuit affirmed that as long as a school board included persons knowledgeable about placement options on an IEP team, it was not required to include an expert in the parents' preferred methodology (*Dong v. Board of Education of the Rochester Community Schools*, 1999). Even so, failure to include a knowledgeable school board representative on an IEP team can be fatal to its recommended program if the omission has the effect of denying parents the opportunity to discuss available resources for their children (*Pitchford ex rel. M. v. Salem-Keizer School District No. 24J*, 2001).

IEPs do not have to be written perfectly in order to pass judicial review. Courts generally allow some flaws as long as they do not compromise the appropriateness of a student's educational program. Courts are ordinarily more forgiving if the missing information was available or provided in another form. For example, the Sixth Circuit affirmed that an IEP that did not specifically contain current levels of performance or the objective criteria for evaluating progress was appropriate because the disputed information was known to all concerned (*Doe v. Defendant I*, 1990). The court was unwilling to exalt form over substance, declaring that the emphasis on procedural safeguards referred to the process by which the IEP was developed, not the myriad technical items that should have been included in the written document. Similarly, the federal trial court in Delaware recognized that even though an IEP had flaws, they did not rise to the level of a violation since they did not hamper the parents' opportunity to participate in its development (*Coale v. State Department of Education*, 2001). Another federal trial court rejected parental contentions to the contrary, decreeing that because an IEP contained present levels of performance and objective evaluation criteria and schedules, it was not defective (*French v. Omaha Public Schools*, 1991).

On the other hand, a federal trial court in California invalidated an IEP that failed to address all areas of a student's disabilities and that contained no statement of the specific services to be provided (*Russell v. Jefferson*, 1985). The court thought that an IEP with those defects would have compromised the integrity of the student's educational program. Similarly, a trial court in New York commented that an IEP containing vague information that did not establish a student's needs with precision was insufficient (*Evans v. Board of Education of the Rhinebeck Central School District*, 1996).

IEPs containing all of the required elements, including specific information, pass judicial muster. By way of illustration, in two separate cases from Kansas, both of which the Tenth Circuit affirmed, the federal trial court observed that IEPs including specific statements of students' present levels of functioning, annual goals adequately describing their anticipated educational performances, measurable short-term objectives, and clearly set criteria for measuring their progress met all federal and state requirements (*Logue v. Shawnee Mission Public School Unified School District No. 512*, 1997, 1998; *O'Toole v. Olathe District Schools Unified School District No. 233*, 1997, 1998). Along the same lines, a federal trial court in Michigan was convinced that an IEP containing a series of tables divided into each academic subject and including short-term objectives, performance criteria, evaluation procedures, and schedules for evaluation was adequate (*Kuszewski v. Chippewa Valley Schools*, 2001).

Another major doctrine of the IDEA is that the placement of children must be based on IEPs, not the other way around. In other words, placements must be developed to fit the unique, individual needs of students rather than the wishes of educators. Courts have invalidated the practice of writing IEPs to fit placements. The Fourth Circuit affirmed that school officials violated the IDEA when they chose to place a student in a county facility, then wrote an IEP to carry out their decision (*Spielberg v. Henrico County Public Schools*, 1988). Moreover, the federal trial court in Connecticut concluded that school board officials violated the IDEA when they proposed a placement without first evaluating a child or writing an IEP (*P.J. v. State of Connecticut Board of Education*, 1992). In like manner, a trial court in New York remarked that school officials who placed a student in a program before they had an IEP in effect violated the IDEA (*Evans v. Board of Education of the Rhinebeck Central School District*, 1996). Conversely, the First Circuit affirmed that school board officials who considered various options along a continuum from least to most restrictive did not finalize a student's placement prior to formulating his IEP (*G.D. v. Westmoreland School District*, 1991).

Notwithstanding disputes over whether school officials made placement decisions in advance, nothing in the IDEA prevents educators from presenting draft IEPs at conferences for the purpose of discussion. The federal trial court in Rhode Island ascertained that presenting parents with a completed IEP at a conference was not an indication that they were denied a meaningful opportunity to participate in its development (*Scituate School Committee v. Robert B.*, 1985, 1986). Subsequently, the First Circuit affirmed that it is acceptable for one person to draft an IEP as long as the parents and other members of an IEP team have the opportunity to provide input into its contents (*Hampton School District v. Dobrowolski*, 1992). Similarly, the Eighth Circuit agreed that nothing in the IDEA or its regulations prohibits school personnel from coming to IEP meetings with tentative recommendations (*Blackmon v. Springfield R-XII School District*, 1999). In another dispute, the Third Circuit affirmed that a draft IEP did not violate the IDEA's parental participation requirement where there was evidence that the parents made suggestions for changes, some of which were incorporated into its final version (*Fuhrmann v. East Hanover Board of Education*, 1993). More recently, the federal trial court in South Carolina reached the same outcome, noting that nothing in the IDEA prevented school officials from creating a draft IEP prior to meeting with parents, as long as parents had the opportunity to provide meaningful input in the process (*Tracy v. Beaufort County Board of Education*, 2004).

Courts frown on attempts by school officials to develop IEPs beforehand and force them on parents without any meaningful discussion of the educational needs of their children. For instance, a federal trial court in Virginia ruled that while school officials must come to IEP conferences with open minds, this did not mean that they had to arrive with blank minds (*Doyle v. Arlington County School Board*, 1992). The court emphasized that even though school board officials cannot finalize placement decisions before IEP meetings, they should give thought to them prior to the meetings. The court made it clear that school board representatives must remain receptive to all parental concerns. In like fashion, the Sixth Circuit ruled that educators could not predetermine a child's placement in an IEP where doing so prevented his parents from having a meaningful opportunity to participate in its development (*Deal v. Hamilton County Board of Education*, 2004, 2005).

School boards sometimes develop interim IEPs for students in order to cover short periods of time while preparing permanent IEPs. This may occur so that children can be placed in special education programs while undergoing evaluations or to cover the short periods of time during which teams prepare permanent IEPs. Yet, such a practice is not consistent with the IDEA. A federal trial court in Alabama asserted that the IDEA does not contain provisions for interim IEPs (*Myles S. v. Montgomery County Board of Education*, 1993). The court pointed out that school boards are required to convene meetings to develop IEPs prior to the beginning of each school year, even if this means gathering over the summer. The federal trial court in Maryland insisted that school board personnel must meet during summer months, if necessary, to develop IEPs within 30 days of the determination that students need special education and related services (*Gerstmyer v. Howard County Public Schools*, 1994).

An exception may exist when students move from one district to another and the board in the latter is unable to implement their existing IEPs immediately. Under these circumstances, a court may allow a temporary placement until the new board can develop a permanent IEP (*Ms. S. ex rel. G. v. Vashon Island School District*, 2003).

The 2004 IDEA amendments make a distinction between students who transfer within a state and those who transfer from another state. When students transfer within a state, receiving school boards must provide services that are comparable to those in students' previous IEPs until such time as school officials either adopt the previous IEPs or develop new IEPs (20 U.S.C. § 1414(d)(2)(C)(i)(I)). On the other hand, when students transfer to districts in other states, the new school boards must provide services comparable to those in the students' previous IEPs until such time as officials decide whether it is necessary to conduct evaluations and develop new IEPs (20 U.S.C. § 1414(d)(2)(C)(i)(II)). Although the difference is slight, this provision recognizes that students who were eligible for services in one state may not necessarily be eligible in another due to differing state standards.

As noted earlier, individualized education programs for students with disabilities must be reviewed and revised, if necessary, at least annually (20 U.S.C. § 1414(d)(4)(A)(i)). IEP teams should provide reviews and revisions more frequently if they are needed. Procedures for reviewing and amending IEPs generally are similar to those for developing initial IEPs. All of the IDEA's regulations' procedural and notification rights apply to meetings convened to review and possibly revise IEPs (34 C.F.R. § 300.324(b)). Naturally, parents must be given the opportunity to provide input into the revision process, just as with initial IEPs.

IEPs should be reviewed if parents express any dissatisfaction with the educational programs of their children. To this end, one court was of the view that a mother's request for a due process hearing put her school board on notice that she was dissatisfied with her daughter's placement status and that officials were obligated to review and possibly revise the child's IEP (*Edwards-White v. District of Columbia*, 1992). In a case that reached the opposite result, the First Circuit affirmed that a school board had no obligation to review and revise an IEP for a student whose parents unilaterally placed him in a private school (*Amann v. Stow School System*, 1992).

There is a limit to the number of times a school board must review a child's IEP. The federal trial court in Connecticut decreed that school officials were justified in refusing to conduct another IEP team meeting when they had convened a large number of meetings in the previous six months and all of the issues raised by the child's guardian had already been discussed and investigated (*Lillbask ex rel. Mauclaire v. Sergi*, 2000).

Although new IEPs should generally be developed if the placements of children are to change, this step is not always necessary. The Ninth Circuit acknowledged that school board officials were not required to write a new IEP for a student who was being transferred temporarily to an off-campus special education program for disciplinary reasons (*Clyde K. v. Puyallup School District No. 3*, 1994). The court observed that the student's IEP could have been fully implemented in the new setting.

PARENTAL RIGHTS

When it enacted the IDEA, Congress intended to make parents partners in the development of appropriate educational programs for their children, whether at school or at home (20 U.S.C. § 1400(c)(5)(B)). In order to accomplish this goal, Congress granted parents unprecedented substantial procedural due process rights. Among the far-reaching rights that the IDEA affords parents is

> an opportunity for the parents of a child with a disability to examine all records relating to such child and to participate in meetings with respect to the identification, evaluation, and educational placement of the child, and the provision of a free appropriate public education to such child, and to obtain an independent educational evaluation of the child. (20 U.S.C. § 1415(b)(1))

In an important addition to the law, the 2004 version of the IDEA expanded the definition of parent. According to the IDEA, the term *parent* now means

> (A) a natural, adoptive, or foster parent of a child (unless a foster parent is prohibited by State law from serving as a parent);
> (B) a guardian (but not the State if the child is a ward of the State);
> (C) an individual acting in the place of a natural or adoptive parent (including a grandparent, stepparent, or other relative) with whom the child lives, or an individual who is legally responsible for the child's welfare; or
> (D) except as used in sections 1415(b)(2) of this title and 1439(a)(5) of this title, an individual assigned under either of those sections to be a surrogate parent. (20 U.S.C. § 1402(23))

The courts recognize the importance Congress placed on parental participation. Accordingly, case law makes it clear that school officials must offer parents opportunities to participate meaningfully in the development of IEPs for their children. In one such case, the Sixth Circuit affirmed that part of an earlier order that found that school officials violated the rights of a child and his parents by having predetermined not to offer him intensive applied behavioral analysis (*Deal v. Hamilton County*, 2004, 2005). The Fifth Circuit, however, explained that the parental right to provide meaningful input does not grant parents veto power over the decisions of IEP teams or the right to dictate outcomes (*White ex rel. White v. Ascension Parish School Board*, 2003).

At the same time, while courts have not insisted on absolute compliance with the letter of the law regarding parental rights, they have been diligent in upholding the rights of parents in the special education process. The courts typically allow school board proposals to stand if procedural violations do not prejudice the process in any way and do not result in a detriment to students, but they do not tolerate egregious violations of parental rights (Osborne, 1993).

Parental Notification

It almost goes without saying that parents cannot exercise rights of which they are unaware. The IDEA stipulates that school boards must inform parents fully of their rights once per year (20 U.S.C. § 1415(d)(1)(A); 34 C.F.R. § 300.504(a)). In addition, the IDEA directs school officials to notify parents on the initial referrals or their first request for evaluations of their children, on the first occurrence when they file IDEA-related complaints, and when they make such a request (20 U.S.C. § 1415(d)(1)(A); 34 C.F.R. § 300.504(a)). In a new provision, the 2004 IDEA and its regulations permit school systems to place notice of the procedural safeguards on their Web sites (20 U.S.C. § 1415(d)(B); 34 C.F.R. § 300.504(b)).

Insofar as the failure of school officials to inform parents of their rights has limited parents' ability to participate in the education of their children, this has led to significant amounts of litigation. Case law recognizes that the purpose of notifying parents of their rights is to provide them with sufficient information to protect their rights, allow them to make informed judgments, and fully participate in due process hearings, if necessary (*Kroot v. District of Columbia*, 1992).

> The purpose of notifying parents of their rights is to provide them with sufficient information to protect those rights, allow them to make informed judgment, and fully participate in due process hearings, if necessary.

The IDEA's regulations identify seven key elements that parental notice must contain. First, notice must describe the action that school officials have proposed or refused to initiate. Second, notice must explain why officials proposed to or refused to act. Third, notice must describe each evaluation, procedure, assessment, record, or report that officials used as a basis for their proposed or refused action. Fourth, notice must include a reminder that parents retain their procedural safeguards. Fifth, notice must include sources for parents to contact if they need assistance in understanding the contents of the notice. Sixth, notice must describe the other options that officials considered and the reasons why they were not pursued. Seventh, notice must be in a language that is understandable to the general public and in the parents' native language unless it is otherwise clearly not feasible to do so. If the native language or other mode of parental communication is not a written language, educational officials must ensure that notice is translated orally or by other means to parents in their native language or other mode of communication, that the parents understand the notice, and that there is written evidence that educators satisfied these requirements (34 C.F.R. § 300.503(b)).

A federal trial court in Illinois declared that the school board's failure to notify a student's parents about meetings at which their son's educational placement was discussed, about their right to review psychological evaluations, and the right to obtain an independent evaluation violated the IDEA (*Max M. v. Thompson*, 1983). The court posited that these procedural violations effectively denied the parents the opportunity to participate in the development of their child's IEP. In another case, the Fourth Circuit affirmed that a school board's failure to notify parents of their rights resulted in the failure to provide a FAPE under *Rowley* (*Hall v. Vance County Board of Education*, 1985). The lower court had discovered that school board officials consistently failed to comply with federal and state statutes requiring them to notify the parents of their rights. The appellate panel reasoned that this failure relegated parental participation to little more than acquiescence to the actions of school officials. More recently, the Sixth Circuit ruled that school officials in Tennessee did not violate a mother's rights when they conferred on an assessment report since she participated fully in the IEP process and was actively involved in evaluating her daughter's eligibility for IDEA services (*N.L. ex rel. Mrs. C. v. Knox County Schools*, 2003).

The purpose of the IDEA's notice requirements is to provide parents with the information necessary to allow them to participate actively in the educational planning process for their children. When parents in the District of Columbia challenged the notice provided by their school board, a federal trial court observed that it was statutorily sufficient (*Smith v. Squillacote*, 1992). The court was satisfied that the notices informed parents about the board's proposed placements for their child and why school officials selected that placement. The court remarked that the information that officials supplied adequately provided the parents with the opportunity to have a meaningful role in the decision-making process and to draw informed conclusions about whether the proposed placement would have conferred an appropriate education on their child. Conversely, the federal trial court in Arizona contended that notice that did not detail the reasons for a school board's proposed action was insufficient (*Magyar v. Tucson Unified School District*, 1997).

Naturally, misleading notice is problematic for school boards. The federal trial court for the District of Columbia indicated that misleading notice violated the procedural rights of parents under the IDEA (*Smith v. Henson*, 1992). The court conceded that although school officials notified the parents that they had 15 days to request a due process hearing, this action was inappropriate because the IDEA did not authorize them to impose such a unilateral time limitation.

A case from Maryland illustrates the principle that notice must be kept up to date. On discovering that school board officials provided parents with an outdated booklet addressing procedural safeguards that did not reflect changes in federal and state law, the federal trial court decreed that it violated the IDEA (*Carnwath v. Board of Education of Anne Arundel County*, 1998). The court decided that the fact that the parents' attorney was aware of those changes did not relieve the board of its obligation to provide them with adequate, up-to-date notice.

Effect of Procedural Errors

Procedural errors on the part of school officials do not necessarily render their recommendations concerning IEPs inappropriate. The Supreme Court, in *Board of Education of the Hendrick Hudson Central School District v. Rowley* (1982), held that to be appropriate, IEPs must be developed in accordance with the procedures outlined in the IDEA. The courts examined the effect of violations to evaluate whether, and to what extent, they interfered with the development of the IEPs for students. If school officials violate the letter of the law but their errors do not interfere with parental participation in the IEP process, courts generally do not annul IEPs. If violations prevent active parental participation in the development of IEPs, though, these errors are generally sufficient to have IEPs invalidated.

Egregious disregard for the IDEA's basic provisions provides courts with sufficient bases to invalidate proposed IEPs. The Fourth Circuit affirmed that a school board that failed both to conduct an annual review of a student's program as required by law and to involve his parents in the IEP process, did not provide an appropriate education (*Board of Education of the County of Caball v. Dienelt*, 1988).

The Sixth Circuit was of the opinion that strict compliance with the IDEA's procedural safeguards is the best way to ensure that its substantive provisions are enforced (*Thomas v. Cincinnati Board of Education*, 1990). Despite this pronouncement, the court did not think that the failure of school officials to provide parents with written notice was prejudicial because the student's mother received adequate oral notice and participated in the IEP conference. Similarly, a federal trial court in New York asserted that a school board's violation of the letter of the law did not prejudice a student or his parents in any way because the parents were involved in planning and executing their child's IEP (*Hiller v. Board of Education of Brunswick Central School District,* 1990). Further, the Eleventh Circuit explained that deficiencies in the notices provided to parents that had no impact on their full and effective participation in the IEP process caused no harm (*Doe v. Alabama State Department of Education,* 1990). In each of these cases, the courts agreed that since the procedural errors did not result in substantive deprivations, they were insufficient to render otherwise appropriate IEPs invalid.

The IEP Conference

IEP conferences provide parents with the best opportunity to partici-pate in the development of appropriate educational programs for their children. At these meetings, team members share evaluation results, develop IEPs, and make placement decisions. Prior to these conferences, parents may have attended meetings where they engaged in discussions of their child's school problems and may have provided information about the child. These earlier meetings aside, IEP conferences are where most decisions about the future education of students are made.

As an initial matter, school officials must take steps to ensure that at least one of a student's parents is present at IEP conferences (34 C.F.R. § 300.322(a)). Further, while school officials are required to notify parents about any meetings in which the IEPs or placements of their children are to be discussed, this does not mean that they must be notified each and every time school personnel confer. In one such case, the Fifth Circuit affirmed that school board officials were not required to notify a child's parents every time one of his teachers discussed his progress with an administrator (*Buser v. Corpus Christi Independent School District,* 1995).

Parental participation is meaningless if parents do not understand the proceedings of IEP conferences. School officials should therefore take the necessary steps to ensure that parents understand what is taking place at IEP meetings. For example, the Second Circuit affirmed that part of an ear-lier order directing school officials to provide sign language interpreters so that parents who were hearing impaired could participate in meetings and conferences that were important to the education of their non-hearing-impaired children. Even though neither of the children in this case needed special education services, and the case was resolved under Section 504 of the Rehabilitation Act (1973), the legal principles are applicable for IEP meetings (*Rothschild v. Grottenthaler,* 1990).

In helping parents to understand IEP meetings and other proceedings, educators may have to go the proverbial "extra mile." In two separate cases, the federal trial court in Connecticut ascertained that parents had the right to tape-record IEP conferences. In the first suit, the court noted that insofar as the child's mother had limited English proficiency, her request to tape-record the proceedings so that she could better understand and follow them was reasonable (*E.H. and H.H. v. Tirozzi*, 1990). In the second case, the court allowed the child's mother to tape-record the proceedings because she could not take notes due to a disabling hand injury (*V.W. and R.W. v. Favolise*, 1990). Both courts agreed that since the IDEA's intent of parental participation meant more than mere presence at IEP conferences, allowing them to make tape recordings afforded them the opportunities to become active and meaningful participants.

School boards also may have the right to make records of IEP proceedings. The First Circuit affirmed that a school board had the right to employ a court reporter at an administrative hearing in order to secure a verbatim record of the proceedings (*Caroline T. v. Hudson School District*, 1990). Although the nature of an administrative hearing is different from that of an IEP conference, in some situations the need for a verbatim record may exist. In situations such as this, courts are likely to grant school boards the right to create verbatim transcripts of meetings.

As noted, procedural errors can create serious problems for school boards since they may cause courts to enter judgments in favor of parents in disagreements involving IEPs. Yet, as a case from the Sixth Circuit indicated, parents may give up some of their rights by failing to participate in the IEP process (*Cordrey v. Euckert*, 1990). The parents here challenged the adequacy of an IEP because all of the required participants were not present at the IEP conference, but then rejected the school board's offer to convene a properly constituted IEP meeting. The court remarked that the parents relinquished their right to a procedurally correct IEP conference by rejecting the board's offer to schedule one.

IEP Revisions

From time to time, along with conducting annual and tri-annual reviews, educators and teams may need to alter IEPs due to changing circumstances within the educational environment or changes in student needs. Minor adjustments that do not result in a change in the student's placement are of little consequence.

Changes that substantially alter IEPs or that result in their not being implemented as written trigger the IDEA's procedural protections. Parents must be notified of any change in a student's educational placement and must be given the opportunity to participate in making the changes (20 U.S.C. § 1415(d)(4)(A)(ii); 34 C.F.R. §§ 300.503(a)(2)). In reviewing IEPs, teams are expected to consider any lack of expected progress toward achieving the students' annual goals, the results of any reevaluation information that was provided to or about them by their parents, their anticipated needs, other matters (34 C.F.R. §§ 300.503(b)(1)(ii)), and/or special factors (34 C.F.R. §§ 300.503(b)(2)). In addition, such a meeting must include a child's regular education teacher (34 C.F.R. §§ 300.503(b)(3)). Moreover, a change in the IDEA and its regulations now permits changes to IEPs to be made by means of video conferences and conference calls (20 U.S.C. § 1414 (f); 34 C.F.R. §§ 300.322(c), 300.328).

> Minor adjustments to IEPs that do not result in a change in student placement are of little consequence. Any changes that alter IEPs substantially or result in their not being implemented as written trigger the IDEA's procedural protections.

The District of Columbia Circuit decided that the school board's failure to notify a surrogate parent of the curtailment of a student's instructional program constituted a denial of an appropriate education (*Abney v. District of Columbia*, 1988). The student lived in a children's hospital and was transported to a school board facility to receive educational services. The record reflected that educators discontinued the child's educational program for several months because medical problems prohibited his being transported. However, the court acknowledged that officials did not provide alternative services and that his surrogate parent was never notified that educational services were no longer being provided. In another case, the Third Circuit affirmed that a school board did not violate the IDEA when officials modified an IEP as a result of discussions that had taken place pursuant to a rejected IEP, even though they had not followed the normal IEP revision process (*Fuhrmann v. East Hanover Board of Education*, 1993). The court agreed with the earlier order that school officials made the modifications in the spirit of compromise.

Noncustodial Parents

In today's world many students do not live with both parents. As discussed below in the section on privacy and student records, the IDEA's parental rights apply to parents who do not have custody of their children due to divorce absent a court order to the contrary. In one such case, the Seventh Circuit declared that a noncustodial parent had standing to sue a school board over his son's IEP (*Navin v. Park Ridge School District*, 2001). Even though the divorce decree gave the custodial mother the right to make educational decisions, the court pointed out that nothing in it stripped the noncustodial father of his parental interest in educational matters.

A recent case from Texas illustrates how judicial proceedings can alter parental rights. The court ruled that a noncustodial father lacked standing to challenge his daughter's placement because a divorce decree awarded full authority for educational decision making to her mother (*Schares v. Katy Independent School District*, 2003). Earlier, the Second Circuit affirmed that under Vermont law, a noncustodial mother lacked standing to demand a hearing under the IDEA on the appropriateness of her daughter's IEP evaluation (*Taylor v. Vermont Department of Education*, 2002). The court posited that the mother lost the right to participate in her daughter's education in a divorce decree that awarded full custody of the child to her father, who opposed the hearing, feeling that it was against his daughter's best interests.

Adult Students

Many students continue to receive special education services after their 18th birthdays. Although these students assume rights of their own on reaching the age of majority, their parents do not lose their rights under the IDEA just because their children have reached this milestone (20 U.S.C. § 1415(m)). Thus, parents are still entitled to notice as to what is taking place with regard to the education of their children even though all other rights associated with the IDEA are transferred to the students.

The Second Circuit noted that the procedural safeguards of the IDEA apply to students between the ages of 18 and 21 even if they have not been declared incompetent (*Mrs. C. v. Wheaton*, 1990). Here, school officials terminated special education services for a 20-year-old student with his consent but without notifying his mother. The court indicated that the termination of services without parental notification violated the IDEA because the mother was entitled to be informed of the change.

Students who are incarcerated in adult prisons are an important subset of children with disabilities whose rights are addressed in the IDEA. Under these provisions, if students with disabilities are convicted as adults under state law and incarcerated in adult prisons, IEP teams may modify their IEPs or placements as long as state officials can demonstrate that they cannot otherwise accommodate bona fide security or compelling penological interests (20 U.S.C. § 1414(d)(7)(B)). In a case from Florida, the Department of Corrections claimed that since a 16-year-old student was incarcerated as an adult, he had the transferred right of majority. The trial court disagreed, clarifying that the rights of majority do not transfer until a child reaches the age of majority under state law (*Paul Y. by Kathy Y. v. Singletary*, 1997).

Student Records and Privacy

In 1974, a year before enacting the Education of All Handicapped Children Act, Congress passed the Family Educational Rights and Privacy Act (FERPA) (20 U.S.C. § 1232g), also known as the Buckley Amendment since its primary sponsor was then-U.S. Senator James Buckley of New York. FERPA, which clarifies the rights of students and their parents with regard to educational records, has two main goals: to grant parents and eligible students access to their educational records and to limit the access of outsiders to these records. FERPA and the IDEA and its regulations have a significant impact on the delivery of special education, and they apply with equal force to parents (20 U.S.C. 1232(g); 34 C.F.R. § 99.4) and eligible students with disabilities. Insofar as parents, rather than special education students, typically exercise the right to access the records of their children, this discussion focuses on parental rights.

Records Covered

FERPA covers all "education records" that contain personally identifiable information relating to students and that are maintained by educational agencies or by persons acting on their behalf (20 U.S.C. § 1232g(a)(4)(A)). Insofar as "educational records" include information about more than one student, parents (20 U.S.C. § 1232g(a)(1)(A)) who review the records of their children can examine only that portion of group data that is specific to their children (20 U.S.C. § 1232g(a)(1)(A)).

Two cases highlight the importance of safeguarding student records. In the first, the federal trial court in Connecticut wrote that school officials violated the privacy rights of parents by releasing their names and that of their son to a local newspaper following a due process hearing (*Sean R. v. Board of Education of the Town of Woodbridge*, 1992). The Eighth Circuit, noting that public policy favors protection of the privacy of minors where sensitive matters are concerned, affirmed that judicial proceedings under the IDEA can be closed to the public (*Webster Groves School District v. Pulitzer Publishing Co.*, 1990). The court pointed out that the IDEA restricts the release of information concerning students with disabilities without parental permission. In order to safeguard the information at issue while preventing the stigmatization of the student, the court declared that access to the courtroom could be restricted and the files sealed.

Another form of records that school systems preserve is so-called directory information, which includes each child's

> name, address, telephone listing, date and place of birth, major field of study, participation in officially recognized activities and sports, weight and height of members of athletic teams, degrees and awards received, and the most recent previous educational agency or institution attended by the student. (20 U.S.C. § 1232g(a)(5)(A))

Before school officials can release directory information about current students, they must provide parents with public notice of the categories of records that are designated as directory and afford parents a reasonable time to request that the material not be released without their consent (20 U.S.C. § 1232g(a)(5)(B); 34 C.F.R. § 99.37). Insofar as the disclosure provisions relating to directory information do not apply to former students, school officials can release such data without obtaining any prior approvals (34 C.F.R. § 99.37(b)).

FERPA requires school officials to notify parents of their annual right to inspect and review, request amendment of, and consent to disclosure of educational records as well as to file complaints with the federal Department of Education alleging failures to comply with the statute's dictates (34 C.F.R. §§ 99.7, 300.612). Typically, parents receive a single notice by a means that is reasonably likely to inform them of their rights, such as school newsletters, student handbooks, notes home, local access TV, e-mail, or some other method or combination of means designed to ensure that they receive notice.

The comprehensiveness of FERPA aside, four major exceptions mean that a variety of documents are not classified as educational records (34 C.F.R. § 99.3(b)) subject to the act's mandatory disclosure provisions. First, records made by educational personnel that are in the sole possession of their makers and are not accessible by or revealed to any other persons except temporary substitutes are not subject to release (20 U.S.C. § 1232g (a)(4)(B)(1)). Second, records kept separately by law enforcement units of educational agencies that are used only for their own purposes cannot be accessed by third parties (20 U.S.C. § 1232g(a)(4)(B)(2)). Third, records that are made in the ordinary course of events relating to individuals who work at, but who do not attend, educational institutions, and that refer exclusively to their capacity as employees and are not available for any other purpose are not subject to disclosure (20 U.S.C. § 1232g(a)(4)(B)(3)). Fourth, records relating to students who are 18 years of age or older, or who attend postsecondary educational institutions, that are made by physicians, psychiatrists, psychologists, or other professionals or paraprofessionals for use in their treatment and are not available to others, except at the request of the students, cannot be released (20 U.S.C. § 1232g(a)(4)(B)(4)).

Access Rights

As noted, pursuant to FERPA, parents have the right to inspect and review records containing personally identifiable information relating to the education of their children (20 U.S.C. § 1232g(a)(1)(A); 34 C.F.R. § 300.613). It is important to recognize that absent court orders or applicable state law, FERPA grants noncustodial parents the same right of access to educational records as custodial parents (34 C.F.R. § 99.4). Where court orders are in effect or if state laws prohibit disclosure to noncustodial parents, school officials would be wise to consider keeping files in two separate locations. Put another way, in order to avoid the risk of mistakenly granting access to noncustodial parents or their representatives, educators should place essentially blank files in the main set of student records directing individuals who need to see them to a second, more secure location. Along with access rights, FERPA requires school officials to provide parents with reasonable interpretations and explanations of information contained in the records of their children (34 C.F.R. § 99.10(c)).

Under FERPA, parental permission or consent is transferred to eligible students who reach their 18th birthday or who attend postsecondary institutions (20 U.S.C. § 1232g(d); 34 C.F.R. § 300.625(b)). In an important exception relating to special education, school officials can take the age and types or severity of students' disabilities into account when considering whether to grant rights of access (34 C.F.R. §§ 300.574, 300.625(a)). Other restrictions of interest are that postsecondary institutions do not have to permit students to inspect financial records in their files that include information about the resources of their parents (20 U.S.C. § 1232g(a)(1)(B); 34 C.F.R. § 99.12(b)(1)) or letters of recommendation where they waived their rights of access (20 U.S.C. § 1232g(a)(1)(C); 34 C.F.R. § 99.37(b)(2)(3)), typically by checking off such an item on a recommendation form. Further, school officials are not required to grant access to records pertaining to individuals who were not or never were students at their institutions (20 U.S.C. § 1232g(a)(6)).

Third parties generally can access school records, other than directory information, only if parents provide written consent (20 U.S.C. §§ 1232g(b)(1), 1232g(b)(2)(A)). In order to assist in the smooth operation of schools, especially as officials in different systems interact with one another, FERPA contains nine major exceptions where parental permission is not required before officials can review educational records.

First, school employees with legitimate educational interests can access student records (20 U.S.C. § 1232g(b)(1)(A)); for example, at the end of a school year, or over a summer, a third grade teacher can read the records of second grade children who will be in her class in the fall in order to prepare classes and other lessons, but she would be unlikely to have a legitimate need to see the files of a child entering fifth grade that she would not be instructing or interacting with in any official capacity.

Second, officials representing schools to which students applied for admission can access their records as long as parents receive proper notice that the information has been sent to the receiving institutions (20 U.S.C. § 1232g(b)(1)(B)).

Third, authorized representatives of the U.S. Comptroller General, the Secretary of the Department of Education, and state and local education officials who are authorized to do so by state law can view student records for law enforcement purposes (20 U.S.C. § 1232g(b)(1)(C)(E)).

Fourth, persons who are responsible for evaluating the eligibility of students for financial aid can review appropriate educational records (20 U.S.C. § 1232g(b)(1)(D)).

Fifth, members of organizations conducting studies on behalf of educational agencies or institutions developing predictive tests or administering aid programs and improving instruction can view records as long as doing so does not lead to the release of personal information about students (20 U.S.C. § 1232g(b)(1)(F)).

Sixth, individuals acting in the course of their duties for accrediting organizations can review student records (20 U.S.C. § 1232g(b)(1)(G)).

Seventh, parents of dependent children can access student records pertaining to their own children (20 U.S.C. § 1232g(b)(1)(H)).

Eighth, in emergency situations, persons who protect the health and safety of students or other persons can view records (20 U.S.C. § 1232g(b)(1)(I)).

Ninth, written permission is not necessary if student records are subpoenaed or otherwise sought via judicial orders except that the parents must be notified in advance of compliance by school boards (20 U.S.C. §§ 1232g(b)(1)(J), 1232g(b)(2)(B)). Even so, prior to ordering the release of information, courts weigh the need for access against the privacy interests of students. FERPA adds that its provisions do not prohibit educational officials from disclosing information concerning registered sex offenders who are required to register by federal law. Of course, in any of these situations educational officials cannot release or quote any personally identifiable information relating to students without parental consent.

A third party seeking disclosure of student records must have written consent from parents specifying the record(s) to be released, the reason(s) for the proposed release, and to whom the information is being given (34 C.F.R. § 99.30). FERPA further specifies that parents have the right to receive copies of the materials to be released (20 U.S.C. § 1232g(b)(2)(A)). In addition, school officials must keep records of all individuals or groups, except exempted parties, who request or obtain access to student records (20 U.S.C. § 1232g(b)(4)(A)). These records must not only explain the legitimate interests of those who were granted access to the educational files but must also be kept with the records of the student in question (20 U.S.C. § 1232g(b)(4)(A); 34 C.F.R. § 300.614).

Educational agencies that maintain student records must comply with parental requests for review without unnecessary delay. More specifically, unless parents agree otherwise, officials must grant them access no later than 45 days after receiving their requests (20 U.S.C. § 1232g(a)(1)(A); 34 C.F.R. § 99.10(b)). Needless to say, nothing prohibits school officials from granting parental requests for access to student records more quickly. Agencies that receive parental requests for access to records cannot charge fees to search for or to retrieve student records (34 C.F.R. §§ 99.11(b), 300.614(b)). Once materials are located, school officials can charge parents for copies as long as a payment does not effectively prevent parents from exercising their rights to inspect and review the educational records of their children (34 C.F.R. §§ 99.11(a), 300.614(a)).

Amending Records

Parents who disagree with the content of the educational records of their children can ask school officials to amend the disputed information (34 C.F.R. § 99.20(a), 300.618(a)). If officials refuse to grant requests to amend records within a reasonable time (34 C.F.R. §§ 99.20(b)(c), 300.618(b)-(c)), parents are entitled to hearings at which hearing officers evaluate whether the challenged material is accurate and appropriately contained within the educational records of students (34 C.F.R. §§ 99.21, 300.619). Hearing officers must both conduct hearings and render decisions within a reasonable time (34 C.F.R. § 99.22). If hearing officers are convinced that contested material is inaccurate, misleading, or otherwise violates the rights of students to privacy, school officials must amend them accordingly and inform students' parents in writing that this has been done (34 C.F.R. §§ 99.21(b)(1), 300.620(a)). In contrast, if hearing officers are satisfied that the materials in educational records are not inaccurate or misleading, or do not otherwise violate the privacy rights of students the records need not be removed or amended (34 C.F.R. §§ 99.21(b)(2), 300.620(b)). Parents who remain concerned over the content of the educational records of their children, even after hearing officers decide that they are acceptable, can add a statement explaining their objections to the records. This statement must be kept with the contested information for as long as it is kept on file (34 C.F.R. §§ 99.21(c), 300.620(c)).

Destruction of Records

The amount of records in the files of students who are in special education placements can multiply rapidly, so it should not be surprising that the IDEA's regulations also discuss the destruction of information that is no longer needed. Although neither the IDEA nor its regulations define the term, the latter stipulate that records can be destroyed when they are no longer needed to provide children with services (34 C.F.R. § 300.624(a)). This could include, but is not limited to, outdated IEPs and test protocols. The regulation adds that parents must be advised that records are going to be destroyed and that school officials can save, without any time limitation, records including students' names, addresses, phone numbers, grades, attendance records, classes attended, and grade levels completed along with the years they were completed (34 C.F.R. § 300.624(b)).

Enforcement

If parents are denied the opportunity to review the records of their children or if information is released impermissibly (as in the case of students who are over the age of 18 in postsecondary institutions), the educational officials who denied appropriate access or granted inappropriate access can be charged with violating FERPA, thereby triggering its enforcement provisions. As the Supreme Court confirmed in *Gonzaga University v. Doe* (2002), admittedly a case from higher education, an aggrieved party must file a written complaint detailing the specifics of an alleged violation with the federal Department of Education's Family Policy Compliance Office (FPCO) (34 C.F.R. § 99.63).

Complaints must be filed within 180 days of either an alleged violation or the date when claimants knew or reasonably should have known about violations (34 C.F.R. § 99.64). When the FPCO receives complaints, its staff must notify officials at the educational institution in writing, detailing the substance of the alleged violations and asking them to respond before considering whether to proceed with investigations (34 C.F.R. § 99.65). If, after investigations (34 C.F.R. § 99.66) are completed, the FPCO staff agree that violations occurred, the Department of Education can withhold future payments under its programs, issue orders to compel compliance, or ultimately terminate an institution's eligibility to receive federal funding if officials refuse to comply within a reasonable time (34 C.F.R. § 99.67), a draconian solution that has yet to occur.

In the only other Supreme Court case involving FERPA, *Owasso Independent School District v. Falvo* (2002), the Court held that since "peer grading," whereby teachers permit students to grade the papers of classmates, does not turn the papers into educational records covered by FERPA, a school board in Oklahoma did not violate the law by permitting teachers to use the practice over the objection of a mother whose children attended schools in the district (Russo & Mawdsley, 2002). The Court explained that student papers do not become educational records within the meaning of FERPA until such time as they are entered into the grade books of teachers.

CHANGE IN PLACEMENT

Once students with disabilities are evaluated, school officials may not change their placements unless their parents have been notified in writing of planned actions and have been afforded opportunities to contest the proposed modifications (20 U.S.C. § 1415(b)(3)(A)). In addition, the IDEA dictates that while administrative hearings or judicial proceedings are pending, a "child shall remain in the then current placement" unless the parents and school board agree otherwise (20 U.S.C. § 1415(j)). This section of IDEA has become known as the "status quo" or "stay put" provision and has been subject to a great deal of litigation.

Then-Current Placement

Generally, the placements of students at the time that actions arise are considered to be their "then current placements." The Sixth Circuit defined then-current placement as the operative placement actually functioning when a dispute first arises (*Thomas v. Cincinnati Board of Education*, 1990). In this case, the court explained that a proposed placement that never was implemented simply did not qualify as the status quo setting.

On occasion, school officials may make placements that are intended to be temporary. In such situations, officials are obliged to make their intentions clear or the courts will consider placements to be the then-current placements (Mehfoud & Osborne, 1998). Litigation involving the District of Columbia public schools illustrates this point. In one dispute, educators at a private facility developed an IEP for a student that called for a transfer to a residential school. The school board agreed to the new placement, but a year later officials notified the student's parents that they saw no need for continued placement there and would no longer assume financial responsibility for the placement. The federal trial court decided that the residential school was the student's then-current placement because the board assumed responsibility for it and had given no indication at the time that it intended to do so for one year only (*Jacobson v. District of Columbia Board of Education*, 1983). In a separate case, the same court indicated that any limitation on a placement must be spelled out clearly and described in a settlement agreement (*Saleh v. District of Columbia*, 1987). Based on the mutual consent of school officials and the child's parents, the student was placed in a private school pending resolution of a placement dispute. The board argued that the private school was an interim placement only, but the court reasoned that it was the then-current placement since its interim status had not been articulated clearly. Similarly, an appellate court held that a private school placement ceased to be the then-current placement at the end of the school year because a hearing officer's order indicated clearly that it was to be for one year only (*Leonard v. McKenzie*, 1989).

A court in New York pointed out that a private school placement that a hearing officer ordered a school board to fund for one year only was not the then-current placement (*Zvi D. v. Ambach*, 1981, 1982). Conversely, in another case from New York, a federal trial court, after uncovering no evidence that school officials limited funding for a private school placement to one school year, stipulated that the private school was the child's pendant, or current, placement (*Evans v. Board of Education of the Rhinebeck Central School District*, 1996). In another case, the First Circuit, recognizing that a private school placement was never intended to be more than temporary and that a settlement agreement specified that it would terminate at the end of the school year, decreed that a public school placement was the student's then-current placement (*Verhoeven v. Brunswick School Committee*, 1999).

Parentally made unilateral placements can be the then-current placements if school boards fail to propose appropriate programs in a timely fashion. In such a situation, the federal trial court for the District of Columbia was of the opinion that where school officials did not propose a program for a student by the deadline established by a hearing officer, the parents were justified in placing their son in a private school (*Cochran v. District of Columbia*, 1987). The court was thus satisfied that this was the child's current educational placement.

If parents unilaterally remove their children from programs, those settings do not cease to be the then-current placements. For example, the Eighth Circuit maintained that the public school placement of a student whose parents removed him from the school was the status quo (*Digre v. Roseville Schools Independent School District No. 623*, 1988). The parents enrolled their child in another school system, but one month later he was reenrolled in his former district. The student's mother tried to reenroll her son as a regular, rather than special, education student, but the court observed that a one-month term as a regular education student in another school system did not negate the child's special education history. Further, a federal trial court in Illinois wrote that the stay put provision does not apply to students whose parents unilaterally place them in private schools (*Joshua B. v. New Trier Township High School District 203*, 1991).

Figure 4.2   Changing the Placement of a Student With Disabilities

- Prior to changing the placement of students with disabilities, school officials must provide their parents or guardians with written notice of the proposed changes. Notice should include
  - An explanation of the IDEA's due process safeguards
  - A description of the proposed change or other options considered, with an explanation of why other options were rejected
  - A description of all assessments used in making a determination
  - A description of any other relevant factors used in making a determination

Notice must be written in a language understood by the general public and in the parents' or guardians' native language or other mode of communication. If necessary, notice can be provided orally. Notice should be provided within a reasonable time prior to the proposed change in placement.

- If parents or guardians object to proposed changes in placements, they are entitled to due process hearings.

- Until disputes are finally resolved, students are to remain in their then-current educational placements, unless their parents or guardians and school officials agree otherwise or judges or hearing officers order changes in placement. (Note: Exceptions exist for dangerous students. See Chapter 5, "Student Discipline," for explanations.)

Placement Pending Appeals

In an early dispute on placements pending appeals, the First Circuit declared that Congress did not intend to freeze an arguably inappropriate placement for the length of time it takes for review proceedings to culminate (*Doe v. Brookline School Committee*, 1983). This means that parents can be reimbursed for the cost of tuition in a private school as long as a court agrees that it is the then-current placement (*Spilsbury v. District of Columbia*, 2004, 2005).

A question arises as to when parents or school officials are entitled to make changes in the placements of students with disabilities pursuant to the orders of hearing officers or judges. Some courts believe that changes in placement can occur once administrative orders are issued, even if they are being appealed. In such a case, the Ninth Circuit ruled that once a state educational agency agreed that a parentally chosen placement was correct, it became the then-current placement under the IDEA and the school board was required to keep it in effect pending judicial review (*Clovis Unified School District v. California Office of Administrative Hearings*, 1990). The federal trial court in Massachusetts thought that if a state agency, such as the Bureau of Special Education Appeals, and the student's parent agreed on a placement, the school board's approval was not required to make a change in placement (*Grace B. v. Lexington School Committee*, 1991). In another case, a federal trial court in New York remarked that a school board was not relieved of its obligation to fund an alternative school placement until final administrative review procedures were completed (*Board of Education of the City of New York v. Ambach*, 1985). At the same time, the court was of the view that the school board was financially responsible only until the date the final judgment was handed down, not until the end of the school year.

The IDEA calls for an agreement by either states or local school boards and parents to effectuate changes in placements during the pendency of review proceedings. The U.S. Supreme Court, in dicta, posited that a state-level hearing order in favor of the parents' chosen placement seems to constitute agreement by the state to a change in placement (*Burlington School Committee v. Department of Education of the Commonwealth of Massachusetts*, 1985). Citing *Burlington*, the Second Circuit ascertained that an order for reimbursement predicated on a finding that a proposed IEP is inappropriate constitutes a change in a student's current educational placement (*Board of Education of the Pawling Central School District v. Schutz*, 2002).

Previously, in a like dispute, the Fifth Circuit affirmed that since a review panel's reversal of an order from a hearing officer that had been in favor of a school board's proposed placement constituted an agreement between the state and parents, a residential facility was the pendant placement during all proceedings (*St. Tammany Parish School Board v. State of Louisiana*, 1998). Earlier, a federal trial court acknowledged that a hearing officer's order constituted agreement by the state to a change in placement

(*Board of Education of Montgomery County v. Brett Y.*, 1997). Another federal trial court thought that an adjudication by either a state hearing officer in a one-tier system or a state reviewing officer in a two-tier system constituted an agreement by the state under the IDEA's stay put provision (*Murphy v. Arlington Central School District Board of Education*, 2000).

On the other hand, according to the District of Columbia Circuit, the IDEA's status quo provision requires that a student's placement remain the same until all administrative hearings and trial court actions are completed (*Anderson v. District of Columbia*, 1989). The court noted that the IDEA did not entitle a student to remain in a private school at public expense pending review by an appeals court. Here the hearing officer and federal trial court agreed that the IEPs offered by the school board were appropriate. A year earlier, the federal trial court for the District of Columbia declared that the school board was required to fund a private school placement during the pendency of a parental appeal of a hearing officer's order (*Holmes v. District of Columbia*, 1988). The court added that since it would have been inappropriate, insensitive, and indefensible for it to have called for a change in placement one semester before the student completed his schooling, the board had to pay for the cost of his remaining in the private school until graduation, even though a hearing officer contended that the board's proposed change in placement was appropriate. In an analogous situation, a federal trial court in New York pointed out that the status quo provision prohibited a school board from permitting a student to graduate from high school during the pendency of administrative appeals because doing so would have terminated his rights to additional educational services (*Cronin v. Board of Education of East Ramapo Central School District*, 1988).

Pursuant to the IDEA's status quo provision, during the pendency of appeals over students who are seeking initial admission to public schools and until all appeals are completed, children are to be placed in public school programs (20 U.S.C. § 1415(j)). However, since the IDEA does not clarify whether these placements should be in general education classrooms or special education programs, litigation has ensued. In such a case, a federal trial court in Wisconsin ordered the immediate termination of a child's placement on the basis that it was inappropriate (*Tammy S. v. Reedsburg School District*, 2003). The court ruled that the immediate termination of the placement was the appropriate remedy since the child's parents and school officials agreed to the change.

Students whose school boards have yet to place them are not protected by the status quo provision. In a case on point, a federal trial court in Illinois explained that the IDEA's status quo provision did not apply to a student who was unilaterally placed by his parents before their school board had the opportunity to make a recommendation regarding his education (*Joshua B. v. New Trier Township High School District 203*, 1991). The court wrote that while the status quo provision was designed to prevent interruptions in programming for students, it was not intended to protect children who were awaiting placements.

Change in Program Location

The courts agree that the general rule of the IDEA is that the term *change in placement* refers to changes that affect the form of educational instruction provided, not the location where it takes place. For various reasons, such as school closings, school boards sometimes are required to move special education programs from one building to another. Courts share the perspective that transfers of entire classes or programs do not constitute changes in placement triggering the IDEA's due process procedures (*Brown v. District of Columbia Board of Education*, 1978; *Concerned Parents and Citizens for the Continuing Education at Malcolm X. v. New York City Board of Education*, 1980; *Middlebrook v. School District of the County of Knox, Tennessee*, 1991).

When the physical locations of programs are moved from one place to another, the educational programming for children must remain substantially the same. For instance, the Fourth Circuit interpreted the IDEA's use of the term *educational placement* as referring to the services that children receive, not necessarily the location where they are provided (*AW ex rel. Wilson v. Fairfax County School Board*, 2004). Thus the court affirmed that to the extent that a child's new setting, in the least restrictive environment, duplicated the educational program in his original placement, albeit in a different location, school officials satisfied the IDEA's stay put provision.

As illustrated by a case from New York, the elimination of a major component of a program can be sufficient cause to trigger the IDEA's due process mechanism. A federal trial court in New York asserted that the elimination of the summer component of what had been a year-round residential program was of such critical magnitude that it constituted a change in a child's placement (*Gebhardt v. Ambach*, 1982). In another case, a federal trial court in Pennsylvania nullified the proposed transfer of two students from one program to another that involved a change in the method of instruction (*Visco v. School District of Pittsburgh*, 1988). The court noted that since the students were making progress in their program, any changes had to be considered with caution.

Even when a transfer involves moving a single student, it may not be considered a change in placement if the new program is almost identical to the former one. The District of Columbia Circuit rejected the claim of a surrogate parent that moving a student who was profoundly disabled from a private to a government operated hospital was a change in placement (*Lunceford v. District of Columbia Board of Education*, 1984). The court explained that the claim failed because the surrogate parent was unable to demonstrate that the shift constituted a fundamental change in or the elimination of a basic element in the child's IEP. Subsequently, the Fifth Circuit adopted a similar rationale in expressing the view that a transfer from one school building to another was not a change in placement because the student's IEP was fully implemented following the move (*Weil v. Board of Elementary and Secondary Education*, 1991). Three years later, the Fifth Circuit approved a magistrate judge's transfer of a student from one location to another on the basis that this did not alter her IEP (*Sherri A.D. v. Kirby*, 1992).

The failure of school officials to implement IEPs completely following changes of location can constitute changes in placements. In such a situation, the District of Columbia Circuit maintained that school board officials violated the IDEA's change in placement provisions when they failed to notify a student's surrogate parent that his educational program had been curtailed on account of his medical condition (*Abney v. District of Columbia*, 1988). The court observed that even though the student's medical condition prevented him from being able to be transported to his special education program, school officials were still obligated to make attempts to provide him with services, albeit alternate services.

Changes in locations that render overall programs more restrictive for students generally constitute changes in placements. Even so, this issue is far from settled, particularly when transfers are made for disciplinary purposes. In one such dispute, a trial court in Louisiana treated the moving of a student from a self-contained special education class to an off-campus alternative program as a change in placement because he would not have had contact with students who did not have disabilities in the new placement (*Jonathan G. v. Caddo Parish School Board*, 1994). On the other hand, a trial court in North Carolina refused to interpret the reassignment of a student to a management school as a change in placement because the new placement provided the same curriculum and services that he received in his former program (*Glen III v. Charlotte-Mecklenburg School Board of Education*, 1995).

In a series of judgments, the federal trial court in the District of Columbia asserted that the school board's failure to pay private school tuition on a timely basis violated the IDEA because it created the very real threat that the students would be removed from the schools (*Petties v. District of Columbia*, 1995). According to the court, such an action would have violated the IDEA's prohibition against unilateral changes in placements.

Graduation Is a Change in Placement

As indicated previously, major modifications to student IEPs amount to changes in placements. Moreover, the courts agree that graduation is a change in placement because it terminates all educational services for students. In an illustrative case, the Supreme Judicial Court of Massachusetts concluded that the failure to provide parents with formal written notice of the school board's decision to permit their son to graduate violated the IDEA and a commonwealth statute (*Stock v. Massachusetts Hospital School*, 1984). Using a similar rationale, a federal trial court in New York treated graduation as analogous to an expulsion since it resulted in a student's total exclusion from his educational placement (*Cronin v. Board of Education of East Ramapo Central School District*, 1988).

Adjustments to IEPs

The general rule is that changes to IEPs constitute changes in placement, but that minor adjustments are allowable. As could be expected, this distinction is often subject to differing perspectives. The Third Circuit reasoned that the important element in evaluating whether a change in placement has occurred is whether a change is likely to affect a student's learning in some significant way (*DeLeon v. Susquehanna Community School District*, 1984). Here the court viewed a minor change in the student's transportation arrangements as not being a change in placement but warned that under some circumstances transportation could have a major impact on a child's learning. Two years later, the federal trial court in Massachusetts echoed the Third Circuit's analysis that a child's learning experience must be affected in some significant way when it decided that an adjustment to an IEP that was more superficial than substantive was not a change in placement (*Brookline School Committee v. Golden*, 1986). The federal trial court in Maryland also treated minor modifications in a student's schedule that did not alter the goals and objectives in his IEP or the amount of special education time as not constituting a change in placement (*Cavanagh v. Grasmick*, 1999).

Services Not in IEPs

School boards sometimes provide students with disabilities with auxiliary services that are not called for in their IEPs. If services are not being provided under the terms of IEPs, they can be changed without providing parents with the IDEA's due process safeguards. In such a situation, the Ninth Circuit ruled that since a tutoring program that was not provided under an IEP was not a special education service, a change in tutors was not a change in placement (*Gregory K. v. Longview School District*, 1987). Ironically, the record indicated that tutoring was provided after the student's parents rejected the school board's offer to provide special education services. Similarly, the Sixth Circuit affirmed that school board officials did not violate the IDEA's stay put provision when they refused to leave a student in an extended school year program that was not included in his IEP (*Cordrey v. Euckert*, 1990).

The IDEA's change in placement procedures are inapplicable to placements that are not made pursuant to its provisions. In other words, if state agencies make residential placements for social purposes, the IDEA's change in placement requirements cannot be invoked if officials attempt to transfer students to other facilities or otherwise remove them from residential facilities (*Corbett v. Regional Center for the East Bay, Inc.*, 1988a). The IDEA's change in placement procedures apply only to services specified in IEPs. As such, a service provider cannot invoke the IDEA's change in placement provision in license revocation proceedings (*Corbett v. Regional Center for the East Bay, Inc.*, 1988b).

Programs That Are No Longer Appropriate

A special problem regarding the IDEA's status quo provision exists when it is no longer appropriate for students to remain in programs they have attended. This may occur for a variety of reasons: private schools can lose their state approval, private schools can be found to be lacking in quality, students may be too old for their programs, or programs may no longer be able to serve children. Generally, courts approve placements in similar facilities. Once again, and as reflected in the following cases, the key element is that new programs must be able to implement student IEPs fully to pass muster under the status quo provision.

In New York, a federal trial court was of the opinion that the transfer of students from a private school that was found to be lacking to alternate facilities was not a change in placement (*Dima v. Macchiarola*, 1981). The court noted that the school board terminated its contract with the private school after an audit disclosed several problems with the school, including mismanagement of funds and serious educational deficiencies. A year later, in a second case from New York, the Second Circuit affirmed, but slightly modified, an order in favor of a student and his parents, declaring that their school board had to leave him in a facility that had lost its state approval until such time as officials were able to offer an appropriate alternative (*Vander Malle v. Ambach*, 1982).

The Sixth Circuit affirmed that the transfer of several students from a closed treatment facility to dissimilar alternate facilities was a change in placement (*Tilton v. Jefferson County Board of Education*, 1983). At the same time, the court acknowledged that since the closing occurred for financial reasons, the IDEA's procedural safeguards did not apply. The court added that the students could contest their new placements through the IDEA's administrative hearing process. In another case where a private school closed, the federal trial court for the District of Columbia upheld a hearing officer's order for the school board to fund a placement at another private school (*Block v. District of Columbia*, 1990). When the private school closed, the board offered the student a public school placement but failed to execute a complete IEP. The facts revealed that when school officials failed to present the child's parents with an IEP by the start of the next school year, they unilaterally enrolled their son in another private school.

In two separate cases the District of Columbia Circuit indicated that when officials in private schools determine that they can no longer serve students, school boards are obligated to locate and fund similar programs (*Knight v. District of Columbia*, 1989; *McKenzie v. Smith*, 1985). In the former case, even though the private school placement was no longer available, the court allowed the board to make an interim placement in a public school program that was not inherently dissimilar until it was able to offer a final placement.

A school board in New Hampshire proposed a placement in a public high school for a student who was too old to continue at the private residential school he attended at public expense. The federal trial court was convinced that since such a transfer would have fundamentally altered the student's educational program, it was a change in placement (*Henry v. School Administrative Unit #29*, 1999). The court concluded that the private school selected by the parents would have provided a substantially similar experience to the one in their son's former placement.

Annual Reviews and Reevaluations

As noted earlier, the IDEA requires school officials to review the IEPs of students with disabilities at least annually (20 U.S.C. § 1414(d)(4)) and to conduct reevaluations at least once every three years, unless they and the parents agree that reevaluations are unnecessary (20 U.S.C. § 1414(a)(2)). Nonetheless, parents still retain the right to request reevaluations sooner than every three years (20 U.S.C. § 1414(a)(2)(A)(ii)). Accordingly, hearing officers and courts cannot order school boards to maintain given placements for longer than one year. Of course, each year's IEP is subject to the IDEA's due process requirements. The federal trial court for the District of Columbia denied a parental request to prohibit the school board from changing a private school placement for two years. The court stated that school board officials had to be free during that time frame to consider whether the private school was still appropriate (*Kattan v. District of Columbia*, 1988).

At least one court ordered a school board to update evaluations before making significant changes in placements (*Brimmer v. Traverse City Area Public Schools*, 1994). Here school board officials proposed a change in placement for several hearing-impaired students from a state school for the deaf to a program within the public schools. Where this change would have fundamentally altered the students' educational programs, the court reasoned that the reevaluations were warranted. Yet, in another case the court made it clear that even though graduation is generally considered to be a change in placement, a reevaluation was not required before a student's services were discontinued due to his graduation (*T.S. v. Independent School District No. 54*, 2001). The court affirmed that the student was not entitled to a due process hearing where he claimed that he was denied services because he did not ask for a hearing until after he graduated, at which time he was no longer protected by the IDEA.

Figure 4.3   Frequently Asked Questions

Q: What are the required components of IEPs?

A: The IDEA dictates that IEPs must contain statements of the current level of academic achievement and functional performance of students; measurable annual goals for children, including academic and functional goals; a description of how officials plan to measure the progress of children toward meeting their annual goals, as well as when such periodic reports are to be provided; statements of special education and related services as well as supplementary aids and services, based on peer-reviewed research to the extent practicable; statements of the special education and related services, as well as supplementary aids and services, that children are to receive; explanations of the extent, if any, to which children are not going to participate in regular classes with peers who are not disabled; statements of the individual appropriate accommodations that are necessary to measure the academic achievement and functional performance of students on state and district assessments; the projected dates of initiation and duration of special education services that children are to receive; starting no later than the first IEP that is to be in effect for students who are 16 years old, statements of appropriate measurable postsecondary education goals, to be updated annually, and transition services; and at least one year before students reach the age of majority, they must be provided with statements that they have been informed of their rights, if any, that will transfer at the age of majority (20 U.S.C.A. § 1414(d)).

Q: If students are promoted from one level to another (i.e., elementary to middle school), does this constitute a change in placement?

A: No, as long as new programs provide substantially the same educational benefits as the previous ones did. Although the IDEA permits minor adjustments that reflect changes to the new levels, the amounts and types of services must remain the same.

Q: Are school boards required to implement the findings and recommendations of independent evaluators?

A: No, the IDEA requires school boards to consider the findings and recommendations of independent evaluators. In other words, this does not require adoption. IEP teams can satisfy the requirement to consider these results by reading and discussing the reports of independent evaluators at IEP meetings with the parents.

Q: What rights do noncustodial parents have in the IEP process?

A: Unless there is a court order or state law stating otherwise, noncustodial parents retain all of the rights of custodial parents. This is true even if noncustodial parents do not live within a school district's boundaries. Thus, noncustodial parents have the right to challenge proposed IEPs. However, as the answer to this question may be affected by state law, school administrators should consult the requirements of state law. For example, state law may specify how noncustodial parents are to be notified of IEP meetings and may require custodial parents to be notified whenever noncustodial parents request information.

Q: Must school officials review IEPs each and every time a parent requests a review?

A: No, though school officials must address parental concerns and dissatisfaction with IEPs. Once school officials have dealt with an issue, they are not required to review it repeatedly every time parents voice a concern.

RECOMMENDATIONS

The IDEA and its regulations provide students with disabilities and their parents with specific procedural rights. Those rights are included in the statute because Congress intended parents to be equal partners with school officials in the development of appropriate educational programs for their children. The U.S. Supreme Court ruled that in enacting the IDEA Congress was well aware that school boards had all too often denied students with disabilities an appropriate education, without consulting their parents. In order to remedy the situation relating to children with disabilities, Congress emphasized the importance and necessity of parental participation throughout the IDEA (*Honig v. Doe,* 1988). The following recommendations were gleaned from the numerous court cases interpreting the IDEA and its regulations. Individual states may provide students and their parents with additional rights. State laws and regulations should be consulted as well. School officials should

- Make sure to complete fair assessments of students with disabilities.
- Guarantee parental input into the evaluation and placement process.
- Ensure that all testing and evaluation materials and procedures are selected and administered in a manner that is not racially or culturally biased.
- Include assessments in all areas of suspected disability in the multidisciplinary evaluation.
- Consult state laws and regulations for timelines for completing evaluations and making placements.
- Develop and implement policies and procedures to avoid the overidentification or disproportionate representation based on race and ethnicity of students with disabilities.
- Develop and implement policies and procedures to seek to ensure that the rate of long-term suspensions and expulsions of students with disabilities does not evidence significant discrepancies based on race and ethnicity.
- Carefully review and discuss the results of independent evaluations, keeping in mind that educators do not have to adopt all findings of independent evaluators.
- Ensure parental participation in the IEP development, even if this requires extraordinary steps such as home visits or telephone conference calls.
- Avoid the use of boilerplate text in IEPs; IEPs that are not individually tailored to meet the unique needs of the student run the risk of being invalidated.
- Ensure that at least one person who has knowledge of various placement options participates as a member of IEP teams.
- Be diligent in ensuring that IEPs contain all of the required elements, particularly students' current levels of functioning, annual goals

and measurable short-term objectives, clearly stated performance criteria, evaluation procedures, and schedules for evaluation.

- Come to IEP meetings with proposals and even a draft IEP, but ensure that parents have input into the IEP process.
- Provide parents with interpreters for IEP meetings and any progress conferences if their primary mode of communication is not English
- Allow parents to tape-record IEP meetings if doing so will assist them in participating in the process.
- Consistent with state law, provide noncustodial parents with their rights with respect to the IEP process.
- Take all necessary steps to protect the privacy of special education students.
- Ensure that student placements are based on IEPs and that IEPs are not written to fit placements.
- State in unequivocal terms in IEPs that placements are intended to be only temporary if this is the case.
- Ensure that a representative of the school board attends all IEP meetings convened in private schools for students who attend private schools at public expense.
- Check with state officials to determine whether their states have been approved for pilot three-year IEPs.
- Consider taking steps to reduce paperwork, regardless of whether state officials choose to participate in the pilot national program.
- Implement all of the IDEA's procedural safeguards before making substantial changes to the IEPs or placements of students.
- Schedule review meetings if parents express dissatisfaction with IEPs or the progress of their children.
- Notify parents any time their school boards propose to act on the placement of or a refusal to initiate actions for students with disabilities.
- Make changes in placement only when parents agree to them or changes in placement are ordered by hearing officers or courts, keeping in mind that unilateral changes in placement cannot be made while appeals are pending.
- Ensure that IEPs can be fully implemented in new locations if changes in location for the delivery of services are required.
- Locate new programs that are substantially similar to current programs and that can implement student IEPs if the current program of students closes or becomes unavailable.
- Be diligent in ensuring that parents are afforded all of the rights and protections that they are guaranteed by the IDEA.

REFERENCES

Abney v. District of Columbia, 849 F.2d 1491 (D.C. Cir. 1988).
Amann v. Stow School System, 982 F.2d 644 (1st Cir. 1992).

Anderson v. District of Columbia, 877 F.2d 1018 (D.C. Cir. 1989).

Andress v. Cleveland Independent School District, 64 F.3d 176 (5th Cir. 1995).

AW ex rel. Wilson v. Fairfax County School Board, 372 F.3d 674 (4th Cir. 2004).

Big Beaver Falls Area School District v. Jackson, 615 A.2d 910 (Pa. Commw. Ct. 1992).

Blackmon v. Springfield R-XII School District, 198 F.3d 648 (8th Cir. 1999).

Block v. District of Columbia, 748 F. Supp. 891 (D.D.C. 1990).

Board of Education of Montgomery County v. Brett Y., 959 F. Supp. 705 (D. Md. 1997).

Board of Education of Murphysboro Community Unit School District No. 186 v. Illinois State Board of Education, 41 F.3d 1162 (7th Cir. 1994).

Board of Education of the City of New York v. Ambach, 612 F. Supp. 230 (E.D.N.Y. 1985).

Board of Education of the County of Caball v. Dienelt, 843 F.2d 813 (4th Cir. 1988).

Board of Education of the Hendrick Hudson Central School District v. Rowley, 458 U.S. 176 (1982).

Board of Education of the Pawling Central School District v. Schutz, 290 F.3d 476 (2d Cir. 2002).

Bonadonna v. Cooperman, 619 F. Supp. 401 (D.N.J. 1985).

Briley v. Board of Education of Baltimore County, 87 F. Supp.2d 441 (D. Md. 1999).

Brimmer v. Traverse City Area Public Schools, 872 F. Supp. 447 (W.D. Mich. 1994).

Brookline School Committee v. Golden, 628 F. Supp. 113 (D. Mass. 1986).

Brown v. District of Columbia Board of Education, EHLR 551:101 (D.D.C. 1978).

Burlington School Committee v. Department of Education of the Commonwealth of Massachusetts, 471 U.S. 359 (1985).

Buser v. Corpus Christi Independent School District, 51 F.3d 490 (5th Cir. 1995).

Carnwath v. Board of Education of Anne Arundel County, 33 F. Supp.2d 431 (D. Md. 1998).

Caroline T. v. Hudson School District, 915 F.2d 752 (1st Cir. 1990).

Cavanagh v. Grasmick, 75 F. Supp.2d 446 (D. Md. 1999).

Chris D. v. Montgomery County Board of Education, 753 F. Supp. 922 (M.D. Ala. 1990).

Clovis Unified School District v. California Office of Administrative Hearings, 903 F.2d 635 (9th Cir. 1990).

Clyde K. v. Puyallup School District No. 3, 35 F.3d 1396 (9th Cir. 1994).

Coale v. State Department of Education, 162 F. Supp.2d 316 (D. Del. 2001).

Cochran v. District of Columbia, 660 F. Supp. 314 (D.D.C. 1987).

Code of Federal Regulations (C.F.R.), as cited (2006).

Concerned Parents and Citizens for the Continuing Education at Malcolm X. v. New York City Board of Education, 629 F.2d 751 (2d Cir. 1980).

Cone v. Randolph County Schools, 103 Fed. Appx. 731 (4th Cir. 2004), *cert. denied*, 125 S. Ct. 1077 (2005).

Corbett v. Regional Center for the East Bay, Inc., 676 F. Supp. 964 (N.D. Cal. 1988a).

Corbett v. Regional Center for the East Bay, Inc., 699 F. Supp. 230 (N.D. Cal. 1988b).

Cordrey v. Euckert, 917 F.2d 1460 (6th Cir. 1990).

Cronin v. Board of Education of East Ramapo Central School District, 689 F. Supp. 197 (S.D.N.Y. 1988).

Daugherty v. Hamilton County Schools, 21 F. Supp.2d 765 (E.D. Tenn. 1998).

Deal v. Hamilton County Board of Education, 392 F.3d 840 (6th Cir. 2004), *rehearing and rehearing en banc denied* (No. 03-5396) (6th Cir. 2005).

DeLeon v. Susquehanna Community School District, 747 F.2d 149 (3d Cir. 1984).

Digre v. Roseville Schools Independent School District No. 623, 841 F.2d 245 (8th Cir. 1988).

Dima v. Macchiarola, 513 F. Supp. 565 (E.D.N.Y. 1981).

Doe v. Alabama State Department of Education, 915 F.2d 651 (11th Cir. 1990).

Doe v. Brookline School Committee, 722 F.2d 910 (1st Cir. 1983).

Doe v. Defendant I, 898 F.2d 1186 (6th Cir. 1990).

Dong v. Board of Education of the Rochester Community Schools, 197 F.3d 793 (6th Cir. 1999).

Doyle v. Arlington County School Board, 806 F. Supp. 1253 (E.D. Va. 1992).

Edwards-White v. District of Columbia, 785 F. Supp. 1022 (D.D.C. 1992).

E.H. and H.H. v. Tirozzi, 735 F. Supp. 53 (D. Conn. 1990).

Evans v. Board of Education of the Rhinebeck Central School District, 921 F. Supp. 1184, 930 F. Supp. 83 (S.D.N.Y. 1996).

Evans v. District No. 17, Douglas County, 841 F.2d 824 (8th Cir. 1988).

Evanston Community Consolidated School Dist. Number 65 v. Michael M., 356 F.3d 798 (7th Cir. 2004).

Family Educational Rights and Privacy Act, 20 U.S.C. § 1232g (1974).

French v. Omaha Public Schools, 766 F. Supp. 765 (D. Neb. 1991).

Fuhrmann v. East Hanover Board of Education, 993 F.2d 1031 (3d Cir. 1993).

G.D. v. Westmoreland School District, 930 F.2d 942 (1st Cir. 1991).

Gebhardt v. Ambach, EHLR 554:130 (W.D.N.Y. 1982).

Gerstmyer v. Howard County Public Schools, 850 F. Supp. 361 (D. Md. 1994).

Glen III v. Charlotte-Mecklenburg School Board of Education, 903 F. Supp. 918 (W.D.N.C. 1995).

Gonzaga University v. Doe, 536 U.S. 273 (2002).

Grace B. v. Lexington School Committee, 762 F. Supp. 416 (D. Mass. 1991).

Gregory K. v. Longview School District, 811 F.2d 1307 (9th Cir. 1987).

Hall v. Vance County Board of Education, 774 F.2d 629 (4th Cir. 1985).

Hampton School Dist. v. Dobrowolski, 976 F.2d 48 (1st Cir. 1992).

Henry v. School Administrative Unit #29, 70 F. Supp.2d 52 (D.N.H. 1999).

Hiller v. Board of Education of Brunswick Central School District, 743 F. Supp. 958 (N.D.N.Y. 1990).

Holland v. District of Columbia, 71 F.3d 417 (D.C. Cir. 1995).

Holmes v. District of Columbia, 680 F. Supp. 40 (D.D.C. 1988).

Honig v. Doe, 484 U.S. 305 (1988).

Hudson v. Wilson, 828 F.2d 1059 (4th Cir. 1987).

Individuals with Disabilities Education Act, 20 U.S.C. § 1400 *et seq.* (2005).

Jacobson v. District of Columbia Board of Education, 564 F. Supp. 166 (D.D.C. 1983).

Johnson ex rel. Johnson v. Olathe District Schools Unified School District. No. 233, Special Services Division, 316 F. Supp.2d 960 (D. Kan. 2003).

Johnson v. Duneland School Corporation, 92 F.3d 554 (7th Cir. 1996).

Jonathan G. v. Caddo Parish School Board, 875 F. Supp. 352 (W.D. La. 1994).

Joshua B. v. New Trier Township High School District 203, 770 F. Supp. 431 (N.D. Ill. 1991).

Kattan v. District of Columbia, 691 F. Supp. 1539 (D.D.C. 1988).

Knight v. District of Columbia, 877 F.2d 1025 (D.D.C. 1989).

Kroot v. District of Columbia, 800 F. Supp. 977 (D.D.C. 1992).

Kuszewski v. Chippewa Valley Schools, 131 F. Supp.2d 926 (E.D. Mich. 2001).

Lenhoff v. Farmington Public Schools, 680 F. Supp. 921 (E.D. Mich. 1988).

Leonard v. McKenzie, 869 F.2d 1558 (D.C. Cir. 1989).

Lillbask ex rel. Mauclaire v. Sergi, 117 F. Supp.2d 182 (D. Conn. 2000).

Logue v. Shawnee Mission Public School Unified School District No. 512, 959 F. Supp. 1338 (D. Kan. 1997), *affirmed* 153 F.3d 727 (10th Cir. 1998) (mem.).

Lora v. Board of Education of the City of New York, 456 F. Supp. 1211 (E.D.N.Y. 1978), *affirmed in part* 623 F.2d 248 (2d Cir. 1980), final order 587 F. Supp. 1572 (E.D.N.Y. 1984).

Lunceford v. District of Columbia Board of Education, 745 F.2d 1577 (D.C. Cir. 1984).

Magyar v. Tucson Unified School District, 956 F. Supp. 1423 (D. Ariz. 1997).

Max M. v. Thompson, 566 F. Supp. 1330 (N.D. Ill. 1983).

McKenzie v. Smith, 771 F.2d 1527 (D.C. Cir. 1985).

Mehfoud, K. S., & Osborne, A. G. (1998). Making a successful interim placement under the IDEA. *Education Law Reporter, 124*, 7–12.

Middlebrook v. School District of the County of Knox, Tennessee, 805 F. Supp. 534 (E.D. Tenn. 1991).

M.L. v. Federal Way School District, 394 F.3d 634 (9th Cir. 2005a), *cert. denied*, 125 S. Ct. 2941 (2005b).

Mrs. C. v. Wheaton, 916 F.2d 69 (2d Cir. 1990).

Ms. S. ex rel. G. v. Vashon Island School District, 337 F.3d 1115 (9th Cir. 2003).

Murphy v. Arlington Central School District Board of Education, 86 F. Supp.2d 354 (S.D.N.Y. 2000).

Myles S. v. Montgomery County Board of Education, 824 F. Supp. 1549 (M.D. Ala. 1993).

Navin v. Park Ridge School District, 270 F.3d 1147 (7th Cir. 2001).

N.L. ex rel. Mrs. C. v. Knox County Schools, 315 F.3d 688 (6th Cir. 2003).

Osborne, A. G. (1993). Parental rights under the IDEA. *Education Law Reporter, 80*, 771–777.

O'Toole v. Olathe District Schools Unified School District No. 233, 963 F. Supp. 1000 (D. Kan. 1997), *affirmed* 144 F.3d 692 (10th Cir. 1998).

Owasso Independent School District v. Falvo, 534 U.S. 426 (2002).

Patricia P. v. Board of Education of Oak Park and River Forest High School District No. 200, 8 F. Supp.2d 801 (N.D. Ill. 1998), *affirmed* 203 F.3d 462 (7th Cir. 2000).

Paul Y. by Kathy Y. v. Singletary, 979 F. Supp. 1422 (S.D. Fla. 1997).

Petties v. District of Columbia, 881 F. Supp. 63, 888 F. Supp. 165. 894 F. Supp. 465, 897 F. Supp. 626 (D.D.C. 1995).

Pitchford ex. rel M. v. Salem-Keizer School District No. 24J, 155 F. Supp.2d 1213 (D. Or. 2001).

P.J. v. State of Connecticut Board of Education, 788 F. Supp. 673 (D. Conn. 1992).

Poolaw v. Bishop, 67 F.3d 830 (9th Cir. 1995).

Raymond S. v. Ramirez, 918 F. Supp. 1280 (N.D. Iowa 1996).

Rehabilitation Act of 1973, Section 504, 29 U.S.C. § 794.

R.L. ex rel. Mr. L. v. Plainville Board of Education, 363 F.Supp.2d 222 (D. Conn. 2005).

Rothschild v. Grottenthaler, 907 F.2d 286 (2d Cir. 1990).

Russell v. Jefferson, 609 F. Supp. 605 (N.D. Cal. 1985).

Russo, C. J., & Mawdsley, R. D. (2002). *Owasso Independent School District v. Falvo*: The Supreme Court upholds peer-grading. *School Business Affairs, 68*(5), 34–36.

Russo C. J., & Talbert-Johnson, C. (1997). The over-representation of African American children in special education: The resegregation of educational programming? *Education and Urban Society, 29*(2), 136–148.

Saleh v. District of Columbia, 660 F. Supp. 212 (D.D.C. 1987).

Schares v. Katy Independent School District, 252 F. Supp.2d 364 (S.D. Tex. 2003).

Scituate School Committee v. Robert B., 620 F. Supp. 1224 (D.R.I. 1985), *affirmed* 795 F.2d 77 (1st Cir. 1986) (mem.).

Sean R. v. Board of Education of the Town of Woodbridge, 794 F. Supp. 467 (D. Conn. 1992).

Seattle School District No. 1 v. B.S., 82 F.3d 1493 (9th Cir. 1996).

Sherri A.D. v. Kirby, 975 F.2d 193 (5th Cir. 1992).

Smith v. Henson, 786 F. Supp. 43 (D.D.C. 1992).

Smith v. Squillacote, 800 F. Supp. 993 (D.D.C. 1992).

Spielberg v. Henrico County Public Schools, 853 F.2d 256 (4th Cir. 1988).

Spilsbury v. District of Columbia, 307 F. Supp. 22 (D.D.C. 2004), 377 F.Supp.2d 1 (D.D.C. 2005).

St. Tammany Parish School Board v. State of Louisiana, 142 F.3d 776 (5th Cir. 1998).

Stock v. Massachusetts Hospital School, 467 N.E.2d 448 (Mass. 1984).

Tammy S. v. Reedsburg School District, 302 F.Supp.2d 959 (W.D. Wis. 2003).

Taylor v. Vermont Department of Education, 313 F.3d 768 (2d Cir. 2002).

Thomas v. Cincinnati Board of Education, 918 F.2d 618 (6th Cir. 1990).

Tilton v. Jefferson County Board of Education, 705 F.2d 800 (6th Cir. 1983).

Tracy v. Beaufort County Board of Education, 335 F.Supp.2d 675 (D.S.C. 2004).

T.S. v. Independent School District No. 54, 265 F.3d 1090 (10th Cir. 2001).

T.S. v. Ridgefield Board of Education, 808 F. Supp. 926 (D. Conn. 1992), *affirmed sub nom. T.S. v. Board of Education of the Town of Ridgefield*, 10 F.3d 87 (2d Cir. 1993).

Vander Malle v. Ambach, 673 F.2d 49 (2d Cir. 1982).

Verhoeven v. Brunswick School Committee, 207 F.3d 1 (1st Cir. 1999).

Visco v. School District of Pittsburgh, 684 F. Supp. 1310 (W.D. Pa. 1988).

V.W. and R.W. v. Favolise, 131 F.R.D. 654 (D. Conn. 1990).*Warren G. v. Cumberland County School District*, 190 F.3d 80 (3d Cir. 1999).

Webster Groves School District v. Pulitzer Publishing Co., 898 F.2d 1371 (8th Cir. 1990).

Weil v. Board of Elementary and Secondary Education, 931 F.2d 1069 (5th Cir. 1991).

Werner v. Clarksville Central School District, 363 F. Supp.2d 656 (S.D.N.Y. 2005).

W.G. and B.G. v. Board of Trustees of Target Range School District No. 23, Missoula, Montana, 789 F. Supp. 1070 (D. Mont. 1991), *affirmed* 960 F.2d 1479 (9th Cir. 1992).

White ex rel. White v. Ascension Parish School Board, 343 F.3d 373 (5th Cir. 2003).

Zvi D. v. Ambach, 520 F. Supp. 196 (E.D.N.Y. 1981), *affirmed* 694 F.2d 904 (2d Cir. 1982).

5

Student Discipline

INTRODUCTION

As originally enacted, even though the Individuals with Disabilities Education Act (IDEA) did not specifically mention discipline, many of its provisions had implications that could have been applied to situations involving the disciplining of students with disabilities. Early court cases recognized that students with disabilities had additional due process rights when faced with such disciplinary sanctions as expulsions or long-term suspensions because such actions could have denied them the free appropriate public education (FAPE) that they were entitled to under the IDEA.

When the U.S. Congress approved the most comprehensive amendments to the IDEA to date in 1997, for the first time it included provisions governing the disciplinary process that applied to students with disabilities. Consistent with their ordinary manner of doing business, Congress and the Department of Education refined and reorganized these provisions as part of the 2004 IDEA amendments (20 U.S.C. § 1415(k)) and their regulations, respectively (34 C.F.R. §§ 300.530–536). As complex as the IDEA's disciplinary requirements are, this chapter reflects that it is possible to extract guiding principles from the statutes, regulations, and numerous court cases dealing with the rights of students with disabilities who are subject to discipline (Dayton, 2002).

This chapter details specific requirements for administering disciplinary penalties to students with disabilities. In order to provide readers with an understanding of how and why many of the current disciplinary provisions of the IDEA came into being, the chapter begins with a historical overview of the case law that developed before the enactment of the

IDEA's 1997 amendments. Now that much of the pre-1997 litigation is incorporated into the IDEA, this review of the early case law provides insight into how the law and regulations should be interpreted. The next sections cover the specific requirements of the current statute and recent litigation. The chapter ends with recommendations for practice.

CASE LAW BEFORE 1997

The IDEA, as originally written, contained no stipulations directly addressing the discipline of students with disabilities, yet courts were often asked to resolve disputes arising out of disciplinary situations involving students with disabilities under the IDEA, and a large body of case law emerged. Even though the IDEA now contains disciplinary provisions, an examination of this case law is instructive because it provides the necessary background for understanding the current version of the law.

Early Decisions

In *Stuart v. Nappi* (1978), school officials in Connecticut unsuccessfully tried to expel a student with disabilities who was involved in several schoolwide disturbances. The student's attorney requested a due process hearing under the IDEA while obtaining an order from the federal trial court that prevented educators from conducting an expulsion hearing. Ruling in favor of the student, the court proclaimed that since an expulsion was a change in placement that was inconsistent with the IDEA's procedures, school officials should have provided the student and his parents with written prior notice before attempting to modify his educational placement (20 U.S.C. § 1415(b)(3)). The court added that school officials could temporarily suspend disruptive students or change their placement to more restrictive settings by complying with the IDEA's procedures.

A year later, a federal trial court in Indiana, in *Doe v. Koger* (1979), overturned the expulsion of a student who was mildly mentally disabled. The court noted that school officials could not expel students whose disruptive conduct was caused by their disabilities. The court implied that students with disabilities could be expelled when there was no relationship between their misconduct and their disabilities, a perspective that became known as the manifestation of the disability doctrine. Further, the court reasoned that disruptive special education students can be transferred to more restrictive settings as long as school officials follow the proper change in placement procedures.

The Fifth Circuit broadened the manifestation of the disability doctrine in *S-1 v. Turlington* (1981) after one of several students who were expelled for a variety of acts of misconduct requested a manifestation hearing. The superintendent of schools concluded that because the student was not classified as emotionally disturbed, the misconduct was not a manifestation of his disability. In overturning the expulsion, the court declared that a manifestation determination must be made by a specialized and knowledgeable group of persons. The court explained that even with an expulsion, school officials could not completely cease serving students with disabilities, even in situations where there was no relationship between their misconduct and disability, and they were properly expelled by following the IDEA's procedures.

A case from the Fourth Circuit, affirming an earlier order from Virginia, illustrates that it is not necessarily all that difficult to establish connections between a student's disability and misconduct. In *School Board of the County of Prince William v. Malone* (1985) a student with a learning disability was involved in several drug transactions. After a committee of special educators was satisfied that there was no causal relationship between the student's disability and his involvement in the drug transactions, he was expelled. On judicial review, a federal trial court found that a relationship did in fact exist because the student's learning disability caused him to have a poor self-image, which in turn led him to seek peer approval by becoming involved in the drug transactions. The court noted that the expulsion was improper because the student's learning disability prevented him from understanding the long-term consequences of his actions.

The early cases permitted school officials to exclude students with disabilities who posed dangers to themselves and/or others as long as they followed proper procedures. For example, in *Jackson v. Franklin County School Board* (1985), the Fifth Circuit affirmed an earlier order supporting a school board's exclusion of a student who was diagnosed as having a psychosexual disorder. A youth court committed the student to a state hospital for treatment, but school officials refused to admit him when he tried to return to school following his release from the hospital. The court agreed with the recommendation of school officials that the student be placed in a private facility because of the danger that he presented to others.

U.S. Supreme Court Decision

In 1988 the U.S. Supreme Court handed down its first, and only, opinion involving discipline under the IDEA in *Honig v. Doe*, a dispute that concerned two special education students identified in court papers as John Doe and Jack Smith. Doe, who was emotionally disturbed with aggressive tendencies, attended a developmental center for children with disabilities. Soon after Doe was placed at the school, he assaulted a peer and broke a school window. Initially Doe was suspended for five days, but was later put on an indefinite suspension pending an expulsion hearing. Doe's counsel unsuccessfully asked school officials to cancel the expulsion hearing and to reconvene a meeting of his individualized education program (IEP) team. Judicial review began after school board representatives ignored the attorney's request. A federal trial court eventually cancelled the expulsion hearing, ordered Doe readmitted to school, and prevented school officials from excluding him while educators sought to place him in an alternative setting.

Smith was also emotionally disturbed and displayed aggressive tendencies. Educators placed Smith in a special education program within a regular school on a trial basis. After he committed a number of acts of misconduct, school authorities reduced Smith's program to a half-day schedule. Although his grandparents agreed to this reduction, they were not advised of their rights or options regarding Smith's IEP. Following an incident wherein he made sexual comments to female students, Smith was suspended for five days and school officials recommended that he be expelled. School officials continued Smith's suspension pending resolution of expulsion proceedings. When Smith's attorney objected to the expulsion hearing, the school board canceled it and offered either to restore the half-day program or provide him with home tutoring. Smith's grandparents chose the home tutoring option.

> In the IDEA, Congress sought to strip school officials of their *unilateral* authority to exclude students with disabilities for disciplinary infractions, particularly children who were emotionally disturbed.

In the litigation initiated by Doe and Smith, now known as *Honig v. Doe* (*Honig*, 1988), a federal trial court in California, the Ninth Circuit, and the Supreme Court agreed that students with disabilities could not be expelled for misbehavior that was related to their disabilities. The Supreme Court acknowledged that in passing the IDEA, Congress intended to limit the authority of school officials to exclude students with disabilities, even for disciplinary purposes:

> We think it clear, however, that Congress very much meant to strip schools of the *unilateral* authority they had traditionally employed to exclude disabled students, particularly emotionally disturbed students, from school. In so doing, Congress did not leave school administrators powerless to deal with dangerous students; it did, however, deny school officials their former right to "self help," and directed that in the future the removal of disabled students could be accomplished only with the permission of the parents or, as a last resort, the courts. (*Honig v. Doe*, 1988, pp. 323–324)

The Court did not leave school officials without recourse; it added that they could suspend students with disabilities for up to 10 days if they posed an immediate threat to the safety of others. The Court suggested that during the 10-day "cooling off" period school officials should seek to reach agreements with parents for alternate placements for their children. In the event that parents adamantly refused to consent to changes in placements, the Court pointed out that school officials could seek judicial aid. Under such circumstances, the Court explained, educators were not required to exhaust administrative remedies prior to seeking judicial relief if they could show that administrative review would have been futile or inadequate. The Court maintained that in appropriate cases the judiciary could temporarily prevent students who were dangerous from attending school. The Court concluded by pointing out that the IDEA created a presumption in favor of students' current educational placements that school officials could overcome only by showing that preserving the status quo was substantially likely to result in injuries to those children and/or others.

Post-*Honig* Lower Court Decisions

Honig cleared up many, but by no means all, issues regarding the discipline of special education students. Accordingly, litigation continued. *Honig* specified that students with disabilities could not be expelled for misbehavior that was related to their disabilities. Moreover, *Honig* suggested that educators could employ ordinary disciplinary sanctions that did not cause changes in placements, such as short-term suspensions.

In 1989 the Tenth Circuit affirmed that short-term disciplinary measures were not changes in placements under the IDEA (*Hayes v. Unified School District No. 377*, 1989). The dispute began when the parents of two students with histories of academic and behavior problems objected to the use of in-school suspensions and time-outs. The court commented that while these short-term measures did not amount to changes in placements, since they were matters relating to the education of the students, they were subject to the IDEA's administrative due process procedures.

By sanctioning suspensions of up to 10 school days, the Supreme Court envisioned a "cooling off" period that would afford school officials and parents time to work together to devise other placements for students if they were needed. Unfortunately, school officials and parents do not always agree, and sometimes other options cannot be agreed on during the 10-day suspension periods. When agreement cannot be reached, disputes are subject to the often lengthy administrative and judicial process.

Honig did give school officials the ability to seek injunctions to remove students with disabilities who are dangerous or who create serious disruptions to the educational process while administrative and judicial proceedings are ongoing. In such a situation, the burden is on school officials to demonstrate that students are truly dangerous and that removal from their then-current educational placements is the only feasible option.

In the face of disruptive behavior by children with disabilities, school boards began filing suits seeking *Honig* injunctions to remove dangerous students. In Virginia, a state court granted an injunction against a 12-year-old student who was involved in a number of fights, struck and yelled obscenities at school officials, and had to be restrained by the police on several occasions (*School Board of the County of Prince William v. Wills*, 1989). A year later another state court in Virginia issued an injunction against a student who set a fire in a school locker, among other infractions (*School Board of the County of Stafford v. Farley*, 1990). Similarly, a federal trial court in Illinois issued an injunction barring a student who violently struck other children and threatened to kill students and staff (*Board of Education of Township High School District v. Kurtz-Imig*, 1989). Finally, a state court in New York declared that school officials met their burden of showing that a student, who ran out of the school waving an iron bar while threatening to kill someone, was likely to endanger other children if he returned to school (*East Islip Union Free School District v. Andersen*, 1994).

Courts have also ordered alternative placements when granting *Honig* injunctions. A federal trial court in Texas prohibited a student who assaulted classmates and teachers, destroyed school property, used profanity, and threatened to kill himself and others, from attending general education classes (*Texas City Independent School District v. Jorstad*, 1990). At the same time, the court decreed that pending the completion of the administrative review process, the student could either attend a behavioral class recommended by school officials or receive home tutoring. In a case from New York, a federal trial court directed school officials to place a student in a special education class pending completion of a due process hearing (*Binghampton City School District v. Borgna*, 1991). The student frequently exhibited aggressive behavior such as punching other children, sticking a pencil in another student's ear, throwing his shoes at staff, hitting faculty, tipping over desks, and throwing chairs. In like fashion, a federal trial court in Florida granted an injunction allowing the school board to transfer a student who had been involved in 43 instances of aggressive behavior to a special education center (*School Board of Pinellas County v. J.M. by L.M.*, 1997).

Not all school boards were successful in their attempts to secure *Honig* injunctions. A federal trial court in Missouri refused to allow the removal of a child who made numerous threats to students and school officials, repeatedly exploded in anger, and threw furniture (*Clinton County R-III School District v. C.J.K.*, 1995). Although another student was injured during one of these outbursts and teachers testified that they were afraid of the student, the court did not think that this was enough to establish that serious personal injury was likely to occur if the student remained in his current placement. In another dispute, a federal trial court in Pennsylvania refused to issue an injunction, observing that school officials failed to show that they had taken every reasonable measure to mitigate the danger that the student at issue posed (*School District of Philadelphia v. Stephan M. and Theresa M.*, 1997).

The Eighth Circuit provided school administrators with practical guidance on the removal of students with disabilities from their then-current educational settings in *Light v. Parkway C-2 School District* (1994). The court allowed the removal of a student with mental disabilities, who exhibited a steady stream of aggressive and disruptive behaviors, from her then-current special education placement. In doing so, the court was of the opinion that children whose misbehaviors flowed directly from their disabilities were subject to removal if they posed a substantial risk of injury to themselves or others. In addition to showing that this student presented such a danger, the court declared that school officials had to demonstrate that they made reasonable efforts to accommodate her disabilities so as to minimize the likelihood that she would injure herself or others. The court emphasized that only a showing of the likelihood of injury was required and that serious harm need not be inflicted before children could be considered likely to cause injury. The court further specified that injury is not defined solely as an infliction that draws blood or sends a victim to an emergency room but includes bruises, bites, and poked eyes.

Another issue that emerged in the years after *Honig* was whether students who were not yet identified as disabled were entitled to the IDEA's protections if they claimed to be disabled. In a case where there was a disagreement over whether a student was qualified for IDEA services, school officials sought to expel him for bringing a gun to school. In *Hacienda La Puente Unified School District of Los Angeles v. Honig* (1992), the Ninth Circuit interpreted *Honig* as requiring school officials to provide all students with disabilities, regardless of whether they were previously identified as such, with the IDEA's procedural protections. The judicial panel thus affirmed a hearing officer's order, and a trial court's refusal to hear the dispute, that the student be readmitted to school because educators had violated his IDEA rights.

Along the same line, in *M.P. by D.P. v. Governing Board of the Grossmont Union High School District* (1994) a federal trial court in California held that the IDEA's procedural safeguards must be applied regardless of whether a student was previously diagnosed as having a disability. The court recognized that a student who was not disabled could attempt to be labeled as disabled solely to gain the benefits of the IDEA, but remarked that the IDEA did not address this possibility. On the other hand, a federal trial court in Virginia decided that a student who was suspended on a weapons violation was not entitled to the protections of the IDEA because the question of her disability was raised well after the infraction (*Doe v. Manning*, 1994). As is addressed later in this chapter, Congress specifically addressed this issue in the 2004 IDEA amendments.

A related issue is whether former special education students who were not receiving services when they committed their disciplinary infractions were entitled to the IDEA's protections. In one case, where a student was removed from special education at his mother's request because he no longer wished to receive special education, a federal trial court in Wisconsin answered in the affirmative. School officials removed the student from a special education class for the emotionally disturbed at his mother's request but against his teacher's recommendation. In *Steldt v. School Board of the Riverdale School District* (1995), the student was expelled for a series of acts that included assaults on peers and school personnel. The court, noting that the mother's request for her son to be removed from special education did not change his status as a student in need of special education, insisted that he was entitled to the IDEA's protections.

A related issue is how school officials should treat students who were evaluated but not classified as disabled. As with most disputes, the answer is based on the unique facts of each case. In one case, a school's IEP team was convinced that a student did not require special education, but his mother contested its recommendation. The Seventh Circuit maintained that the student was not entitled to an injunction barring his expulsion while administrative proceedings were pending (*Rodiriecus L. v. Waukegan School District No. 60*, 1996). The court refused the student's request where school officials lacked either knowledge or reasonable suspicion on which to decide that he was disabled since not one single individual, teacher, guardian, parent, or school official, proposed or suggested that he may have needed special education. In a case such as this the court wrote that educators needed to employ a flexible approach when applying the IDEA's stay put provision and should not apply it automatically to every student who was referred for a placement in special education.

In *Honig*, the Supreme Court held that special education students could be suspended for up to 10 days. Unfortunately, the Court failed to indicate whether the 10-day limit was consecutive or cumulative. The Ninth Circuit, in *Parents of Student W. v. Puyallup School District* (1994), interpreted *Honig* as not supporting the proposition that the 10-day limit referred to 10 total days. The court determined that the school board's suspension guidelines, wherein each suspension triggered an evaluation to consider whether a student was receiving an appropriate education, were lawful. On the other hand, in *Manchester School District v. Charles M.F.* (1994), the federal trial court in New Hampshire decreed that cumulative suspensions totaling more than 10 days constituted a pattern of exclusion that resulted in a change of placement.

In *S-1 v. Turlington* (*Turlington*, 1981), discussed earlier, the Fifth Circuit asserted that even when special education students were properly expelled by following all of the IDEA's due process procedures, a complete cessation of services was not authorized. According to *Turlington*, a school board would still have to provide special education and related services to expelled students with disabilities.

This issue arose again in Virginia in 1992 when commonwealth officials submitted their three-year plan for special education to the U.S. Department of Education (USDOE). The plan included a regulation declaring that students with disabilities could be disciplined in the same manner as those who were not disabled if there was no causal relationship between their misconduct and their disabilities. The USDOE responded by notifying officials in Virginia that they could not discontinue educational services to expelled special education students, even if the discipline resulted from behavior unrelated to the students' disabilities. When officials left the regulation unchanged, the ensuing dispute eventually ended up in the courts. Following years of litigation, the Fourth Circuit, in *Commonwealth of Virginia Department of Education v. Riley (Riley,* 1997), ruled that the IDEA did not require local school boards to discipline disabled students differently from those who were not disabled when their misconduct was unrelated to their disabilities. The court found that the IDEA only required states to provide students with disabilities with access to a FAPE that, as with any right, could be forfeited by conduct antithetical to the right itself. The court concluded that school boards were not required to provide educational services to students with disabilities who forfeited their rights to a FAPE by willfully engaging in conduct so serious as to warrant the ultimate penalty of expulsion.

Later in the same year that the Fourth Circuit resolved *Riley,* the Seventh Circuit reached a similar outcome in *Doe v. Board of Education of Oak Park & River Forest High School District 200 (Oak Park,* 1997). When school officials expelled a student for possession of a pipe and a small amount of marijuana, the board's evaluation team was unconvinced that there was a causal relationship between his disability and misconduct. Under the circumstances, a federal trial court reasoned that the board was not required to provide the student with alternative educational services during the expulsion period. The appeals court agreed, declaring that the IDEA was not intended to shield special education students from the usual consequences of misconduct when their misbehavior was unrelated to their disabilities.

Riley and *Oak Park* can be contrasted with the order of a federal trial court in Arizona. In *Magyar v. Tucson Unified School District* (1997) school officials expelled a student with a learning disability after he gave an assault-style knife to another child. In reinstating the student, the court interpreted the IDEA as requiring school officials to provide all students with disabilities with a FAPE. The court thought that since the use of the word *all* in the IDEA was clear and unequivocal, it did not include an exception for misbehaving students. Again, this situation is addressed in the most recent amendments to the IDEA and its implementing regulations.

Figure 5.1   Procedural Steps and Timelines in the Disciplinary Process

When students with disabilities misbehave, educators should take the following steps (time limitations are in brackets):

- Take whatever measures are necessary to restore order and maintain discipline (immediately)
- Suspend students (for up to 10 school days) by following normal procedures
- Conduct functional behavioral assessments and develop behavior intervention plans if these are not already in place; review the functional behavioral assessments and behavior intervention plans if they are in place (within 10 school days)
- If expulsion is under consideration, complete manifestation determinations (within 10 school days), keeping in mind that
  - If officials determine that student misconduct was a manifestation of their disabilities, the children may not be expelled but may be moved to more restrictive placements by following the IDEA's change in placement procedures
  - If officials decide that there is no relationship between student disabilities and misconduct, the children may be expelled but they must continue to receive special education services during the expulsion period
- If student misconduct involved weapons, drugs, or the infliction of serious bodily injuries, consider placing offenders in interim alternative educational settings (for up to 45 school days)
- Seek hearing officer or judicial orders to change the placements of students (immediately) if they are not expelled or moved to interim alternative educational settings and school personnel are of the opinion that maintaining their then-current placements is likely to result in injuries to the students and/or others
- At the end of the expulsion period or the interim alternative placement, either return students to their former placements or develop new placements by following the IDEA's change in placement procedures

THE 1997 AND 2004 IDEA AMENDMENTS

Against this backdrop of litigation, and amid pressure from advocates for both school boards and students with disabilities, Congress, after debate, added disciplinary provisions to the IDEA in 1997. The 1997 amendments implemented the most far-reaching changes to the IDEA since it was originally enacted in 1975. Some of these provisions simply codified existing case law, others clarified gray areas, and some resolved judicial differences of opinion. Inasmuch as the 1997 amendments did not settle all issues, litigation continued (Daniel, 2001). When Congress amended the IDEA again in 2004, it further refined the disciplinary provisions. The cumulative result of these two amendments is that the IDEA now includes comprehensive guidelines dealing with disciplining of students with disabilities. Consequently, litigation in this area has decreased.

AUTHORITY OF SCHOOL PERSONNEL

The IDEA now outlines the authority and obligations of school officials when they discipline students with disabilities. The current disciplinary language provides school officials with more guidance than at any time in the past. Still, questions do arise that lead to litigation.

Case-by-Case Determination

Recognizing that disciplinary infractions may present school officials with unique situations, Congress inserted a clause into the 2004 version of the IDEA affording school officials some flexibility. The IDEA now explicitly permits educators to consider unique circumstances on case-by-case bases when evaluating whether changes in placements are necessary for students with disabilities who violate school rules (20 U.S.C. § 1415(k)(1)(A); 34 C.F.R. § 300.530(a)).

Suspensions and Placements
in Interim Alternative Educational Settings

The IDEA clearly stipulates that school officials may remove students with disabilities who violate school rules to appropriate interim alternative settings or other settings or suspend them for up to 10 school days (20 U.S.C. § 1415(k)(1)(B); 34 C.F.R. § 300.530(b)). Even so, educators can implement such measures only to the extent that they use similar punishments when disciplining students who are not disabled. In addition, students may be removed to interim alternative educational settings for up to 45 school days under specified circumstances, without regard for whether their misbehaviors are manifestations of their disabilities (20 U.S.C. § 1415(k)(1)(G); 34 C.F.R. § 300.530(g)).

Short-Term Suspensions

The 1997 amendments afforded school officials the authority to suspend special education students for not more than 10 school days as long as similar sanctions would have been applied to students who are not disabled. This language has been carried over into the 2004 version.

The IDEA now affords school personnel the explicit authority to suspend special education students for not more than 10 school days as long as similar sanctions apply to students who are not disabled (20 U.S.C. § 1415(k)(1)(B); 34 C.F.R. § 300.530(b)). Under these circumstances, school officials must conduct functional behavioral assessments of students if they have not already been completed; in addition, this step must be undertaken to address the misconduct of students so that it does not recur (20 U.S.C. § 1415(k)(1)(D)(ii); 34 C.F.R. § 300.530(d)(ii)).

In a related matter, the IDEA's regulations declare that a series of removals of students with disabilities resulting in a pattern of exclusions that cumulate to more than 10 school days may be considered changes in placements (34 C.F.R. § 300.536(a)(2)(i)). According to the regulation, in evaluating whether changes in placements occurred, decision makers must consider such factors as the length of each removal, the total amount of time that students are removed, and the proximity of the exclusions to one another (34 C.F.R. § 300.536(a)(2)(iii)). The regulation adds that if a student is suspended for misbehavior substantially similar to past misbehavior that was determined to be a manifestation of the student's disabilities, a change in placement also has occurred (34 C.F.R. § 300.536(a)(2)).

Suspensions for separate, but dissimilar, acts of misconduct may exceed 10 cumulative days in one school year (34 C.F.R. § 300.530(b)(1)). School board officials are not required to continue special education services for students who are removed for up to 10 cumulative days unless educational services are routinely provided to students who are not disabled under similar circumstances (34 C.F.R. § 300.530(d)(3)). If subsequent suspensions exceed 10 cumulative school days in one year, however, services must begin again after the 10th day (34 C.F.R. § 300.530(b)(2)).

Transfers to Other Settings for Disciplinary Reasons

Beginning with its 1997 amendments, the IDEA allows school officials to place students with disabilities in interim alternative educational settings for up to 45 school days for weapons and drug violations. In an important clarification, this provision now specifies that this period is for 45 school, not calendar days (20 U.S.C. § 1415(k)(1)(G); 34 C.F.R. § 300.530(g)). Specifically, the IDEA and its regulations authorize school officials to transfer students to alternative settings if they carry or possess weapons at school, on school premises, or at school functions (20 U.S.C. § 1415(k)(1)(G)(i); 34 C.F.R. § 300.530(g)(1)). Similarly, the law permits the same transfer for students who possess, use, sell, or solicit drugs under those same circumstances (20 U.S.C. § 1415(k)(1)(G)(ii); 34 C.F.R. § 300.530(g)(2)). The 2004 amendments add that such transfers can occur for students who inflict serious bodily injury on other persons at school, on school premises, or at school functions (20 U.S.C. § 1415(k)(1)(G)(iii); 34 C.F.R. § 300.530(g)(3)).

The IDEA requires school officials to conduct functional behavioral assessments and to implement behavioral intervention plans for any students who are placed in interim alternative settings (20 U.S.C. § 1415(k)(1)(D)(ii); 34 C.F.R. § 300.530(d)(ii)). If parents disagree with the placements in the interim alternative settings and request hearings, students must remain in their interim alternative educational settings pending the decisions of hearing officers or until the expiration of the 45-day period (20 U.S.C. § 1415(k)(4); 34 C.F.R. § 300.533). After the expiration of the 45-day period, students are entitled to return to their former placements even if hearings regarding school board proposals to change their placements are pending (20 U.S.C. § 1415(k)(4)(A)).

School officials have the explicit authority to transfer students with disabilities to appropriate interim alternative placements for up to 45 school days for possession of weapons or possession, use, sale, or solicitation of illegal drugs at school, on school premises, or at school functions. Students who inflict seriously bodily injury on others at school, on school premises, or at school functions are now subject to the same action.

Weapons, Alcohol, and Drugs. School officials have the explicit authority to transfer students with disabilities to appropriate interim alternative placements for up to 45 school days for weapons, drug, and alcohol violations (20 U.S.C. §§ 1415(k)(1)(G)(i), (ii); 34 C.F.R. §§ 300.530(g)(1), (2)). This clause expands the authority that the Gun-Free Schools Act of 1994 granted school officials to exclude students from schools for drug violations. The IDEA defines weapons and illegal drugs by referring to other federal legislation (20 U.S.C. §§ 1415(k)(7)(A), (B); 34 C.F.R. § 300.530(i)). In this regard, the definition of a dangerous weapon is expanded beyond the previous definition enunciated in the Gun-Free Schools Act. Under the new definition, what can be considered a dangerous weapon includes other instruments, devices, materials, and substances capable of inflicting harm in addition to firearms, but does not include small pocket knives (18 U.S.C. § 930(g)(2)). The IDEA defines an illegal drug as a controlled substance, but excludes controlled substances that may be legally prescribed by physicians (20 U.S.C. § 1415(k)(7)(B); 34 C.F.R. § 300.530(i)(1)). The Controlled Substances Act (1999), which is located at 21 U.S.C. § 812(c), and is too lengthy to repeat here, sets forth the full categorization of controlled substances.

Infliction of Serious Bodily Injury. The IDEA allows educators to remove students with disabilities to interim alternative settings for inflicting serious bodily injuries (20 U.S.C. § 1415(k)(1)(G)(iii); 34 C.F.R. § 300.530(g)(3)). The IDEA defines serious bodily injury by referencing another section of the U.S. Code (20 U.S.C. § 1415(k)(7)(C); 34 C.F.R. § 300.530(i)(3)). Serious bodily injury involves a substantial risk of death, extreme physical pain, protracted and obvious disfigurement, or protracted loss or impairment of the function of a bodily member, organ, or mental faculty (18 U.S.C. §

1365(h)(3)). Serious bodily injury may be contrasted with bodily injury, which generally involves only cuts, abrasions, bruises, burns, or other temporary injuries (18 U.S.C. § 1365(h)(4)).

Other Infractions. The IDEA permits school officials to remove students with disabilities from inclusive settings, moving them to interim alternative placements for infractions other than those specifically listed in its provisions (20 U.S.C. § 1415(k)(1)(A); 34 C.F.R. § 300.530(a)). When exercising this case-by-case authority, school officials are likely to be faced with parental challenges. Prior case law indicates that school officials are likely to be upheld as long as they can reasonably justify their actions.

As illustrated by a pre-2004 case from Texas, one such circumstance when school officials might seek to remove a student with disabilities from school could be an act of sexual harassment. In *Randy M. v. Texas City ISD* (2000) school officials recommended the transfer of a special education student to an alternative education program for the remainder of a school year after he, in consort with another child, ripped the pants off a female student. Prior to making this recommendation, the child's IEP team determined that the student's misconduct was not a manifestation of his disability. When the student's parents sought to prevent the transfer, a federal trial court refused their request. In denying the parents' request, the court expressed its view that the disciplinary actions of the school officials were entirely appropriate under the facts of the case. The court explained that school officials were justified in taking stern and aggressive remedial action when faced with such conduct.

Another circumstance that can lead to the removal of a student with disabilities is behavior that may not necessarily have caused serious bodily injury but that, if repeated, has the potential to do so. In such a case, an appellate court in New York approved the removal of a child who hit other students and teachers, after acknowledging that educators had shown that allowing him to return to school was likely to result in injury to himself or others (*Roslyn Union Free School District v. Geffrey W.*, 2002).

Functional Behavioral Assessments and Behavioral Intervention Plans

> The IDEA requires school officials to conduct functional behavioral assessments and implement behavioral intervention plans, if they are not already in place, or review such assessments and plans if they have been implemented for students with disabilities.

The IDEA requires school personnel to conduct functional behavioral assessments (FBAs) and implement behavioral intervention plans (BIPs) under certain circumstances, if they are not already in place, or to review such assessments and plans if they have been implemented for students with disabilities. Specifically, officials must perform FBAs and implement BIPs whenever students with disabilities are removed from their then-current placements for disciplinary reasons for more than 10 school days (20 U.S.C. § 1415(k)(1)(D)(ii); 34 C.F.R. § 300.530(d)(1)(ii)). FBAs and BIPs must also be executed, if they have not already been done, if officials decide that student misbehaviors are not manifestations of their disabilities (20 U.S.C. § 1415(k)(1)(F)(i); 34 C.F.R. § 300.530(f)(1)).

Even though it calls for their creation, neither the IDEA nor its regulations provide much guidance as to what should be included in FBAs or BIPs. As of this writing, there have been few judicial opinions or results of due process hearings dealing with the contents of either FBAs or BIPs. In fact, in one dispute over a school's BIP, the Seventh Circuit held that because there are no substantive requirements for a BIP, the challenged BIP could not have fallen short of criteria that did not exist (*Alex R. v. Forrestville Valley Community Unit School District*, 2004). Nevertheless, the fact that substantive criteria for FBAs and BIPs do not exist, does not mean that developing them is unimportant. One court overturned a school's manifestation determination, in part, where school officials failed to conduct an FBA prior to acting (*Coleman v. Newburgh Enlarged City School District*, 2004). Further, the Eighth Circuit went so far as to comment that a BIP does not need to be written (*School Board of Independent School District No. 11 v. Renollett*, 2006). The Eighth Circuit's position notwithstanding, school officials would be well-advised that the safest course of action is to put both FBAs and BIPs in writing.

Expulsions

The IDEA permits educators to expel students with disabilities as long as the behaviors that gave rise to their violations of school rules were not manifestations of their disabilities. Again, though, under these circumstances expulsions must be treated in the same manner and for the same duration as they would have been for students who are not disabled (20 U.S.C. § 1415(k)(1)(C); 300 C.F.R. § 300.530(c)).

Provision of Special Education Services During Expulsions

> The IDEA, as currently written, makes it perfectly clear that special education services must continue during expulsions of students with disabilities.

The IDEA makes it clear that special education services must continue during expulsions (20 U.S.C. §§ 1412(a)(1)(A), 1415(k)(1)(D)(i); 34 C.F.R. §

530(d)(1)(i)). This provision comports with the position previously taken by the USDOE, effectively reversing judicial orders to the contrary (*Commonwealth of Virginia Department of Education v. Riley*, 1997; *Doe v. Board of Education of Oak Park & River Forest High School District 200*, 1997). The addition of this section to the IDEA ended a controversy that existed among the federal circuits prior to the enactment of the 1997 amendments.

Figure 5.2   Definition of *Manifestation*

Prior to the enactment of the 2004 IDEA amendments, a precise definition of manifestation did not exist. As the IDEA now reads, *manifestation* is defined as conduct that was caused by or had a direct and substantial relationship to student disabilities; or conduct that was the direct result of the failure of school officials to implement the IEPs of students (20 U.S.C.A. § 1415(k)(1)(E)(i)).

Manifestation Doctrine

> When school officials contemplate the expulsion of special education students, the IDEA requires educators first to ascertain whether their misbehaviors are manifestations of their disabilities.

As noted earlier in this chapter, the courts have long recognized that expulsions of students in special education settings constitute changes in placements. Expelling students for misconducts that were manifestations of their disabilities, the courts reasoned, would have been the equivalent of punishing children for behavior over which they had no control. In addition, the courts agreed that expulsions would have resulted in denying students the FAPEs they were entitled to under federal law. When school officials contemplate the expulsion of special education students, the IDEA requires educators first to ascertain whether students' misbehaviors are manifestations of their disabilities. If officials agree that there is no connection between the disabilities of children and their misconduct, they may expel students (20 U.S.C. § 1415(k)(1)(C); 34 C.F.R. § 300.530(c)). Insofar as it is highly likely that parents are apt to challenge the expulsions of their children, it is imperative for school officials to follow proper procedures when making manifestation determinations.

Personnel Making the Manifestation Determination

Whether particular forms of student misconduct are manifestations of their disabilities are judgments for school officials, parents, and relevant members of students' IEP team (20 U.S.C. § 1415(k)(1)(E); 34 C.F.R. §

300.530(e)). Members of IEP teams should have personal knowledge of the students involved and of special education as well as an understanding of the characteristics of the disabilities of the children. The IDEA's regulations stipulate that parents of children with disabilities along with regular and special education teachers, a school board representative who is qualified to provide or supervise special education, a person qualified to interpret evaluation data, and the students (if appropriate) should be included in meetings at which IEPs are developed, reviewed, or revised (34 C.F.R. § 300.321(a)). Other qualified persons, such as current teachers or guidance counselors, may be called in to provide additional information (34 C.F.R. § 300.321(a)(6)).

The parents of students must be invited to attend meetings where manifestation determinations are to be made since the IDEA's regulations afford them the right to attend any meetings in which the educational placements of their children are discussed (34 C.F.R. §§ 300.321, 300.322). Inasmuch as manifestation determinations affect student placements, parents have the right to attend the meetings at which they are made.

Timeline

Manifestation determinations should be made immediately after but no later than 10 days following decisions that are reached that would remove students from their then-current educational placements for more than 10 days (20 U.S.C. § 1415(k)(1)(E)(i); 34 C.F.R. § 300.530(e)(1)). Even so, the federal trial court in Maine pointed out that a delay in conducting a manifestation hearing was of no consequence where the parents were given the opportunity to participate and the delay did not affect its outcome (*Farrin v. Maine School Administrative District No. 59*, 2001). The court observed that the school board's special education director made several unsuccessful attempts to contact the parents in seeking to schedule the hearing within the 10-day time period.

Manifestation as Defined in the IDEA

Prior to 2004 the IDEA did not include a precise definition of the term *manifestation*. The current version of the IDEA specifies that conduct should be considered to be manifestations of students' disabilities if it was caused by or had a direct and substantial relationship to their disabilities or if it was the direct result of failures to implement their IEPs (20 U.S.C. § (k)(1)(E); 34 C.F.R. § 300.530(e)(1)). Earlier case law can provide some guidance on how this new language can be interpreted.

The language that is now included in the IDEA's definition of manifestation is similar to the wording that the Ninth Circuit used in *Doe v. Maher* (1986), the case that, on appeal, became known as *Honig v. Doe*. Here the court acknowledged that manifestation of the disability refers to "conduct that is caused by, or has a direct and substantial relationship" to the student's disability (pp. 1480–1481, n. 8). The court offered further clarification with statements that disabilities must significantly impair students' behavioral controls but does not embrace conduct that "bears only an attenuated relationship" to children's disabilities (pp. 1480–1481, n. 8).

In a judgment that was handed down before the 2004 amendments and the current definition of manifestation became effective, a federal trial court in New York overturned a school panel's finding that a student's misconduct was not a manifestation of his disability. Although it is a pre-2004 amendment opinion, this case illustrates one way that a disability may be deemed to have a direct relationship to a student's misconduct. When the student was disciplined after an altercation with another child, he claimed that his actions were in response to taunting from the other student about the fact that he was in a special education placement. The court was thus satisfied that the student's disability was directly involved in the ensuing altercation for which he was disciplined (*Coleman v. Newburgh Enlarged City School District*, 2004).

In another pre-2004 amendment case, the Fourth Circuit upheld a school board's manifestation determination. Here a student coerced another child into putting a threatening note in the computer file of a third student. The court was convinced that the student was aware of the consequences of sending the threatening note, and even anticipated them by enlisting the services of another child. Uncovering nothing in the student's records indicating that he could not manage his emotional problems, the court agreed that his misconduct was not a manifestation of his disability (*AW ex rel. Wilson v. Fairfax County School Board*, 2004).

Decisions the Manifestation Team Must Make

Along with evaluating whether misconduct was caused by or had a direct and substantial relationship to student disabilities, IEP teams must consider whether behavior was due to IEPs that were not properly implemented (20 U.S.C. § 1415(k)(1)(E)(i)(II); 34 C.F.R. § 300.530(e)(ii)). In reviewing whether placements were appropriate, IEP teams should use the same standards that apply when prospectively evaluating whether a proposed placement is appropriate. Unless state law dictates otherwise, the basic criterion of an appropriate placement is whether it results in conferring "some educational benefit" on a special education student (*Board of Education of the Hendrick Hudson Central School District v. Rowley*, 1982).

If IEP teams decide that students' misconduct is either a manifestation of their disabilities or results from inappropriate placements or IEPs, children may not be expelled or suspended for more than 10 days and school officials must reconsider their then-current placements. At the same time, officials can consider making appropriate nonpunitive changes in placements, such as the use of time-out rooms and study carrels (*Honig v. Doe*, 1988), that can be implemented subject to the IDEA's procedural safeguards and least restrictive environment provisions. Students may be suspended for more than 10 days, or expelled, if their misconduct is not caused by their disabilities or do not result from inappropriate IEPs or placements.

Consideration of the Student's Disability Classification

Manifestation determinations must be individualized. Blanket judgments based on the characteristics generally exhibited by others with the same disability are not allowed. As such, IEP teams must consider whether disabilities, as they affect students, are related to specific misconduct. An important consideration here is the severity of student disabilities (*Elk Grove Unified School District*, 1989). IEP teams should also evaluate whether students have any previously unidentified disabilities that could have caused their wrongdoings (*Modesto City Schools*, 1994). Further, manifestation determinations must refer to specific incidents, as generalizations cannot be the key factor. In other words, IEP teams must consider whether the disabilities exhibited by students could have caused the particular misconduct giving rise to their proposed expulsions.

Consideration of Causes Other Than Disability

IEP teams must also consider other factors that could have caused student misbehavior (*Elk Grove Unified School District*, 1989). When several factors contribute to misbehavior, and a disability is one of them, as long as IEP teams can make a connection between the disability and misconduct, students cannot be expelled.

Reevaluation Requirement

If evaluation data are not up to date, school officials should conduct reevaluations (*In re Child with Disabilities*, 1989). Even though the IDEA requires school officials to conduct reevaluations every three years, reevaluations are warranted earlier if the circumstances surrounding students change. One circumstance that could require an earlier evaluation is sudden changes in the behavior of students. At least one court ruled that a reevaluation is required whenever a significant change in placement is being contemplated (*Brimmer v. Traverse City Area Public Schools*, 1994). A reevaluation should include a psychological assessment designed specifically to elicit data relative to the behavior that led to the disciplinary action. If those who conducted the most recent assessments are not part of the group making the manifestation determination, they should be consulted regarding the specific incident in question. If available evaluation data are more than one year old, school officials are to make sure that reevaluations are completed before convening a manifestation determination meeting.

Making the Decision

According to the revised IDEA and its regulations, IEP teams making manifestation determinations must consider all relevant information, including evaluative and diagnostic results and observations of children (20 U.S.C. § 1415(k)(1)(E)(i); 34 C.F.R. § 300.530(e)(1)). After IEP teams consider all relevant information, they should proceed as they would in making any other identifications, classifications, or placement decisions. IEP teams must thus exercise sound professional judgment. Members of IEP teams must rely on their professional knowledge, knowledge of the students, and understanding of the circumstances that led to the misconduct in making this critical judgment.

Appeals

As are any matters related to the special education programs of students, manifestation determinations are subject to the IDEA's administrative appeals process. The 2004 amendments specify that in the case of manifestation determinations, hearings must be expedited. Expedited hearings must take place within 20 school days of the date on which they were requested and decisions must be rendered within 10 days of the hearing (20 U.S.C. § 1415(k)(4)(B); 34 C.F.R. § 300.532(c)). If parents contest a manifestation determination, school officials must postpone any long-term suspensions or expulsions until hearings have been completed, even though students may remain in interim alternative educational settings (20 U.S.C. § 1415(k)(4)(A); 34 C.F.R. § 300.533).

Authority of Hearing Officers

The IDEA affords hearing officers the authority to issue change in placement orders (20 U.S.C. § 1415(k)(3)(B); 34 C.F.R. § 300.532(b)(2)(ii)). Essentially, when hearing appeals, officers have two options: they may either return students to the placements from which they were removed or order that they be placed in interim alternative settings. If hearing officers choose the latter option, placement may not be for more than 45 school days.

Placement Pending Appeals

When parents challenge the placement decisions of school boards, the IDEA stipulates that their children are to remain in their then-current placements pending the outcome of the hearings (20 U.S.C. § 1415(j)). As stated above, an exception exists when parents challenge the actions of school boards that would place children in interim alternative settings for disciplinary reasons. The IDEA declares that while such appeals are pending, students are to remain in interim alternative settings until hearing officers render judgments or the 45-day limit has expired (20 U.S.C. § 1415(k) (3)(4)(A); 34 C.F.R. § 300.533). In these circumstances, hearings must take place within 20 days and decisions must be rendered within another 10 days (20 U.S.C. § 1415(k)(3)(4)(B); 34 C.F.R. § 300.532(c)).

Injunctions to Allow School Boards to Exclude Dangerous Students

In *Honig* the Supreme Court gave school officials the authority to seek injunctions to exclude dangerous students with disabilities from the regular education environment. Hearing officers now have the authority to order changes in placements to appropriate interim alternative educational settings for periods of up to 45 days, when school officials can demonstrate that keeping students in their then-current placements is substantially likely to result in injuries to the students at issue and/or others (20 U.S.C. § 1415(k)(3)(B)(ii); 34 C.F.R. § 300.532(b)(2)(ii)). Still, this change does not prohibit school officials from seeking injunctive relief to bar students from attending school.

In a case that was litigated prior to the most recent changes in the IDEA and its regulations, a federal trial court in Alabama acknowledged that the IDEA allows school boards to seek orders from hearing officers but does not require that this be done prior to seeking injunctions (*Gadsden City Board of Education v. B.P.*, 1998). The court ruled that since the expedited hearing provision in the amended IDEA is permissive, the exhaustion of administrative remedies is not required if boards choose to seek *Honig* injunctions.

An appellate court in New York, in like fashion, affirmed an injunction that allowed a school board to exclude a student, placing him on homebound instruction after he committed several acts of misconduct, including hitting peers and teachers (*Roslyn Union Free School District v. Geffrey W.*, 2002). The court was satisfied that the evidence presented by school officials clearly demonstrated that allowing the student to return to school was substantially likely to result in injury to himself and/or others.

Rights of Students Not Yet Identified as Disabled

The current version of the IDEA and its regulations requires school boards to provide the statute's protections to students who have not been determined to be eligible for special education, if educators knew that children were disabled before the misbehavior occurred (20 U.S.C. § 1415 (k)(5); 34 C.F.R. § 300.534). The law and regulations also outline the circumstances under which school officials are considered to have knowledge that students are disabled. Factors that give rise to educator knowledge that students have disabilities are written expressed concern from parents that their children may require special education or requests for evaluations; prior behavioral and academic performance of students; and expressed concern from teachers about the performance of students (20 U.S.C. § 1415(k)(5)(B); 34 C.F.R. § 300.534(b)). If school officials conducted evaluations but did not conclude that students had disabilities, then boards are not considered to have knowledge of disabilities under these provisions. Further, if parents refused permission for evaluations or declined offered special education services, school officials are not deemed to have knowledge of student disabilities (20 U.S.C. § 1415(k)(5)(C); 34 C.F.R. § 300.534(c)).

If school board officials lack prior knowledge that students are disabled, children may be disciplined in the same manner as peers who are not disabled (20 U.S.C. § 1415(k)(5)(D)(i); 34 C.F.R. § 300.534(d)(1)). Moreover, any request for an evaluation that is made during a time period in which a disciplinary sanction has been imposed must be conducted in an expedited manner (20 U.S.C. § 1415(k)(5)(D)(ii); 34 C.F.R. § 300.534(d)(2)). Unlike guidelines for conducting expedited hearings, however, neither the IDEA nor its regulations specify a time period within which such evaluations must be completed. Until these evaluations are completed, students are to remain in the educational placements selected by school officials, which can be suspensions or expulsions without the receipt of educational services (34 C.F.R. § 300.534(d)(2)(ii)). If, following the evaluations, school officials are convinced that students do have disabilities, then they are entitled to special education and related services (34 C.F.R. § 300.534(d)(2)(iii)).

In an interesting case, *Colvin v. Lowndes County, Mississippi, School District* (1999), a federal trial court held that parents had not shown that their son had a disability even though they had made requests for an evaluation. The court did observe that school officials violated the IDEA by failing to provide some assessment procedure to evaluate whether the student was a child with a disability.

In contrast, the federal trial court in Connecticut, in *J.C. v. Regional School District No. 10* (2000), decided that a student whose parents expressed concern over his poor performance and requested evaluations was entitled to the protections of the IDEA when faced with expulsion. In this case, the student was evaluated, but school officials did not think that he was entitled to an IEP because he was not disabled. When the student again faced expulsion, he was reevaluated at his parents' request; this time the school board agreed that the student was eligible for special education. Similarly, the federal trial court in Massachusetts overturned the expulsion of a student who failed all of her courses. Prior to conducting the student's expulsion hearing, school officials evaluated her and agreed that she was not disabled. Her attorney requested a due process hearing to contest that outcome. Noting that the evaluation team's finding that the student was not disabled was not final and was subject to the pending hearing, the court reasoned that since the student sufficiently stated a claim that school officials had knowledge that she was disabled, educators should have afforded her the protections of the IDEA (*S.W. and Joanne W. v. Holbrook Public Schools*, 2002).

Effect of the IDEA on the Juvenile Court and Law Enforcement Authorities

The IDEA maintains that nothing in its provisions can be interpreted as prohibiting school officials from reporting crimes committed by special education students to the proper authorities or to impede law enforcement and judicial authorities carrying out their responsibilities (20 U.S.C. § 1415(k)(6); 34 C.F.R. § 300.535). Further, if school officials do report a crime, the IDEA provides that they must furnish the special education and disciplinary records of students to the appropriate authorities.

In a case from Massachusetts, an appellate court emphasized that a juvenile court proceeding did not constitute a change in placement under the IDEA even when the proceeding took place as a consequence of misconduct that occurred at school (*Commonwealth v. Nathaniel N.*, 2002). The court, in upholding the student's adjudication as a delinquent for possession of marijuana in school, pointed out that the IDEA clearly authorized school officials to report criminal activities to the proper authorities.

Some court proceedings may trigger the IDEA's change in placement provisions. In such a case, school officials in New York unsuccessfully initiated proceedings to have an eight-year-old student declared to be a person in need of services due to his tardiness, absenteeism, and misconduct. In dismissing the request in favor of the student, the court explained that before initiating their action, which would have changed the child's placement, school officials failed to review his IEP to see whether additional interventions had been warranted (*In re Doe*, 2002).

RECOMMENDATIONS

Under the amended IDEA, students with disabilities are subject to the disciplinary process when they misbehave. To the extent that the IDEA entitles students with disabilities to a FAPE, additional due process may be required if disciplinary actions can result in substantial losses of educational opportunities. No area of special education law is more contentious than that caused by the imposition of disciplinary sanctions on students with disabilities.

The current provisions of the IDEA, along with case law, seem to strike an appropriate balance. School officials may take disciplinary actions against students with disabilities by following the IDEA's procedures. This

Figure 5.3   Frequently Asked Questions

Q: Does the IDEA create a dual system of discipline?

A: No. The IDEA does not prevent school officials from disciplining students with disabilities. The IDEA does provide for additional procedural protections to ensure that students with disabilities are not disciplined for behavior over which they have no control and that the disciplinary process cannot be used to circumvent the obligations of school officials to provide special education and related services.

Q: Is the 10-day limit on a suspension consecutive or cumulative?

A: Unless state law dictates otherwise, this limit refers to 10 consecutive days. However, a series of suspensions that total more than 10 days in a school year could constitute a pattern of exclusion that could be considered the equivalent of an expulsion. Factors that are considered in evaluating whether multiple suspensions constitute a pattern of exclusion include the length of each suspension, the proximity of suspensions to each other, and the total amount of time the student has been excluded from school.

Q: Can the parents of students who have not been identified as disabled thwart the disciplinary process by claiming that their children are disabled and requesting evaluations?

A: School officials are required to provide the IDEA's protections to students who were previously not identified as disabled if they either knew, or should have known, that the children were disabled. Factors that officials should consider in this regard include prior parental concerns that children might require special education, requests for evaluations, behavioral and academic performances, and expressed concerns by teachers about the performance of students. If parents previously refused evaluations or services, school officials are not required to provide the IDEA's protections in disciplinary situations. Unfortunately, the IDEA's process can be abused and may be used to slow down the disciplinary process, but it cannot be used by students who do not have disabilities to avoid disciplinary sanctions.

Q: Does the IDEA prevent school officials from referring misbehaving students to law enforcement authorities?

A: No. The IDEA specifically states that nothing within it can be interpreted as prohibiting school officials from reporting crimes or impeding law enforcement or judicial authorities from carrying out their duties. Thus, when special education students are reported for suspicion of having committed crimes, school officials must furnish their special education and disciplinary records to the proper authorities.

Q: What do school officials need to do to obtain injunctions or orders from hearing officers in order to prevent dangerous students from attending school?

A: School officials must show that maintaining students in their then-current placements is likely to result in injury to them and/or others. Further, school officials must demonstrate that they have taken reasonable steps to control the behavior of students and that less restrictive alternatives are not feasible. For this purpose, thorough documentation of the history of student misconduct and the response of school officials is a must.

---

balance allows educators to discipline misbehaving students while removing the possibility that these students can be deprived of educational opportunities for behavior that stems from their disabilities. The recommendations below have been developed from the IDEA and case law. Even so, readers are cautioned to also consult state law in this area since many jurisdictions impose additional requirements on school officials when disciplining students with disabilities.

School officials should

- Impose normal minor disciplinary actions such as detentions or time-outs by following their usual procedures.
- Follow the usual procedures when suspending students with disabilities for periods of up to 10 school days.
- Immediately initiate the IDEA's due process protections whenever disciplinary sanctions may involve expulsions or transfers to other educational settings such as alternative schools.
- Determine whether students' misconduct was a manifestation of their disabilities.
- Render manifestation determinations within 10 school days of decisions to change students' placements.
- Ensure that manifestation determinations are made by school personnel, including student IEP teams in conjunction with a child's parents.
- Ensure that parents are invited to participate in manifestation determination meetings and are notified of their rights.
- Ensure that the teams making manifestation determinations examine whether the misconduct in question was either caused by or had a direct and substantial relationship to a student's disability.
- Ensure that the teams making the manifestation determinations consider whether a student's IEP was properly implemented.
- Ensure that all evaluation data are current or conduct reevaluations if they are not.
- Provide special education services during expulsion periods for students who have been properly expelled.
- Propose new placements if IEP teams determine that since the then-current placements of students did not meet their needs, this may have been a contributing factor in their misbehavior.
- Provide expedited hearings to parents who disagree with the results of manifestation determinations.
- Immediately remove students who are charged with the possession of weapons or drugs on school property or at school functions by following the normal suspension procedures.
- Place students who are charged with the possession of weapons or drugs on school property or at school functions in interim alternative settings for 45-day periods following their initial 10-day suspensions.

- Consider whether students who caused serious bodily harm should be removed to interim alternative settings for 45-day periods.
- Ensure that the alternative setting allows students to progress in the general education curriculum and permits the delivery of their special education services.
- Seek judicial or hearing officer orders to remove students whose presence in school could cause a danger to themselves and/or others or could substantially interrupt the education process.
- When seeking injunctions to exclude students from their educational programs, be prepared to show that everything possible has been done to mitigate the danger or chance of disruption and that there is no less restrictive alternative than removal.
- Conduct functional behavioral assessments and develop behavioral intervention plans as part of the annual IEP process for all students with disabilities who have a history of misbehavior.
- Review functional behavioral assessments and behavioral intervention plans when students are faced with serious disciplinary action or manifestation determinations are scheduled.
- Include the following elements in functional behavioral assessments: observations of students, documenting aspects of their behavior; analysis of the situations that trigger misbehavior; review of the effectiveness of previous interventions; medical, psychological, and social data that could affect behavior; and any other information that could provide insight into the behaviors.
- Include the following elements in behavioral intervention plans: strategies for dealing with students' behavior (both strategies for dealing with the behavior at the time it surfaces and long-term strategies for preventing future occurrences), supportive services that can be provided to the students to help them to deal with the situations that tend to precipitate the unwanted behavior, expected behaviors, a description of inappropriate behaviors, and a statement of the positive and negative consequences for any behavior.
- Provide the IDEA's protections to students who have not been identified as having disabilities but who may, in fact, be disabled.
- Provide special education and disciplinary records of students to the appropriate authorities if school personnel report crimes in which students were involved.
- Carefully and completely document all misbehavior and all actions taken in response to the misbehavior of students.

REFERENCES

Alex R. v. Forrestville Valley Community Unit School District, 319 F.3d 446 (7th Cir. 2004).
AW ex rel. Wilson v. Fairfax County School Board, 372 F.3d 674 (4th Cir. 2004).

Binghampton City School District v. Borgna, 17 EHLR 677 (N.D.N.Y. 1991).

Board of Education of the Hendrick Hudson Central School District v. Rowley, 458 U.S. 176 (1982).

Board of Education of Township High School District v. Kurtz-Imig, 16 EHLR 17 (N.D. Ill. 1989).

Brimmer v. Traverse City Area Public Schools, 872 F. Supp. 447 (W.D. Mich. 1994).

Child with Disabilities, In re, 16 EHLR 207 (SEA Cal. 1989).

Clinton County R-III School District v. C.J.K., 896 F. Supp. 948 (W.D. Mo. 1995).

Code of Federal Regulations (C.F.R.), as cited.

Coleman v. Newburgh Enlarged City School District, 319 F. Supp.2d 446 (S.D.N.Y. 2004).

Colvin v. Lowndes County, Mississippi, School District, 114 F. Supp. 504 (N.D. Miss. 1999).

Commonwealth of Virginia Department of Education v. Riley, 106 F.3d 559 (4th Cir. 1997).

Commonwealth v. Nathaniel N., 764 N.E.2d 883 (Mass. Ct. App. 2002).

Controlled Substances Act, 21 U.S.C. § 812 (1999).

Daniel, P. T. K. (2001). Discipline and the IDEA reauthorization: The need to resolve inconsistencies. *Education Law Reporter, 142,* 591–607.

Dayton, J. (2002). Special education discipline law. *Education Law Reporter, 163,* 17–35.

Doe, In re, 753 N.Y.S.2d 656 (N.Y. Fam. Ct. 2002).

Doe v. Board of Education of Oak Park & River Forest High School District 200, 115 F.3d 1273 (7th Cir. 1997).

Doe v. Koger, 480 F. Supp. 225 (N.D. Ind. 1979).

Doe v. Maher, 793 F.2d 1470 (9th Cir. 1986), *affirmed Honig v. Doe,* 484 U.S. 305 (1988).

Doe v. Manning, 1994 WL 99052, 21 IDELR 357 (W.D. Va. 1994).

East Islip Union Free School District v. Andersen, 615 N.Y.S.2d 852 (N.Y. Sup. Ct. 1994).

Elk Grove Unified School District, 16 EHLR 622 (SEA Cal. 1989).

Farrin v. Maine School Administrative District No. 59, 165 F. Supp.2d 37 (D. Me. 2001).

Gadsden City Board of Education v. B.P., 3 F. Supp.2d 1299 (N.D. Ala. 1998).

Gun-Free Schools Act of 1994, 20 U.S.C. § 8921 (1994).

Hacienda La Puente Unified School District of Los Angeles v. Honig, 976 F.2d 487 (9th Cir. 1992).

Hayes v. Unified School District No. 377, 877 F.2d 809 (10th Cir. 1989).

Honig v. Doe, 484 U.S. 305 (1988).

Individuals with Disabilities Education Act, 20 U.S.C. § 1400 *et seq.* (2005).

Jackson v. Franklin County School Board, 765 F.2d 535 (5th Cir. 1985).

J.C. v. Regional School District No. 10, 115 F. Supp. 297 (D. Conn. 2000), *reversed on other grounds* 278 F.3d 119 (2d Cir. 2002).

Light v. Parkway C-2 School District, 41 F.3d 1223 (8th Cir. 1994).

Magyar v. Tucson Unified School District, 958 F. Supp. 1423 (D. Ariz. 1997).

Manchester School District v. Charles M.F., 1994 WL 485754, 21 IDELR 732 (D.N.H. 1994).

Modesto City Schools, 21 IDELR 685 (SEA Cal. 1994).

M.P. by D.P. v. Governing Board of the Grossmont Union High School District, 858 F. Supp. 1044 (S.D. Cal. 1994).

Parents of Student W. v. Puyallup School District, 31 F.3d 1489 (9th Cir. 1994).

Randy M. v. Texas City ISD, 93 F. Supp.2d 1310 (S.D. Tex. 2000).

Rodiriecus L. v. Waukegan School District No. 60, 90 F.3d 249 (7th Cir. 1996).

Roslyn Union Free School District v. Geffrey W., 740 N.Y.S.2d 451 (N.Y. App. Div. 2002).

S-1 v. Turlington, 635 F.2d 342 (5th Cir. 1981).

School Board of Independent School District No. 11 v. Renollett, 440 F.3d 1007 (8th Cir. 2006).

School Board of Pinellas County v. J.M. by L.M., 957 F. Supp. 1252 (M.D. Fla. 1997).

School Board of the County of Prince William v. Malone, 762 F.2d 1210 (4th Cir. 1985).

School Board of the County of Prince William v. Wills, 16 EHLR 1109 (Va. Cir. Ct. 1989).

School Board of the County of Stafford v. Farley, 16 EHLR 1119 (Va. Cir. Ct. 1990).

School District of Philadelphia v. Stephan M. and Theresa M., 1997 WL 89113 (E.D. Pa. 1997).

Steldt v. School Board of the Riverdale School District, 885 F. Supp. 1192 (W.D. Wis. 1995).

Stuart v. Nappi, 443 F. Supp. 1235 (D. Conn. 1978).

S.W. and Joanne W. v. Holbrook Public Schools, 221 F. Supp.2d 222 (D. Mass. 2002).

Texas City Independent School District v. Jorstad, 752 F. Supp. 231 (S.D. Tex. 1990).

6

Dispute Resolution

INTRODUCTION

As discussed throughout this book, the Individuals with Disabilities Education Act (IDEA) (2005) is designed to afford parents and school officials opportunities to work together to develop individualized educational programs (IEPs) for students with disabilities. Yet, in recognizing that parents and educators may not agree in all situations, Congress included dispute resolution provisions in the IDEA (20 U.S.C. § 1415).

Parents of students with disabilities may request mediation (20 U.S.C. § 1415(e)) or due process hearings (20 U.S.C. § 1415(f)) if they disagree with any actions of school boards regarding proposed IEPs or of the provision of a free appropriate public education (FAPE) for their children. After having exhausted administrative remedies, parents may seek judicial review in federal or state courts (20 U.S.C. § 1415(i)(2)(A)). Courts can waive the exhaustion requirement only when it clearly is futile to pursue additional administrative remedies (*Honig v. Doe*, 1988). Students must remain in their then-current placements while administrative or judicial actions are pending unless school officials and parents agree to other arrangements (20 U.S.C. § 1415(j)), hearing officers order changes (20 U.S.C. § 1415(k)(3)(B)), or judicial decrees call for new placements (*Honig v. Doe*, 1988).

The IDEA empowers the judiciary to review the records of administrative proceedings, to hear additional evidence, and to "grant such relief as the court determines is appropriate" based on a preponderance of the evidence (20 U.S.C. § 1415(i)(2)(C)(iii)). Even so, the U.S. Supreme Court cautioned judges not "to substitute their own notions of sound educational policy for those of the authorities which they review" (*Board of Education of Hendrick Hudson Central School District v. Rowley*, 1982, p. 206). In examining dispute resolution, it is important to note that most of the cases in this chapter are older than those in the rest of the book since the majority of the IDEA's dispute resolution procedures are essentially settled law.

> The U.S. Supreme Court cautioned judges not "to substitute their own notions of sound educational policy for those of the authorities which they review" (*Board of Education of the Hendrick Hudson Central School District v. Rowley*, 1982, p. 206).

MEDIATION

In order to provide parents with an alternative remedy in disputes over the placements of their children, the IDEA (20 U.S.C. § 1415(e)(1)) and its accompanying regulations (Assistance to the States for the Education of Children with Disabilities, 2006, 34 C.F.R. § 300.506(a)) direct states and school officials to offer mediation, at public expense (20 U.S.C. § 1415(e)(2)(D)), as an option when due process hearings may be possible. To date, these provisions have been subject to little litigation.

The IDEA specifies that mediation must be voluntary on the part of the parties; cannot be used to deny or delay parental rights to due process hearings or to deny any other rights under the IDEA; and must be conducted by trained, qualified, impartial mediators (20 U.S.C. § 1415(e)(2)(A)(iii); 34 C.F.R. § 300.506(b)(1)) whose names are on state-maintained lists of qualified mediators in special education (20 U.S.C. § 1415(e)(2)(C)).

Mediators cannot be employees of states, school boards, or other agencies that provide direct services to students who are subject to the mediation process nor can they have personal or professional conflicts of interest (34 C.F.R. § 300.506(c)(1)). Individuals who otherwise qualify as mediators are not considered employees of states or boards solely by virtue of being paid to serve as mediators (34 C.F.R. § 300.506(c)(2)).

Mediation sessions must be scheduled in a timely manner in locations convenient to the parties (20 U.S.C. § 1415(e)(2)(E)). Any agreements that the parties reach as a result of mediation must be formalized in writing (20 U.S.C. § 1415(e)(2)(F)). Discussions that occur during mediation must be kept confidential and cannot be used as evidence in subsequent due process hearings or civil proceedings; the parties may also be required to sign a confidentiality pledge prior to the commencement of such process (20 U.S.C. § 1415(e)(2)(G)). A new regulatory subsection makes it clear that the results of mediation agreements can be enforced in federal or state courts (34 C.F.R. § 300.506(b)(7)).

Insofar as the mediation process is voluntary, if parents choose not to participate in mediation, states may establish procedures allowing them to meet at convenient times and locations with disinterested third parties who are under contract with parent training and information centers, community parent resource centers, or appropriate alternative dispute resolution entities to encourage the use of, and explain the benefits of, the process (20 U.S.C. § 1415(e)(2)(B)).

RESOLUTION SESSIONS

A new provision of the IDEA requires school board officials to convene meetings between parents and relevant members of the IEP teams of their children (34 C.F.R. § 300.510(a)(4)) within 15 days of parental requests for due process hearings in an attempt to resolve placement disputes (20 U.S.C. § 1415(f)(1)(B)(i); 34 C.F.R. § 300.510(a)). If educators do not convene requested resolution sessions within 15 days, parents can seek the intervention of hearing officers to begin this process (34 C.F.R. § 300.510(b)(5)).

Resolution sessions must include a school board representative with decision-making authority on its behalf (34 C.F.R. § 300.510(a)(i)) but may not include board attorneys unless parents are also accompanied by counsel (34 C.F.R. § 300.510(a)(ii)). However, if school officials are unable to get parents to participate in resolution sessions within a 30-day period, and can document their reasonable efforts to secure parental participation, hearing officers can dismiss the parents' complaints (34 C.F.R. § 300.510(b)(4)). The parties need not attend resolution sessions if they agree, in writing, to waive their meetings and agree to mediation (34 C.F.R. § 300.510(a)(3)).

If parties do not resolve their disputes within 30 days, they should schedule due process hearings (20 U.S.C. § 1415(f)(1)(B)(ii); 34 C.F.R. § 300.510(b)). If the parties do resolve their differences at resolution sessions, they must execute and sign legally binding settlement agreements (20 U.S.C. § 1415(f)(1)(B)(iii); 34 C.F.R. § 300.510(c)). Settlement agreements are enforceable in state or federal courts, but either party may void such agreements within three business days (20 U.S.C. § 1415(f)(1)(B)(iv); 34 C.F.R. § 300.510(d)).

DUE PROCESS HEARINGS

Pursuant to the IDEA, parents have the right to request due process hearings on any matters concerning the delivery of a FAPE to their children, including identification, evaluation, and placement (20 U.S.C. § 1415(f)). School board officials may ask for hearings if parents refuse to consent to evaluations (34 C.F.R. § 300.300(a)(3)) and must provide parents with proper notice of their rights when school personnel make requests to evaluate their children (34 C.F.R. § 300.503(a)). Of course, while administrative or judicial actions are pending, students must remain in their then-current placements unless parents and school officials agree to other settings (20 U.S.C. § 1415(j)), hearing officers order changes (20 U.S.C. § 1415(k)(3)(B)), or judicial decrees mandate changes in placements (*Honig v. Doe*, 1988).

It is up to parents to choose whether to have their children present at hearings (34 C.F.R. § 300.512(c)(1)) and whether hearings should be open to the public (34 C.F.R. § 300.512(c)(2)). If no parents can be identified, their whereabouts cannot be discovered, or children are wards of the state, surrogate parents who are appointed to safeguard the educational interests of children can request hearings (34 C.F.R. § 300.30(a)(5)). The IDEA regulations specify that the appointing agency ensure that surrogate parents are not employees of school boards or state educational agencies, cannot have personal or professional conflicts of interest with regard to the interest of the children involved, and have the knowledge and skill to act in this capacity (34 C.F.R. § 300.519(d)(2)). State laws and regulations govern other qualifications for surrogate parents.

Parties filing due process complaints must forward copies of them to their state education agencies (34 C.F.R. § 300.508(a)(2)). Complaints must include the names and addresses of the children, their schools, and, if children are homeless, available contact information. In addition, complaints must include descriptions of the nature of the problems relating to the proposed or refused initiations or changes in the placements of the children, including facts relating to the problems and proposed resolutions to the extent known and available to the parties (34 C.F.R. § 300.508(b)).

A regulation specifies that due process hearings cannot take place until one of the parties, or its attorney, files a sufficient complaint (34 C.F.R. § 300.508(c)). Complaints are to be deemed sufficient unless the party receiving them notifies the hearing officer and the other party in writing, within 15 days of receipt of the complaints, that they are insufficient (34 C.F.R. § 300.508(d)(1). Within five days of receipt of this response, hearing officers must evaluate whether complaints are sufficient on their face and must immediately notify the parties of their decisions (34 C.F.R. § 300.508(d)(2)).

Parties may amend due process complaints only if the opposing parties consent in writing, are given the opportunity to resolve the underlying disputes through resolution sessions, or hearing officers grant permission no later than five days before hearings begin (34 C.F.R. § 300.508(d)(3)). If parties file amended complaints, the timelines for the resolution sessions to resolve the dispute begin anew (34 C.F.R. § 300.508(d)(4)).

Assuming, as is almost always the case, that parents requested due process hearings, school officials must respond within 10 days of receiving complaints. Responses must include explanations of why school officials proposed or refused to take the actions raised in the complaints; a description of other options that IEP teams considered and the reasons why they were rejected; a description of each evaluation procedure, assessment, record, or report they relied on as the basis for the proposed or refused actions; and a description of the other factors that were relevant to their proposed or refused actions. The regulations go on to stipulate that responses cannot be interpreted as precluding school officials from asserting, if appropriate, that parental due process complaints are insufficient (34 C.F.R. § 300.508(e)).

Depending on the law in a given jurisdiction, either the state-level or local school boards may conduct due process hearings (20 U.S.C. § 1415(f)(1)(A)). If local boards conduct initial hearings, either party may initiate state-level appeals (20 U.S.C. § 1415(g)). States are free to establish either a one- or two-tiered administrative due process mechanism. While procedures vary from state to state, most jurisdictions have created two-tiered systems that begin with hearings in front of individual hearing officers and provide for appeals to review panels. In two-tiered systems, both procedures cannot be at the state level (*Burr v. Ambach*, 1988, 1989a, 1989b, 1990).

In states with two-tiered administrative hearing systems, some courts agreed that appeals heard by the head of state educational agencies fail to meet the IDEA's impartiality requirements. For example, the Third Circuit ruled that Pennsylvania's Secretary of Education was not an impartial third-party decision maker (*Muth v. Central Bucks School District*, 1988; *Johnson v. Lancaster-Lebanon Intermediate Unit No. 13, Lancaster City School District*, 1991). In an earlier case, the same court maintained that employees of the Delaware Department of Public Instruction were forbidden to serve as state-level review officers (*Grymes v. Madden*, 1982). Similarly, courts in New York held that the State Commissioner of Education was not impartial (*Antkowiak v. Ambach*, 1988; *Burr v. Ambach*, 1988, 1989a, 1989b, 1990; *Holmes v. Sobol*, 1988; *Louis M. v. Ambach*, 1989). Yet, a state court in New York agreed that review officers who were appointed to oversee adjudications of local hearing officers were impartial even though they were subordinate to the Commissioner (*Board of Education of the Baldwin Union Free School District v. Commissioner of Education*, 1994).

In the past, the IDEA did not contain a statute of limitations for requesting administrative due process hearings. Thus, time limitations needed to be either mandated by state law or borrowed from analogous state statutes. Congress remedied this situation with the passage of the 2004 IDEA amendments by instituting a two-year limitations period for requesting hearings (20 U.S.C. § 1415(f)(3)(C)). At the same time, if state laws create other limitations periods, they prevail (34 C.F.R. § 300.507(a)(2)). Moreover, the federal timeline is to be stayed if parents can show that school officials misrepresented that they resolved the problems or if they withheld pertinent information from parents (20 U.S.C. § 1415(f)(3)(D)).

Subject Matter of Hearings

Parents can request due process hearings on any matter relating to the education of their children with disabilities (20 U.S.C. § 1415(f)(1)(A)). For instance, parents have the right to ask for hearings if school officials refuse to assess whether their children have disabilities (*Hacienda La Puente Unified School District of Los Angeles v. Honig*, 1992), if they disagree with findings or recommendations offered by school officials (*Dong v. Board of Education*, 1999), or if they are dissatisfied with the content or implementation of the IEPs of their children (*Kuszewski v. Chippewa Valley Schools*, 2000). State laws and regulations may provide parents with additional rights over the content and structure of due process hearings.

If parents whose children either are enrolled in public schools or seeking to enroll them fail, or refuse, to respond to requests to provide consent for initial evaluations, school officials may, but are not required to, request due process hearings to pursue initial evaluations, if appropriate, except to the extent that doing so would be inconsistent with state laws relating to parental consent (34 C.F.R. § 300.300(a)(3)(i)). If school officials choose not to pursue evaluations under the circumstances, parents may not accuse them of violating their duties under the IDEA (34 C.F.R. § 300.300(a)(3)(ii)). School officials can request hearings if parents refuse to consent to evaluations (34 C.F.R. § 300.300(a)(3)), but not if parents refuse to consent to the provision of services for their children (34 C.F.R. § 300.300(b)(2)).

Another circumstance under which parents can request due process hearings is after the eligibility of their children to receive special education ends, because students may be entitled to compensatory educational services if courts agree that they were denied a FAPE. In such a case, the Supreme Court of Ohio held that a student was entitled to a hearing even though the request for it was submitted one day before the student's eligibility for special education services ended under state law (*Board of Education of Strongville City School District v. Theado*, 1991). The record reflected that school board officials objected to the hearing since the student was no longer eligible for services. Reversing in favor of the student, the court disagreed, reasoning that insofar as it was possible to award compensatory services to children who were denied an appropriate education, he was entitled to the hearing.

According to an important new limitation, parties requesting due process hearings pursuant to the IDEA are precluded from raising issues that were not included in the complaints that they filed to initiate the proceedings unless the other party agrees otherwise (20 U.S.C. § 1415(f)(3)(B); 34 C.F.R. § 300.511(d)).

Impartiality of Hearing Officers

Hearing officers, typically selected pursuant to provisions in state law (*Cothern v. Mallory*, 1983), must be impartial, meaning that they cannot be employees of the states or districts involved in the education of the children whose cases appear before them or have personal or professional interests in these students (20 U.S.C. § 1415(f)(3)(A); 34 C.F.R. § 300.511(c)). Individuals who otherwise qualify as hearing officers are not considered employees of states or local school boards solely by virtue of being paid to serve in this capacity (34 C.F.R. § 300.511(c)(2)). State education agencies are required to keep lists of qualified hearing officers along with explanations of their qualifications (34 C.F.R. § 300.511(c)(3)).

The fact that hearing officers may be employed by other school boards does not automatically make them biased. In a representative challenge to the impartiality of a hearing officer, the Tenth Circuit reiterated the rule that an officer's being employed by another school district did not violate the IDEA's prohibition against working for the district involved in a hearing (*L.B. and J.B. ex rel. K.B. v. Nebo School District*, 2004). Further, the court confirmed that a hearing officer must not have any personal or professional interest that would conflict with his or her objectivity.

Authority of Hearing Officers

In due process hearings, hearing officers must sort out what took place and apply the law to the facts in a manner similar to that of trial court judges. Like judges, hearing officers are empowered to issue orders and grant equitable relief regarding the provision of a FAPE for students with disabilities.

There are limitations on the power of hearing officers. Hearing officers generally do not have the authority to provide remedies when broad policies or procedures that affect a large number of students are challenged or to address matters of law since they lack the ability to consider a statute's constitutionality. Rather, the power of hearing officers is limited to the facts of the disputes at hand. In such a case, the Ninth Circuit ruled that a hearing officer lacked the power to address the legislature's failure to appropriate sufficient funds for special education programs (*Kerr Center Parents Association v. Charles*, 1990). Along the same lines, a federal trial court in Indiana concluded that a hearing officer did not have the authority to rule on the legality of a state-required application review process for students who needed residential placements or to provide a remedy (*Bray v. Hobart City School Corporation*, 1993). In addition, the IDEA limits the awarding of attorneys fees to prevailing parents in special education disputes to the discretion of federal courts (20 U.S.C. §1415(i)(3)(B)).

The question remains open whether hearing officers can grant awards of compensatory services to students who were denied a FAPE. While the Third Circuit noted that the hearing process was powerless to address the question of compensatory education (*Lester H. v. Gilhool*, 1990), the Second Circuit reached the opposite result (*Burr v. Ambach*, 1988, 1989a, 1989b, 1990). Moreover, the federal trial court in New Hampshire asserted that a hearing officer erred in writing that he lacked the authority to award compensatory services. The court thought that in light of the importance Congress placed on the process, such power was coextensive with that of the courts (*Cocores v. Portsmouth, New Hampshire School District*, 1991). To the extent that hearing officers can grant awards of tuition reimbursement, it seems logical that they should have the authority to award compensatory educational services as well.

Training of Hearing Officers

The IDEA and its regulations require hearing officers to be impartial and have no personal or professional interest in the outcome of the disputes before them (34 C.F.R. § 300.511(c)). Insofar as these provisions do not contain specific language regarding the other qualifications of hearing officers, these criteria are left up to the states to establish. In one of the few cases on point, the federal trial court in Connecticut held that a state's failure to train hearing officers was not a violation of the IDEA (*Canton Board of Education v. N.B. and R.B.*, 2004).

Burden of Proof

Until recently, since the IDEA and its regulations were silent as to which party bore the burden of proof in due process hearings, such determinations were based on state laws or judicial discretion, leading to a great deal of disagreement, and inconsistency, over this important question. Not surprisingly, two distinct perspectives emerged. On the one hand, the Fourth (*Weast v. Schaffer*, 2004), Fifth (*Alamo Heights Independent School District v. State Board of Education*, 1986), Sixth (*Doe v. Board of Education of Tullahoma City Schools*, 1993), and Tenth (*Johnson v. Independent School District No. 4*, 1990) Circuits agreed that the parties challenging IEPs bore the burden of proof. These courts assigned presumptions in favor of IEPs as long as they were developed according to the procedures outlined in the IDEA.

Conversely, the Second (*Grim v. Rhinebeck Central School District*, 2003), Third (*Carlisle Area School v. Scott P.*, 1995), Seventh (*Beth B. v. Van Clay*, 2002), Eighth (*Blackmon v. Springfield R-XII School District*, 1999), Ninth (*Seattle School District No. 1 v. B.S.*, 1996), and District of Columbia (*McKenzie v. Smith*, 1985) Circuits placed the burden of proof on school boards, regardless of whether they or parents wished to alter IEPs. These courts contended that since school boards had the duty of providing a FAPE for students with disabilities, school officials should have been better able to meet the burden of proof due to their better access to relevant information, coupled with parental lack of expertise in formulating an appropriate IEP.

In 2005 the U.S. Supreme Court stepped into the fray and resolved the controversy over who had the burden of proof in *Schaffer v. Weast* (2005).

In conceding that arguments could be made on both sides of the issue, the Court saw no reason to depart from the usual rule that the party seeking relief bears the burden of persuasion. In IDEA cases, this is generally the parents (Osborne & Russo, 2005). The issue was important because the assignment of the burden of proof can well determine the final outcome in close cases (Wenkart, 2004). Under the Court's ruling, parents who challenge proposed IEPs must now demonstrate that IEPs are deficient unless state laws provide otherwise (Russo & Osborne, 2006).

Exhaustion of Administrative Remedies

> The IDEA requires parties to exhaust administrative remedies before filing suit unless it clearly is futile to do so.

Based on congressional desire for reasonably quick resolution of disputes over the placements of students with disabilities, the IDEA requires parties to exhaust administrative remedies before filing suits unless it clearly is futile to do so (*Honig v. Doe*, 1988). Exhaustion of administrative remedies may also be excused if school officials either deny parental requests for due process hearings or frustrate parental attempts to challenge the results of hearings (*Abney ex rel. Kantor v. District of Columbia*, 1988; *Independent School District No. 623 v. Digre*, 1990) or if it is impossible for parents to obtain adequate relief through hearings (*Padilla v. School District No. 1*, 2000). Exhaustion is not required to enforce final administrative orders, except that these cases must be filed under the Civil Rights Act of 1871, Section 1983 (42 U.S.C. § 1983)(see *Robinson v. Pinderhughes*, 1987), a statute that is discussed later in this chapter. Put another way, as reviewed in the next section, because parties may not file suit until administrative appeals are pursued, courts refuse to address issues that were not subject to complete exhaustion (*T.S. v. Ridgefield Board of Education*, 1993).

Exhaustion Required

Courts have long refused to hear cases where the party bringing suit had not exhausted administrative remedies (*Riley v. Ambach*, 1981; *Christopher W. v. Portsmouth School Committee*, 1989; *Cox v. Jenkins*, 1989; *Doe v. Smith*, 1989; *Gardener v. School Board of Caddo Parish*, 1992; *T.S. v. Ridgefield Board of Education*, 1993; *Doe v. Arizona Department of Education*, 1997; *N.B. v. Alachua County School Board*, 1996; *D.C. ex rel. S.K. v. Hamamoto*, 2004). Exhaustion is required for a variety of reasons. By way of illustration, since judges consider themselves generalists when reviewing the educational needs of students with disabilities and hearing officers more experienced in these matters (*Crocker v. Tennessee Secondary School Athletic Association,* 1989), they want to be able to review complete records that have been developed by professionals with competence in this complex area of the law. In one dispute, where a student sought damages over a board's alleged failure to provide IDEA services, the Second Circuit decided that this did not entitle her to sidestep the exhaustion requirement because the real problem was the lack of specificity in her IEP rather than the board's failure to comply with its content (*Polera v. Board of Education of the Newburgh Enlarged City School District,* 2002).

Most courts treat class action suits, wherein one person or a small group of individuals files a case on behalf of a larger group of similarly aggrieved individuals challenging policies and/or procedures with widespread application, as being subject to the exhaustion requirements (*Hoeft v. Tucson Unified School District,* 1992). One court went so far as to declare that all members of a class had to exhaust administrative remedies prior to bringing suit (*Jackson v. Fort Stanton Hospital and Training School,* 1990). Other courts have pointed out that filing representative claims served the purposes of exhaustion (*Association for Retarded Citizens of Alabama v. Teague,* 1987; *Association for Community Living in Colorado v. Romer,* 1993).

The Tenth Circuit stated that the issue of whether a state's policies denied students with disabilities a FAPE entailed a factually intensive inquiry into the circumstances of their cases and was the type of issue the administrative process was designed to address (*Association for Community Living in Colorado v. Romer,* 1993). A federal trial court in Indiana reached a different result in positing that plaintiffs representing a class need not exhaust administrative remedies because class action administrative hearings are not permitted (*Evans v. Evans,* 1993).

Insofar as litigants must exhaust administrative remedies, parties cannot file suit based on issues that have not already been addressed at due process hearings. In this regard, the Second Circuit wrote that a student's attorney could not claim on his request for compensatory education that a school board committed procedural violations since the issue had not been raised at a due process hearing (*Garro v. State of Connecticut,* 1994). A federal court in New York also explained that parents could not raise the issue of the appropriateness of an evaluation facility because they failed to challenge the hearing officer's recommendation on the issue in the presence of a state-level review officer (*Stellato v. Board of Education of the Ellenville Central School District,* 1994).

Parties must exhaust administrative remedies when claims are made under statutes other than the IDEA (*Torrie v. Cwayna,* 1994), when classroom procedures are challenged (*Hayes v. Unified School District No. 377,* 1989), or when seeking enforcement of administrative orders if state regulations provide for this through the administrative process (*Norris v. Board of Education of Greenwood Community School Corporation,* 1992).

Exhaustion Not Required

Courts generally agree that parents are not required to exhaust administrative remedies under a variety of circumstances (Clark, 2002). In the first of two cases on point, the Ninth Circuit agreed that parents were able to skip a due process hearing when their complaint was that they were denied access to that process (*Kerr Center Parents Association v. Charles*, 1990). In the second, the federal trial court in Arizona indicated that exhaustion would have been futile where a parent claimed that she was denied meaningful access to the IDEA's due process procedures (*Begay v. Hodel*, 1990).

Parties may also not be required to exhaust administrative remedies when complaints allege systemic failures. In one such case, the Second Circuit acknowledged that a school board's alleged failure to prepare and implement IEPs, notify parents of meetings, provide parents with required progress reports, perform timely evaluations, provide adequate procedural safeguards, carry out their required responsibilities in a timely fashion, and offer appropriate training for staff members were systemic failures that could not be remedied through the administrative hearing process (*J.S. ex rel. N.S. v. Attica Central Schools*, 2004).

Challenges to school board policies that could violate the IDEA may not be subject to the administrative process. As such, the Ninth Circuit was convinced that a claim that the school day for specified special education students was shorter than for regular education pupils was not subject to the exhaustion requirement because it had nothing to do with individual IEPs (*Christopher S. ex rel. Rita S. v. Stanislaus County Office of Education*, 2004).

Courts have considered exhaustion to be futile when hearing officers lacked authority to grant the requested relief. The Second Circuit decided that a parent's complaint about the method by which hearing officers were selected was not subject to exhaustion since a sole hearing officer lacked the authority to alter the procedure (*Heldman v. Sobol*, 1992). Federal trial courts in New York also found that exhaustion was not required when the requested relief was that a child be placed in a school that was not on the state's list of approved placements because the hearing officer could not order a student to attend classes in an unapproved facility (*Straube v. Florida Union Free School District*, 1992) or in challenging an adjudication of officials of the state education department who rejected a parental request but declined to make an exception to general procedures (*Vander Malle v. Ambach*, 1987).

The previous section discussed cases wherein courts subjected class action suits to the exhaustion of remedies requirement. Yet, since not all courts agree, exhaustion may not be necessary in class action suits where the claims of plaintiffs are systemic in nature and hearing officers would not have the authority to order relief. In such a case, the Second Circuit remarked that exhaustion was not required when a hearing officer could not order a systemwide change to correct the alleged wrongs (*J.G. v. Board of Education of the Rochester City School District*, 1987).

Exhaustion may be unnecessary in emergency situations if it would cause severe or irreparable harms to students. Nevertheless, the Third Circuit specified that since mere allegations of irreparable harm are insufficient to excuse exhaustion, a plaintiff must present actual evidence to support such a claim (*Komninos v. Upper Saddle River Board of Education*, 1994).

When litigation involves issues that are purely legal rather than factual, exhaustion may not be required (*Lester H. v. Gilhool*, 1990). Similarly, exhaustion may not be necessary if a state persistently fails to render expeditious decisions regarding a student's educational placement (*Frutiger v. Hamilton Central School District*, 1991).

Finally, courts have refused to apply the exhaustion requirement when students do not need special education. To this end, courts agree that parents do not have to exhaust administrative remedies in cases under Section 504 if their children are not receiving services under the IDEA, even if they are disabled (*Doe v. Belleville Public School District No. 118*, 1987; *Robertson v. Granite City Community Unit School District No. 9*, 1988).

Rights of Parties to a Hearing

Parties involved in due process hearings have the right to be accompanied and advised by counsel with special knowledge concerning the education of students with disabilities (20 U.S.C. § 1415(h)(1)). In one case, the Supreme Court of Delaware held that the IDEA does not authorize non-attorneys to represent parents at hearings (*In re Arons*, 2000). Consequently, the court affirmed an order forbidding non-attorneys with special knowledge and training with respect to the problems of students with disabilities to represent parents at due process hearings.

As quasi-judicial proceedings, the parties may present evidence, compel the attendance of witnesses, and cross-examine witnesses during hearings (20 U.S.C. § 1415(h)(1)(2)). The parties can prohibit the introduction of evidence that is not disclosed at least five business days prior to hearings (34 C.F.R. § 300.512(a)(3)). At the same time, the parties have the right to obtain a written or, at the option of the parents, an electronic verbatim record of the hearing, as well as findings of fact and decisions (20 U.S.C. § 1415(h)(3), (4)).

In a procedural matter, the federal trial court in New Jersey observed that an indigent parent who could not afford to pay for it was entitled to receive a written transcript of a hearing at public expense so that she could challenge its results (*Militello v. Board of Education of the City of Union City*, 1992). The court contended that a copy of the transcript of the lengthy and complex hearing was an essential tool for the mother's effective and efficient review of its outcome. In a slightly different case, the First Circuit ruled that educational officials could provide either a written transcript or an electronic record of the administrative hearings to indigent parents (*Edward B. v. Paul*, 1987).

According to the IDEA, hearing officers must render final decisions within 45 days of requests for hearings (34 C.F.R. § 300.515(a)). Even so, hearing officers can grant requests from the parties for extensions or continuances (34 C.F.R. § 300.515(c)). The adjudications of hearing officers are final unless they are appealed (20 U.S.C. § 1415(i)(1)(A)).

In states with two-tiered due process hearing systems, officials must ensure that final decisions, based on the record, are reached within 30 days of requests for review (34 C.F.R. § 300.515(b)). At least one court decreed that the IDEA's finality requirement precludes a hearing officer from taking any action that interferes with rendering a final adjudicative order. The federal trial court in Delaware asserted that a hearing panel may not refer a case to some other body for review (*Slack v. State of Delaware Department of Public Instruction*, 1993). In this case, a hearing panel commented that a student was entitled to a residential placement but did not order the child to be moved to such a setting. Instead, the panel commented that a mechanism should have been established to evaluate options. The court concluded that referring the case for additional review did not comport with the IDEA's finality requirements, thereby undermining the concern for prompt resolution of placement disputes.

Once administrative review is complete, aggrieved parties may file suit in federal or state courts (20 U.S.C. § 1415(i)(2)(A)). Aggrieved parties are generally considered to be the losing parties or the ones who did not obtain the relief sought. While prevailing parties are ordinarily not viewed as aggrieved, the federal trial court in Delaware permitted parents who won on the legal issues but did not obtain the relief they sought to be treated as the aggrieved party so that they could seek judicial review (*Slack v. State of Delaware Department of Public Instruction*, 1993).

JUDICIAL REVIEW

As reflected in Figure 6.1, and as mentioned earlier, under the IDEA, either party can appeal the results of due process hearings to federal or state courts once the party has exhausted administrative remedies. As important as this issue is, though, the IDEA is silent on whether cases are to be submitted to juries. Insofar as due process hearings generate their own record, the courts generally do not conduct trials *de novo*. In other words, courts ordinarily do not repeat investigations that occurred administratively. Rather, the courts examine the records of hearings and hear new or additional testimony when necessary before ruling. Due to the importance

Figure 6.1   Dispute Resolution Under the IDEA

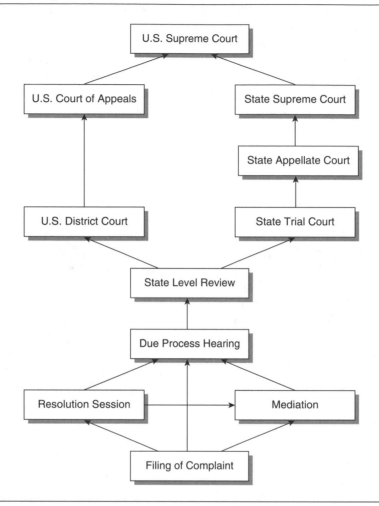

Congress placed on the administrative process, courts are required to give due weight to the results of due process hearings and overturn adjudication only when they are convinced that it was clearly erroneous.

Pro Se Parents

As a preliminary matter, while parents have the right to have attorneys represent them at trial and parents who are lawyers can represent themselves, the issue of attorney fees aside, questions arise over whether parents who are not attorneys can represent their children in judicial proceedings. Consistent with many other areas under the IDEA, the courts are split on the question of whether parents who are not attorneys can act as pro se plaintiffs, literally, "on behalf of the self," in disputes over the education of their children who are in special education placements. Courts are on what can be described as a kind of sliding scale from letting parents represent their children in all circumstances, to doing so in some situations, to prohibiting them from acting at all.

On the one hand, the First Circuit held, as a matter of first impression, that parents can be aggrieved parties within the meaning of the IDEA. Accordingly, the court concluded that parents could sue their school system on behalf of the child regardless of whether the rights at issue were substantive or procedural (*Maroni v. Pemi-Baker Regional School District*, 2003).

In a midway position, the Third Circuit found that Congress expressly permitted parents to represent their children in administrative proceedings pursuant to the IDEA. Still, the court declared that since Congress did not specifically permit parents to represent their children in court, they could act only in administrative proceedings (*Collinsgru v. Palmyra Board of Education*, 1998). Further, the Eleventh Circuit interpreted the IDEA as allowing parents to sue on behalf of their children but not to act as counsel at trial since the statute does not confer authority on nonlawyers to represent their children pro se in judicial proceedings (*Devine v. Indian River County School Board*, 1997).

Conversely, federal trial courts in New York and Oregon as well as the Second, Third, Sixth, and Seventh Circuits agreed that parents cannot appear pro se on behalf of their children in IDEA judicial actions. A federal trial court in New York ruled that since the IDEA requires non-attorney parents to be represented by counsel when bringing actions on behalf of their children, a father could not file a pro se suit in a disagreement over the placement of his son (*Fauconier v. Committee on Special Education*, 2003). The court in Oregon reached the same outcome, declaring that non-attorney parents could not act pro se in suits representing their children with disabilities (*C.O. v. Portland Public Schools*, 2005).

The Second Circuit explained that it saw no reason to deviate from its own rule (*Wenger v. Canastota Central School District*, 1998, 1999) that the IDEA was designed to protect the legal interests of children, not their parents (*Tindall v. Poultney High School District*, 2005). In the first of two unpublished cases that render them of limited precedential value (*Carpenter v. Pennell School District Elementary Unit*, 2003a, 2003b) the court affirmed that a father who was neither a lawyer nor custodian of his daughters could not file suit pro se on their behalf because he had no substantive rights to protect. The same court also vacated an earlier order permitting a mother to represent her son in place of an attorney on the basis that she lacked the authority to do so (*Montclair Board of Education v. M.W.D.*, 2006). The Sixth Circuit reached the same outcome in two separate cases. In the first, the court noted that since, by definition, *pro se* means to appear on one's own behalf, it follows that one cannot appear pro se on another person's behalf. The court added that because students with disabilities do not share their rights to a free appropriate public education with their parents, non-attorney parents cannot represent their children in IDEA suits (*Cavanaugh ex rel. Cavanaugh v. Cardinal Local School District,* 2005).

In a case that is headed to the Supreme Court, the Sixth Circuit, relying on the opinion of the Third Circuit (*Collinsgru v. Palmyra Board of Education,* 1998), reasoned that while parents can act on behalf of their children in administrative proceedings, they have no right to act pro se in judicial matters because they do not have their own substantive rights at issue (*Winkelman v. Parma City School District,* 2005). In the case from the Seventh Circuit, the court simply declared that a noncustodial father who was not a lawyer had no authority to appear as his son's legal representative in his suit against their school board under the IDEA (*Navin v. Park Ridge School District,* 2001, 2002a, 2002b).

Insofar as the Supreme Court has agreed to hear an appeal on the case from Sixth Court, it will be interesting to see whether, and to what extent, it clarifies both whether non-attorney parents can act pro se on behalf of their children and whether they have enforceable rights apart from those of their children.

Standing

In order to file suit, parties must have standing, or a legitimate interest, in the issues litigated. Put another way, parties must be able to show that they were faced with threatened injuries or deprivations of rights. As most of the cases in this chapter, and book, reveal, the vast majority of cases litigated on behalf of students with disabilities are filed by their parents; moreover, surrogate parents can file suits to protect the rights of these children (34 C.F.R. § 300.30(a)(5)). For example, the Second Circuit acknowledged that the father of a student with disabilities had standing to sue over the methods by which hearing officers were selected (*Heldman v. Sobol,* 1992). The court added that since the father had an enforceable right to an impartial hearing on behalf of his son, he had standing to challenge how hearing officers are selected.

Parents can lose their standing if they are no longer the legal guardians of their children. In such a case, the Fifth Circuit maintained that under state law, a child's managing conservator, not her father, had the authority to file suit on her behalf (*Susan R.M. v. Northeast Independent School District,* 1987). In another dispute, where a divorce decree gave a mother the sole custody of her daughter, a federal trial court in Pennsylvania concluded that the father did not have standing to sue (*Carpenter v. Pennell School District Elementary Unit,* 2002; 2003a, 2003b).

In a case seeking reimbursement for the partial depletion of health insurance benefits that were used to procure special education services, the Fourth Circuit agreed with the student that she had standing (*Shook v. Gaston County Board of Education*, 1989). The court noted that since using her insurance benefits to pay for special education diminished the student's resources because the policy capped her available benefits, she had a legitimate interest in the outcome of the litigation. In two separate actions, a federal trial court in Pennsylvania explained that an insurance company lacked standing under the IDEA when attempting to compel a board to provide services it had been paying for under health insurance policies (*Allstate Insurance Co. v. Bethlehem Area School District*, 1987; *Gehman v. Prudential Property and Casualty Insurance Company*, 1989). The court dismissed the cases on the basis that only aggrieved parents or school boards had access to the IDEA's due process mechanism.

The IDEA permits school officials to ask for hearings if parents refuse to consent to evaluations (34 C.F.R. § 300.300(a)(3)). Unfortunately, the courts do not agree on whether states can be aggrieved parties that challenge the results of due process hearings. Along these lines, the Ninth Circuit declared that a board could file such a suit (*Clovis Unified School District v. California Office of Administrative Hearings*, 1990). Similarly, the Seventh Circuit asserted that a nonprofit corporation that operated a licensed child care facility had standing to advocate for the rights of students with disabilities placed in its custody (*Family & Children's Center v. School City of Mishawaka*, 1994). The court indicated that the corporation had standing because the denial of the students' IDEA rights would have deprived it of money to which it otherwise would have been entitled. According to the court, the corporation was an aggrieved party in light of the outcome of a due process hearing.

On the other hand, the Eleventh Circuit wrote that a school board lacked standing to seek to compel the state educational agency to provide special education services (*Andrews v. Ledbetter*, 1989). The court was convinced that the IDEA was designed to resolve disputes about particular IEPs and that nothing in it permits local boards to sue states to compel them to fulfill their statutory duties. In like fashion, federal trial courts in New York (*Board of Education of the Seneca Falls Central School District v. Board of Education of the Liverpool Central School District*, 1990) and Indiana (*Metropolitan School District v. Buskirk*, 1997) agreed that school boards lacked standing to sue each other in disputes under the IDEA.

Burden of Proof

While the U.S. Supreme Court resolved who bears the burden of proof in challenging IEPs in due process hearings, the IDEA and its regulations remain silent on who bears the burden of proof in judicial disputes. As such, this is a question left for judicial discretion (Osborne, 2001). Insofar as the courts are unable to agree on who bears the burden of proof in judicial proceedings, two perspectives have emerged.

The First (*Doe v. Brookline School Committee*, 1983), Fourth (*Barnett v. Fairfax County School Board*, 1991), Fifth (*Christopher M. v. Corpus Christi Independent School District*, 1991), Sixth (*Dong v. Board of Education*, 1999), Seventh (*Board of Education of Community Consolidated School District v. Illinois State Board of Education*, 1991), Tenth (*Johnson v. Independent School District No. 4*, 1990), and Eleventh Circuits (*Devine v. Indian River*, 2001) agree that the party challenging an IEP or the result of a due process hearing bears the burden of proof. These courts are generally of the same opinion that although the outcome of due process hearings is entitled to a degree of deference, the parties seeking to set aside administrative orders must demonstrate that the final results were inappropriate. In addition, the courts reasoned that since the IDEA creates a presumption in favor of then-current placements, the parties attacking their terms must prove that they were inappropriate.

Conversely, the Third Circuit (*Oberti v. Board of Education of the Borough of Clementon School District*, 1993) and a federal trial court in Virginia (*Board of Education v. Michael M.*, 2000) placed the burden of proof on school boards. These courts agreed that since school boards bear the ultimate responsibility for providing special education, they should have to prove that proposed IEPs are appropriate. The courts also recognized the advantage school officials have over parents in proceedings brought pursuant to the IDEA. This approach has gained strength in suits in which compliance with the IDEA's least restrictive environment provision was the issue (*Oberti v. Board of Education of the Borough of Clementon School District*, 1993; *Mavis v. Sobol*, 1994).

Due to the fact that litigation may take more than a year, IEPs that are being challenged may have expired by the time courts act. In the meantime, the parties may have initiated challenges to more recently developed IEPs. In cases such as this, courts ordinarily treat the losing parties in disputes over original IEPs as bearing the burden of producing evidence of changed circumstances that rendered initial IEPs inappropriate (*Town of Burlington v. Department of Education, Commonwealth of Massachusetts*, 1984, 1985). When this happens, there is a presumption in favor of the placements that were ordered as a result of the first, disputed IEPs unless parties can prove that the circumstances have changed.

Judicial Deference

In line with the Supreme Court's position that judges should not substitute their views for those of school authorities (*Board of Education of the Hendrick Hudson Central School District v. Rowley*, 1982), most jurists defer to educators on matters dealing with appropriate instructional methodologies as long as school officials followed procedural requirements. The

Fourth Circuit thus reiterated the widely accepted notion that neither it nor a trial court should have disturbed an IEP simply because judges disagreed with its contents since the judiciary owes deference to educators as long as IEPs meet the IDEA's basic requirements (*Tice v. Botetourt County School Board*, 1990). Due to its having found that school officials failed to follow proper procedures in developing the IEP, the court refused to grant deference to the hearing officer's order.

> Most judges defer to educators on matters about appropriate methodology as long as procedural requirements are followed.

The Supreme Court (*Board of Education of the Hendrick Hudson Central School District v. Rowley*, 1982) and other federal courts (*Roncker v. Walter*, 1983; *Briggs v. Board of Education of Connecticut*, 1989; *Kerkham v. Superintendent, District of Columbia Schools*, 1991) agree that the IDEA's mandate requiring courts to review the records of due process hearings implies that their results must be given due weight. Still, it is unclear how much weight is due to these results. In *Rowley* the Court added that questions of methodology are for resolution by the states, clarifying that the judiciary should defer to hearing officers on questions of the content of IEPs and instructional methodology.

The First Circuit declared that a trial court must reach its own independent judgment based on the record of the due process hearing as supplemented at trials (*Town of Burlington v. Department of Education, Commonwealth of Massachusetts*, 1984, 1985). The court specified that while the amount of weight to be afforded the result of hearings is left to the discretion of trial courts, judges must consider the records carefully and endeavor to respond to administrative resolutions of all material issues. In another dispute, the First Circuit held that a trial court did not err in failing to overlook or misconstrue evidence where its judgment was based on a supportable finding that an IEP was reasonably calculated to address a student's needs (*Lenn v. Portland School Committee*, 1993).

In a related matter, federal trial courts in California (*Bertolucci v. San Carlos Elementary School District*, 1989) and New Jersey (*Woods v. New Jersey Department of Education*, 1993) rejected the notion that judges have broad power to overturn the orders of hearing officers. These courts shared the view that the IDEA's mandate for judicial review is not an open invitation for judges to substitute their views of sound educational policy for those of school officials. The Fourth Circuit also posited that a court is bound by an administrative record and additional evidence as produced at trial, but must act independently (*Burke County Board of Education v. Denton*, 1990). Conversely, the Fifth Circuit stated that courts need not defer to hearing officers when their own reviews reveal that officers erroneously assessed the facts or misapplied the law (*Teague Independent School District v. Todd D.,* 1993).

The District of Columbia Circuit acknowledged that courts overturning the results of due process hearings must explain their grounds for doing so (*Kerkham v. McKenzie,* 1988). In addition, a trial court in the same jurisdiction pointed out that judges may reverse the orders of hearing officers only when they are satisfied that school officials have proved that the officers erred (*Block v. District of Columbia,* 1990). The federal trial court in Massachusetts also noted that while a hearing officer's order must be accorded some deference, it is not entitled to great deference on matters of law (*Puffer v. Raynolds,* 1988).

In a two-tiered due process hearing scheme, courts defer to final orders (*Karl v. Board of Education of the Genesco Central School District,* 1984; *Thomas v. Cincinnati Board of Education,* 1990). Moreover, if review procedures are flawed, courts defer to initial adjudications (*Puffer v. Raynolds,* 1988). In such a case, the Fourth Circuit reasoned that a hearing officer's judgment should not have been accorded any weight since he discredited a witness he had not seen or heard testify while a local hearing officer relied on the credibility of the same witness (*Doyle v. Arlington County School Board,* 1991). On remand, a trial court considered the fact that all of the parents' witnesses had a record of testifying against the school board in evaluating the record of the due process hearing (*Doyle v. Arlington County School Board,* 1992). The Fourth Circuit again affirmed, but it did so without a written opinion (*Doyle v. Arlington County School Board,* 1994).

Admission of Additional Evidence

The IDEA permits courts to hear additional evidence at the request of one of the parties (20 U.S.C. § 1415(i)(2)(C)(ii)). Even so, courts can limit the amount and kind of extra evidence they are willing to admit, especially if it had not been introduced prior to judicial review. In the first of two cases, the Eleventh Circuit affirmed that a trial court was within its discretion in refusing to receive and consider evidence that a school board wished to offer in addition to the record of a due process hearing (*Walker County School District v. Bennett,* 2000). In the second, the Sixth Circuit commented that a trial court erred in relying on additional evidence to address issues beyond those presented at a due process hearing over the appropriateness of a student's IEP (*Metropolitan Board of Public Education v. Guest,* 1999).

The First Circuit affirmed that a party seeking to admit additional evidence must justify its request (*Roland M. v. Concord School Committee,* 1990). Here, a trial court refused to hear the testimony of witnesses for parents who could have testified at a due process hearing but whose testimony was deliberately withheld by their attorney. The panel determined that the trial court did not abuse its discretion in refusing to allow the witnesses to testify. In addition, a federal trial court in Illinois refused to admit evaluation materials that school officials had not previously submitted to the hearing officer (*Board of Education of the Paxton-Buckley-Loda Unit School District No. 10 v. Jeff S.*, 2002). Noting that withholding this information from the hearing officer severely undercut the role of the administrative hearing, the court also pointed out that such action deprived the court of the hearing officer's expertise on the matter.

On the other hand, the Sixth Circuit expressed the view that a lower court was justified in admitting additional evaluation materials (*Metropolitan Board of Public Education of the Metropolitan Government of Nashville and Davidson County v. Bellamy*, 2004). In this case, the court recognized that the parents had neither the opportunity nor resources to procure additional evaluations before the due process hearing took place.

A party wishing to present additional evidence must make its intention to do so clearly known to a court. In such an instance, the Seventh Circuit judged that if neither party makes its intention to submit additional evidence known, a court is entitled to assume that they wish to have the case resolved on the basis of the administrative record (*Hunger v. Leininger*, 1994).

The Sixth Circuit affirmed that it is appropriate for a trial court to consider evidence that a hearing officer failed to review (*Metropolitan Government of Nashville and Davidson County v. Cook*, 1990). The court stressed that the admission of additional evidence did not undercut the administrative process. In a case that was along the same line, the Fifth Circuit agreed that a trial court gave due weight to the result of a due process hearing but was free to take additional evidence into consideration (*Teague Independent School District v. Todd D.*, 1993).

Due to the delay that often occurs between the time that placements are finalized and judicial review is initiated, additional evidence may be available about how students progressed in the disputed settings. It is not clear whether a court should admit evidence that develops after a disputed placement is made. The Ninth Circuit held that a trial court has the discretion to admit additional evidence concerning relevant events occurring after an administrative hearing (*Ojai Unified School District v. Jackson*, 1993). A federal trial court in Wisconsin also admitted evidence concerning progress a student had made in a home-based program during the time between the hearing and court review (*Konkel v. Elmbrook School District*, 2004). On the other hand, the Third Circuit affirmed that IEPs and placements should be reviewed from the perspective of the information that was available when the initial action was taken (*Fuhrmann v. East Hanover Board of Education*, 1993). While the court recognized that events that occur after a placement is made may be relevant, it concluded that they cannot be substituted for the threshold determination of whether an IEP was reasonably calculated to confer an appropriate education.

Mootness

Courts will not accept cases unless they present live controversies, meaning that the parties have real interests in their outcomes. To this end, courts have rejected cases as moot where they could not grant effective relief due to a student's graduation (*Honig v. Doe*, 1988; *Thomas R.W. v. Massachusetts Department of Education*, 1997) or where relief would have served no purpose because a student moved (*Smith v. Special School District No. 1*, 1999). However, if the controversies that initiated disputed are no longer alive, but they are capable of repetition, courts may still hear the cases. In such a dispute, the Supreme Court ruled that judges may adjudicate ongoing controversies and have jurisdiction if there is a reasonable likelihood that a party will again suffer the deprivation of the rights that initiated the suit (*Honig v. Doe*, 1988).

> Courts will not accept cases unless they present live controversies.

The Fifth Circuit declared a case moot after a school board agreed to provide a student with services (*Lee v. Biloxi School District*, 1992). Similarly, the federal trial court in New Hampshire indicated that a case was moot where a school year ended and there was no reasonable expectation that the controversy would have recurred (*Greene v. Harrisville School District*, 1990). Subsequently, federal trial courts in Indiana (*Merrifield v. Lake Central School Corporation*, 1991) and Texas (*McDowell v. Fort Bend Independent School District*, 1990) rejected claims as moot where students were no longer eligible to receive services because they reached the maximum eligibility age under state law.

Once a student is removed from a disputed setting and receives a new placement, the placement issue is moot (*Robbins v. Maine School Administrative District No. 56*, 1992). Moreover, a case is moot if the parties no longer retain an interest in its outcome (*Stellato v. Board of Education of the Ellenville Central School District*, 1994).

In its only special education case involving mootness, the Supreme Court held that a dispute was not moot for a 20-year-old student who was still eligible to receive services under the IDEA, where there could be a reasonable expectation that he would again be subjected to the deprivation of rights complained about in the litigation (*Honig v. Doe*, 1988). Other courts refused to treat cases as moot where issues were capable of repetition, such as when a school year ended (*Jenkins v. Squillacote*, 1991), when the basic complaint still existed (*Straube v. Florida Union Free School District*, 1992), when the IEP on which the suit was brought was superseded by a new IEP (*DeVries v. Spillane*, 1988), and when parents enrolled their child in a private school (*Daniel R.R. v. State Board of Education*, 1989; *Heldman v. Sobol*, 1992). One federal appellate court went so far as to assert that a case was not moot when parents approved an IEP because the board's past failures to adhere to the IDEA enhanced the probability that future violations would have occurred (*Abney ex rel. Kantor v. District of Columbia*, 1988).

Exchange of Information

Attorneys for the parties in IDEA proceedings generally exchange information prior to trials. Principles of fairness dictate that one side cannot withhold information that is crucial to the other party's case because, just as in due process hearings, the goal is to have all possible evidence available to help measure an IEP's appropriateness rather than to prevail in a dispute just for the sake of winning. For example, the federal trial court for the District of Columbia held that the school board had to provide parents with information about private schools, the qualifications of the teachers in them, and the disabilities of the students attending them since these matters were not privileged (*Fagan v. District of Columbia*, 1991). At the same time, the court acknowledged that the board was not required to provide information about due process hearings and suits challenging other placements since the parents' attorney could obtain this material through normal legal research.

Res Judicata

Based on the principle of res judicata, courts cannot hear cases or render judgments on matters that they have already resolved. *Res judicata* stands for the proposition that a final judgment by a court of competent jurisdiction is conclusive and acts as an absolute bar to a subsequent action involving the same claim. By way of illustration, the Eleventh Circuit, in a case that was before it for the second time, affirmed that, under res judicata, a trial court's decision prior to the first appeal precluded additional consideration of the issues (*Jenkins v. State of Florida*, 1991).

Settlement Agreements

During the course of a dispute parents and school officials often negotiate settlement agreements that effectively end controversies. Settlement agreements are sometimes reached as a result of a mediation process that occurs before due process hearings have started or during litigation. When the parties agree on settlements during litigation, hearing officers or courts may either approve or reject them if they deem their terms to be contrary to public policy or existing law. In a representative case of this nature, the Eleventh Circuit decided that a trial court could vitiate a settlement agreement only if it violates public policy (*In re Smith*, 1991). Thus, where the panel believed that a settlement agreement was not void as against public policy due to its high cost, the court issued an order to enforce its provisions to provide housing for a student with disabilities.

In a case from New Jersey, the federal trial court noted that the existence of a settlement agreement that had been negotiated by parents and school officials during a due process hearing did not bar the court from hearing the case (*Woods v. New Jersey Department of Education*, 1992). The court ascertained that despite the settlement agreement, school officials still had the duty to provide the student with a FAPE. In another case, the same court offered that a settlement agreement reached through mediation formed a contract between the parties, but the court did not allow the school board to avoid its responsibilities under the IDEA (*D.R. v. East Brunswick Board of Education*, 1993, 1997). The court emphasized that there was a presumption that the services agreed to by the parties at the time that they entered into the agreement met the student's special education needs. In addition, the court decreed that the parents had the right to question the terms of the agreement if there was a change in circumstances.

STATUTES OF LIMITATIONS

Earlier versions of the IDEA did not contain a statute of limitations either for requesting due process hearings or filing suits after exhausting administrative remedies (Osborne, 1996, 2004; Zirkel & Maher, 2003). Consequently, in amending the IDEA in 2004 Congress included specific statutes of limitations to govern the timelines for seeking such actions.

The IDEA and its regulations now require parties to request impartial due process hearings within two years of the date they knew or should have known about the actions that form the bases of their complaints (20 U.S.C. § 1415(f)(3)(C); 34 C.F.R. § 300.511(e)). Moreover, if states have explicit time limitations for requesting hearings, these limitations prevail. Limitations periods may be set aside if school boards specifically misrepresented that they resolved the problems forming the basis of complaints or if officials withheld information that they should have provided to parents (20 U.S.C. § 1415(f)(3)(D); 34 C.F.R. § 300.511(f)). After final administrative decisions are rendered, parties have 90 days to file judicial appeals (20 U.S.C. § 1415(g)(2)(B); 34 C.F.R. § 300.516(b)). Again, if state laws provide otherwise, they prevail.

Beginning and Waiving a Limitations Period

Limitations periods generally begin when cases are resolved. In two separate disputes, the federal trial court in New Hampshire clarified that the statute of limitations begins to run on the day decisions are released, not the day the aggrieved parties receive copies of them in the mail (*I.D. v. Westmoreland School District*, 1991; *G.D. v. Westmoreland School District*, 1992). On the other hand, the Seventh Circuit affirmed that where a prevailing parent sought to recover attorneys' fees, the statute of limitations did not begin until after the expiration of the time when the school board could file an appeal of the hearing officer's adjudication (*McCartney C. v. Herrin Community Unit School District No. 4,* 1994). The court remarked that the parent could neither have recovered attorney fees until administrative and judicial proceedings were finished nor have known that the school board would not have appealed the administrative order until after the time period to do so had expired. In cases that did not necessarily involve appeals of due process hearings, courts agree that the clock begins to run on the day that students reach the age of majority (*Shook v. Gaston County Board of Education,* 1989), their eligibility for services ends (*Hall v. Knott County Board of Education,* 1991), or they graduate (*Richards v. Fairfax County School Board,* 1992).

Occasionally, difficulties ensue when parents are not fully aware of their procedural rights under the IDEA. A federal trial court in Illinois commented that a case filed after the statute of limitations expired was not untimely where parents were unaware of the limitations period and were not apprised of the deadline for challenging the results of a due process hearing (*Board of Education of the City of Chicago v. Wolinsky,* 1993). The court interpreted the IDEA as requiring state officials to inform parents of the full range of available procedural avenues. In addition, the federal trial court in New Hampshire declared that a case that was filed after the statute of limitations expired was not time-barred since the hearing officer failed to inform the parents of how much time they had to file an appeal (*Hebert v. Manchester, New Hampshire, School District,* 1993).

The First Circuit held that a suit that was filed after the statute of limitations expired was not barred where the parental delay was not unreasonable because in the interim they attempted to resolve their differences with the school board (*Murphy v. Timberlane Regional School District,* 1992). On remand, the federal trial court in New Hampshire found (*Murphy v. Timberlane Regional School District,* 1993), and the First Circuit affirmed (*Murphy v. Timberlane Regional School District,* 1994), that the case was not barred by the doctrine of laches, which applies when a party fails to assert a right, along with a lapse of time and other circumstances that put the other party at a disadvantage. The court conceded that school board officials failed to show that witnesses were unavailable or had failed memories. In a conceptually related dispute, the Eleventh Circuit was of the opinion that since school officials never raised the issue of a suit's being time-barred, they waived the right to use the statute of limitations as a defense (*J.S.K. v. Hendry County School Board,* 1991).

Limitations periods may be tolled, or suspended, for good reason. For example, the federal trial court in Connecticut tolled the limitations period because a parent requested clarification of a hearing officer's order (*R.M. ex rel J.M. v. Vernon Board of Education,* 2002). In like fashion, the trial court in the District of Columbia tolled the limitations period where a parent requested reconsideration of a hearing officer's adjudication (*R.S. v. District of Columbia,* 2003). In another suit from the District of Columbia, the same court tolled the statute of limitations because school board officials failed to inform the parents of the limitations period (*Abraham v. District of Columbia*, 2004).

CASES UNDER OTHER STATUTES

The IDEA is the primary federal statute protecting the rights of students with disabilities. Even so, parents can seek protection for the educational rights of their children with disabilities under other federal statutes and, in particular, under state laws that may provide greater protection than the IDEA (*Geis v. Board of Education*, 1985). To this end, the IDEA specifies that none of its provisions can be interpreted as restricting, or limiting, the rights, procedures, and remedies available under the Constitution, Title V of the Rehabilitation Act of 1973, or other federal statutes protecting the rights of students with disabilities (20 U.S.C. § 1415(1)). The IDEA further stipulates that before a suit can be filed under one of these other laws, all available administrative remedies must be exhausted (20 U.S.C. § 1415(i)(A); *Quackenbush v. Johnson City School District*, 1983).

Most cases seeking relief under statutes other than the IDEA are filed pursuant to Section 1983 of the Civil Rights Act of 1871 (42 U.S.C. § 1983), an expansive law used to enforce rights secured by federal law or the Constitution. A variety of courts have agreed that Section 1983 may be used to enforce the results of a due process hearing (*Robinson v. Pinderhughes*, 1987; *Reid v. Board of Education, Lincolnshire-Prairie View School District 103*, 1990; *Grace B. v. Lexington School Committee*, 1991) or to remedy a deprivation of due process or other rights secured by the IDEA (*Digre v. Roseville Schools Independent School District No. 623*, 1988; *Hiller v. Board of Education of the Brunswick Central School District*, 1988; *Mrs. W. v. Tirozzi*, 1989). Yet, courts have made it clear that cases filed under Section 1983 must be predicated on more than re-allegations of claims presented under the IDEA (*Barnett v. Fairfax County School Board*, 1991), that Section 1983 cases are not viable when adequate remedies exist under other laws (*Fee v. Herndon*, 1990), and that Section 1983 cannot be used to expand the rights of students under the IDEA (*Crocker v. Tennessee Secondary School Athletic Association*, 1992).

Pursuant to Section 1983, school officials acting under the color of state law, meaning that they acted as if they had the official authority to act as they did, may be liable for actions that have the effect of depriving students (or their parents) of rights secured by federal law. In such a case, a federal trial court in Indiana posited that an attorney hired to represent a school board in a special education case could be sued under Section 1983 (*Bray v. Hobart City School Corporation*, 1993). The student's parents successfully claimed that the advice the attorney gave the board led officials to deprive their son of his IDEA rights.

Section 504 of the Rehabilitation Act of 1973 prohibits discrimination against individuals with disabilities in programs receiving federal assistance (29 U.S.C. § 794). As might have been expected, parties frequently file suit alleging discrimination under Section 504 and the deprivation of rights under the IDEA. If a dispute can be settled under the IDEA's provisions, however, courts will not turn to Section 504 for relief. A case from Pennsylvania is illustrative (*Gaudiello v. Delaware County Intermediate Unit*, 1992). The parents of a student with physical disabilities requested a due process hearing after school officials refused to permit him to have his service dog accompany him to class unless he moved to a less restrictive placement. After a hearing officer maintained that the student could be educated in the less restrictive environment, his parents filed suit under Section 504 rather than challenge the hearing officer's order. In denying the parents' claim, a federal trial court concluded that the IDEA was the exclusive avenue through which they could bring an equal protection claim on behalf of their child's right to a FAPE. If relief is not available under the IDEA, a case may proceed under Section 504 (*University Interscholastic League v. Buchannan*, 1993).

The bottom line is that if school officials comply with the IDEA, courts are generally satisfied that they will have met the dictates of Section 504 (*Cordrey v. Euckert*, 1990; *Doe v. Alabama State Department of Education*, 1990; *Barnett v. Fairfax County School Board*, 1991). In addition, at least one court declared that a party cannot rely on Section 504 to expand the rights available under the IDEA (*Carey v. Maine School Administrative District 17*, 1990).

RECOMMENDATIONS

In light of the IDEA's extensive mechanism for dispute resolution, educators should

- Familiarize themselves with the dispute resolution provisions in both federal and state law. This is important because procedures vary from state to state, especially, for example, when it comes to due process hearings, since even though the majority of states have two levels of review, others are restricted to one.
- Take formal steps to notify parents of and explain to them all of their rights to challenge any aspect of the education of their children.
- Make sure to inform parents that they may request mediation, which remains optional, or due process hearings if disputes cannot be resolved.
- Notify parents of their obligation to exhaust administrative remedies unless exhaustion clearly is not feasible.
- Pay careful attention, in consultation with their attorneys, to the date restrictions in the IDEA and state law with regard to initiating

Figure 6.2   Frequently Asked Questions

Q: What is the advantage of using the mediation process as opposed to going directly to due process hearings?

A: Unfortunately, due process hearings can be very adversarial. Mediation, on the other hand, can be a nonadversarial process that helps the parties to communicate better and resolve their dispute in a manner that is acceptable to both sides. The adversarial nature of due process hearings often causes permanent breakdowns in the relationships between parents or guardians and school officials. Conversely, mediation may help to maintain a working relationship between parents or guardians and school officials.

Q: Since many special education disputes end up in court, why is it necessary to exhaust administrative remedies? Would disputes be settled faster if the parties could go directly to court?

A: Exhaustion has two primary purposes: First, exhaustion allows for fact-finding by hearing officers who are familiar with special education; second, exhaustion provides a factual record for the courts to review. While the results of many hearings are appealed to the courts, the majority are not. The administrative process provides a fairly expedient means of settling disputes. If disputes are appealed to the courts, judicial review can be rendered more quickly because factual records exist and the court does not need to engage in fact-finding.

Q: How long do the losing parties to administrative hearings have to file judicial appeals?

A: The losing parties to administrative hearings have 90 days to file appeals unless state law dictates otherwise. Insofar as statutes of limitations may vary considerably from state to state, it is important for school administrators to check state law in this regard.

Q: Which party bears the burden of proof in court?

A: Again, this varies by jurisdiction. Some courts have ruled that the parties bringing the appeals bear the burden of proof while others decided that those challenging IEPs or the status quo have the burden of showing why they are inappropriate. Yet other courts have reasoned that the burden is always on school boards to show that their proposed IEPs and placements are appropriate. It is important for school officials to be aware of how courts within their jurisdictions place the burden of proof.

Q: Can parents bypass the IDEA by filing suit under other statutes such as Section 504 or Section 1983?

A: The IDEA specifically states that none of its provisions can be interpreted to restrict or limit the remedies available under the Constitution, Section 504, or other statutes protecting the rights of students with disabilities. Thus, parents or guardians may file suits under statutes other than the IDEA. Even so, parents or guardians must exhaust all administrative remedies under the IDEA if it makes relief available.

---

a due process hearing and statutes of limitations, which will vary significantly from state to state.

- Comply with the IDEA's requirement of sharing all information with parents within five days of due process hearings when preparing for hearings.
- Keep careful records of all materials relating to student placements since this information is most useful in due process hearings and judicial proceedings.
- Remind parents that they may safeguard the rights of their children under other federal and state laws in addition to the IDEA.

REFERENCES

Abney ex rel. Kantor v. District of Columbia, 849 F.2d 1491 (D.C. Cir. 1988).

Abraham v. District of Columbia, 338 F. Supp.2d 113 (D.D.C. 2004).

Alamo Heights Independent School District v. State Board of Education, 790 F.2d 1153 (5th Cir. 1986).

Allstate Insurance Co. v. Bethlehem Area School District, 678 F. Supp. 1132 (E.D. Pa. 1987).

Andrews v. Ledbetter, 880 F.2d 1287 (11th Cir. 1989).

Antkowiak v. Ambach, 838 F.2d 635 (2d Cir. 1988).

Arons, In re, 796 A.2d 867 (Del. 2000).

Assistance to the States for the Education of Children with Disabilities, 34 C.F.R. §§ 300.1–300.818. (2005).

Association for Community Living in Colorado v. Romer, 992 F.2d 1040 (10th Cir. 1993).

Association for Retarded Citizens of Alabama v. Teague, 830 F.2d 158 (11th Cir. 1987).

Barnett v. Fairfax County School Board, 927 F.2d 146 (4th Cir. 1991), *cert. denied,* 502 U.S. 859 (1991).

Begay v. Hodel, 730 F. Supp. 1001 (D. Ariz. 1990).

Bertolucci v. San Carlos Elementary School District, 721 F. Supp. 1150 (N.D. Cal. 1989).

Beth B. v. Van Clay, 282 F.3d 493 (7th Cir. 2002).

Blackmon v. Springfield R-XII School District, 198 F.3d 648 (8th Cir. 1999).

Block v. District of Columbia, 748 F. Supp. 891 (D.D.C. 1990).

Board of Education of Community Consolidated School District v. Illinois State Board of Education, 938 F.2d 712 (7th Cir. 1991).

Board of Education of Strongville City School District v. Theado, 566 N.E.2d 667 (Ohio 1991).

Board of Education of the Baldwin Union Free School District v. Commissioner of Education, 610 N.Y.S.2d 426 (N.Y. Sup. Ct. 1994).

Board of Education of the City of Chicago v. Wolinsky, 842 F. Supp. 1080 (N.D. Ill. 1993).

Board of Education of the Hendrick Hudson Central School District v. Rowley, 458 U.S. 176 (1982).

Board of Education of the Paxton-Buckley-Loda Unit School District No. 10 v. Jeff S., 184 F. Supp.2d 790 (C.D. Ill. 2002).

Board of Education of the Seneca Falls Central School District v. Board of Education of the Liverpool Central School District, 728 F. Supp. 910 (W.D.N.Y. 1990).

Board of Education v. Michael M., 95 F. Supp.2d 600 (S.D. W. Va. 2000).

Bray v. Hobart City School Corporation, 818 F. Supp. 1226 (N.D. Ind. 1993).

Briggs v. Board of Education of Connecticut, 882 F.2d 688 (2d Cir. 1989).

Burke County Board of Education v. Denton, 895 F.2d 973 (4th Cir. 1990).

Burr v. Ambach, 863 F.3d 1071 (2d Cir. 1988), *vacated sub nom. Sobol v. Burr*, 492 U.S. 902 (1989a), *affirmed* 888 F.2d 258 (2d Cir. 1989b), *cert. denied*, 494 U.S. 1005 (1990).

Canton Board of Education v. N.B. and R.B., 343 F. Supp.2d 123 (D. Conn. 2004).

Carey v. Maine School Administrative District 17, 754 F. Supp. 906 (D. Me. 1990).

Carlisle Area School v. Scott P., 62 F.3d 520 (3d Cir. 1995).

Carpenter v. Pennell School District Elementary Unit, 2002 WL 1832854 (E.D. Pa. 2002), *aff'd sub nom. Carpenter v. Children for Youth Services*, 64 Fed.Appx. 850 (3d Cir. 2003a) (table), *cert. denied*, 540 U.S. 819 (2003b)

Cavanaugh ex rel. Cavanaugh v. Cardinal Local School District, 409 F.3d 753 (6th Cir. 2005).

Christopher M. v. Corpus Christi Independent School District, 933 F.2d 1285 (5th Cir. 1991).

Christopher S. ex rel. Rita S. v. Stanislaus County Office of Education, 384 F.3d 1205 (9th Cir. 2004).

Christopher W. v. Portsmouth School Committee, 877 F.2d 1089 (1st Cir. 1989).

Civil Rights Act of 1871, Section 1983, 42 U.S.C. § 1983.

Clark, S. G. (2002). Administrative remedy under IDEA: Must it be exhausting? *Education Law Reporter, 163*, 1–15.

Clovis Unified School District v. California Office of Administrative Hearings, 903 F.2d 635 (9th Cir. 1990).

C.O. v. Portland Public Schools, 406 F. Supp.2d 1157 (D. Or. 2005).

Cocores v. Portsmouth, New Hampshire School District, 779 F. Supp. 203 (D.N.H. 1991).

Code of Federal Regulations (C.F.R.), as cited.

Collinsgru v. Palmyra Board of Education, 161 F.3d 225 (3d Cir. 1998).

Cordrey v. Euckert, 917 F.2d 1460 (6th Cir. 1990).

Cothern v. Mallory, 565 F. Supp. 701 (W.D. MO.1983).

Cox v. Jenkins, 878 F.2d 414 (D.C. Cir. 1989).

Crocker v. Tennessee Secondary Schools Athletic Association, 873 F.2d 933 (6th Cir. 1989), 980 F.2d 382 (6th Cir. 1992).

Daniel R.R. v. State Board of Education, 874 F.2d 1036 (5th Cir. 1989).

D.C. ex rel. S.K. v. Hamamoto, 97 Fed. Appx. 736 (9th Cir. 2004).

Devine v. Indian River County School Board, 121 F.3d 576 (11th Cir. 1997)

Devine v. Indian River, 249 F.3d 1289 (11th Cir. 2001).

DeVries v. Spillane, 853 F.2d 264 (4th Cir. 1988).

Digre v. Roseville School Independent School District No. 623, 841 F.2d 245 (11th Cir. 1988).

Doe v. Alabama State Department of Education, 915 F.2d 651 (11th Cir. 1990).

Doe v. Arizona Department of Education, 111 F.3d 678 (9th Cir. 1997).

Doe v. Belleville Public School District No. 118, 672 F. Supp. 342 (S.D. Ill. 1987).

Doe v. Board of Education of Tullahoma City Schools, 9 F.3d 455 (6th Cir. 1993).

Doe v. Brookline School Committee, 722 F.2d 910 (1st Cir. 1983).

Doe v. Smith, 879 F.2d 1340 (6th Cir. 1989).

Dong v. Board of Education, 197 F.3d 793 (6th Cir. 1999).

Doyle v. Arlington County School Board, 953 F.2d 100 (4th Cir. 1991), *on remand* 806 F. Supp. 1253 (E.D. Va. 1992), *affirmed* 39 F.3d 1176 (4th Cir. 1994) (mem.).

D.R. v. East Brunswick Board of Education, 838 F. Supp. 184 (D.N.J. 1993), *reversed on other grounds* 109 F.3d 896 (3d Cir. 1997).

Edward B. v. Paul, 814 F.2d 52 (1st Cir. 1987).

Evans v. Evans, 818 F. Supp. 1215 (N.D. Ind. 1993).

Fagan v. District of Columbia, 136 F.R.D. 5 (D.D.C. 1991).

Family & Children's Center v. School City of Mishawaka, 13 F.3d 1052 (7th Cir. 1994).

Fauconier v. Committee on Special Education, 2003 WL 21345549 (S.D.N.Y. 2003).

Fee v. Herndon, 900 F.2d 804 (5th Cir. 1990).

Frutiger v. Hamilton Central School District, 928 F.2d 68 (2d Cir. 1991).

Fuhrmann v. East Hanover Board of Education, 993 F.2d 1031 (3d Cir. 1993).

Gardener v. School Board of Caddo Parish, 958 F.2d 108 (5th Cir. 1992).

Garro v. State of Connecticut, 23 F.3d 734 (2d Cir. 1994).

Gaudiello v. Delaware County Intermediate Unit, 796 F. Supp. 849 (E.D. Pa. 1992).

G.D. v. Westmoreland School District, 783 F. Supp. 1532 (D.N.H. 1992).

Gehman v. Prudential Property and Casualty Insurance Company, 702 F. Supp. 1192 (E.D. Pa. 1989).

Geis v. Board of Education, 774 F.2d 575 (3d Cir. 1985).

Grace B. v. Lexington School Committee, 762 F. Supp. 416 (D. Mass. 1991).

Greene v. Harrisville School District, 771 F. Supp. 1 (D.N.H. 1990).

Grim v. Rhinebeck Central School District, 346 F.3d 377 (2d Cir. 2003).

Grymes v. Madden, 672 F.2d 321 (3d Cir. 1982).

Hacienda La Puente Unified School District of Los Angeles v. Honig, 976 F.2d 487 (9th Cir. 1992).

Hall v. Knott County Board of Education, 941 F.2d 402 (6th Cir. 1991).

Hayes v. Unified School District No. 377, 877 F.2d 809 (10th Cir. 1989).

Hebert v. Manchester, New Hampshire, School District, 833 F. Supp. 80 (D.N.H. 1993).

Heldman v. Sobol, 962 F.2d 148 (2d Cir. 1992).

Hiller v. Board of Education of the Brunswick Central School District, 674 F. Supp. 73 (N.D.N.Y. 1987), 687 F. Supp. 735 (N.D.N.Y. 1988).

Hoeft v. Tucson Unified School District, 967 F.2d 1298 (9th Cir. 1992).

Holmes v. Sobol, 690 F. Supp. 154 (W.D.N.Y. 1988).

Honig v. Doe, 484 U.S. 305 (1988).

Hunger v. Leininger, 15 F.3d 664 (7th Cir. 1994), *cert. denied*, 513 U.S. 839 (1994).

I.D. v. Westmoreland School District, 788 F. Supp. 632 (D.N.H. 1991).

Independent School District No. 623 v. Digre, 893 F.2d 987 (8th Cir. 1990).

Individuals with Disabilities Education Act, 20 U.S.C. § 1400 *et seq.* (2005).

Jackson v. Fort Stanton Hospital and Training School, 757 F. Supp. 1243 (D.N.M. 1990).

Jenkins v. Squillacote, 935 F.2d 303 (D.C. Cir. 1991).

Jenkins v. State of Florida, 931 F.2d 1469 (11th Cir. 1991).

J.G. v. Board of Education of the Rochester City School District, 830 F.2d 444 (2d Cir. 1987).

Johnson v. Independent School District No. 4, 921 F.2d 1022 (10th Cir. 1990), *cert. denied*, 500 U.S. 905 (1991).

Johnson v. Lancaster-Lebanon Intermediate Unit No. 13, Lancaster City School District, 757 F. Supp. 606 (E.D. Pa. 1991).

J.S. ex rel. N.S. v. Attica Central Schools, 386 F.3d 107 (2d Cir. 2004).

J.S.K. v. Hendry County School Board, 941 F.2d 1563 (11th Cir. 1991).

Karl v. Board of Education of the Genesco Central School District, 736 F.2d 873 (2d Cir. 1984).

Kerkham v. McKenzie, 862 F.2d 884 (D.C. Cir. 1988).

Kerkham v. Superintendent, District of Columbia Schools, 931 F.2d 84 (D.C. Cir. 1991).

Kerr Center Parents Association v. Charles, 897 F.2d 1463 (9th Cir. 1990).

Komninos v. Upper Saddle River Board of Education, 13 F.3d 775 (3d Cir. 1994).

Konkel v. Elmbrook School District, 348 F. Supp.2d 1018 (E.D. Wis. 2004).

Kuszewski v. Chippewa Valley Schools, 117 F. Supp. 646 (E.D. Mich. 2000).

L.B. and J.B. ex rel. K.B. v. Nebo School District, 379 F.3d 966 (10th Cir. 2004).

Lee v. Biloxi School District, 963 F.2d 837 (5th Cir. 1992).

Lenn v. Portland School Community, 998 F.2d 1083 (1st Cir. 1993).

Lester H. v. Gilhool, 916 F.2d 865 (3d Cir. 1990).

Louis M. v. Ambach, 714 F. Supp. 1276 (N.D.N.Y. 1989).

Maroni v. Pemi-Baker Regional School District, 346 F.3d 247 (1st Cir. 2003).

Mavis v. Sobol, 839 F. Supp. 968 (N.D.N.Y. 1994).

McCartney C. v. Herrin Community Unit School District No. 4, 21 F.3d 173 (7th Cir. 1994).

McDowell v. Fort Bend Independent School District, 737 F. Supp. 386 (S.D. Tex. 1990).

McKenzie v. Smith, 771 F.2d 1527 (D.C. Cir. 1985).

Merrifield v. Lake Central School Corporation, 770 F. Supp. 468 (N.D. Ind. 1991).

Metropolitan Board of Public Education of the Metropolitan Government of Nashville and Davidson County v. Bellamy, 116 Fed. Appx. 570 (6th Cir. 2004).

Metropolitan Board of Public Education v. Guest, 193 F.3d 457 (6th Cir. 1999).

Metropolitan Government of Nashville and Davidson County v. Cook, 915 F.2d 232 (6th Cir. 1990).

Metropolitan School District v. Buskirk, 950 F. Supp. 899 (S.D. Ind. 1997).

Militello v. Board of Education of the City of Union City, 803 F. Supp. 974 (D.N.J. 1992).

Montclair Board of Education v. M.W.D., 182 Fed.Appex. 136 (3d Cir. 2006).

Mrs. W. v. Tirozzi, 706 F. Supp. 164 (D. Conn. 1989).

Murphy v. Timberlane Regional School District, 973 F.2d 13 (1st Cir. 1992), *on remand,* 819 F. Supp. 1127 (D.N.H.1993), *affirmed* 22 F.3d 1186 (1st Cir. 1994), *cert. denied,* 513 U.S. 987 (1994).

Muth v. Central Bucks School District, 839 F.2d 113 (3d Cir. 1988), *affirmed on other grounds sub nom. Dellmuth v. Muth,* 491 U.S. 223 (1989).

Navin v. Park Ridge School District, 270 F.3d 1147 (7th Cir. 2001), *on remand,* 2002 WL 774300 (N.D. Ill. 2002a), aff'd 49 Fed. Appx. 69 (7th Cir. 2002b).

N.B. v. Alachua County School Board, 84 F.3d 1376 (11th Cir. 1996).

Norris v. Board of Education of Greenwood Community School Corporation, 797 F. Supp. 1452 (S.D. Ind. 1992).

Oberti v. Board of Education of the Borough of Clementon School District, 995 F.2d 1204 (3d Cir. 1993).

Ojai Unified School District v. Jackson, 4 F.3d 1467 (9th Cir. 1993), *cert. denied,* 513 U.S. 825 (1994).

Osborne, A. G. (1996). Statutes of limitations for filing a lawsuit under the Individuals with Disabilities Education Act. *Education Law Reporter, 106,* 959–970.

Osborne, A. G. (2001). Proving that you have provided a FAPE under IDEA. *Education Law Reporter, 151,* 367–372.

Osborne, A. G. (2004). Statutes of limitations for filing a lawsuit under the IDEA: A state by state analysis. *Education Law Reporter, 191,* 545–556.

Osborne, A. G., & Russo, C. J. (2005). The burden of proof in special education hearings: *Schaffer v. Weast. Education Law Reporter, 200,* 1–12.

Padilla v. School District No. 1, 233 F.3d 1268 (10th Cir. 2000).

Polera v. Board of Education of the Newburgh Enlarged City School District, 288 F.3d 478 (2d Cir. 2002).

Puffer v. Raynolds, 761 F. Supp. 838 (D. Mass. 1988).

Quackenbush v. Johnson City School District, 716 F.2d 141 (2d Cir. 1983).

Rehabilitation Act of 1973, Section 504, 29 U.S.C. §§ 792, 794 (1998).

Reid v. Board of Education, Lincolnshire-Prairie View School District 103, 765 F. Supp. 965 (N.D. Ill. 1990).

Richards v. Fairfax County School Board, 798 F. Supp. 338 (E.D. Va. 1992).

Riley v. Ambach, 668 F.2d 635 (2d Cir. 1981).

R.M. ex rel J.M. v. Vernon Board of Education, 208 F. Supp.2d 216 (D. Conn. 2002).

Robbins v. Maine School Administrative District No. 56, 807 F. Supp. 11 (D. Me. 1992).

Robertson v. Granite City Community Unit School District No. 9, 684 F. Supp. 1002 (S.D. Ill. 1988).

Robinson v. Pinderhughes, 810 F.2d 1270 (4th Cir. 1987).

Roland M. v. Concord School Community, 910 F.2d 983 (1st Cir. 1990), *cert. denied* 499 U.S. 912 (1991).

Roncker v. Walter, 700 F.2d 1058 (6th Cir. 1983).

R.S. v. District of Columbia, 292 F. Supp.2d 23 (D.D.C. 2003).

Russo, C. J., & Osborne, A. G. (2006). The Supreme Court clarifies the burden of proof in special education due process hearings: *Schaffer ex rel. Schaffer v. Weast. Education Law Reporter, 208,* 705–717.

Schaffer v. Weast, 546 U.S. 49 (2005).

Seattle School District No. 1 v. B.S., 82 F.3d 1493 (9th Cir. 1996)

Shook v. Gaston County Board of Education, 882 F.2d 119 (4th Cir. 1989).

Slack v. State of Delaware Department of Public Instruction, 826 F. Supp. 115 (D. Del. 1993).

Smith, In re, 926 F.2d 1027 (11th Cir. 1991).

Smith v. Special School District No. 1, 184 F.3d 764 (8th Cir. 1999).

Stellato v. Board of Education of the Ellenville Central School District, 842 F. Supp. 1512 (N.D.N.Y. 1994).

Straube v. Florida Union Free School District, 801 F. Supp. 1164 (S.D.N.Y. 1992).

Susan R.M. v. Northeast Independent School District, 818 F.2d 455 (5th Cir. 1987).

Teague Independent School District v. Todd D., 999 F.2d 127 (5th Cir. 1993).

Thomas R.W. v. Massachusetts Department of Education, 130 F.3d 477 (1st Cir. 1997).

Thomas v. Cincinnati Board of Education, 918 F.2d 618 (6th Cir. 1990).

Tice v. Botetourt County School Board, 908 F.2d 1200 (4th Cir. 1990).

Tindall v. Poultney High School District, 414 F.3d 281 (2d Cir. 2005).

Torrie v. Cwayna, 841 F. Supp. 1434 (W.D. Mich. 1994).

Town of Burlington v. Department of Education, Commonwealth of Massachusetts, 736 F.2d 773 (1st Cir. 1984), *affirmed on other grounds sub nom., Burlington School Committee v. Department of Education of the Commonwealth of Massachusetts,* 471 U.S. 359 (1985).

T.S. v. Ridgefield Board of Education, 10 F.3d 87 (2d Cir. 1993).

University Interscholastic League v. Buchannan, 848 S.W.2d 298 (Tex. App. 1993).

Vander Malle v. Ambach, 667 F. Supp. 1015 (S.D.N.Y. 1987).

Walker County School District v. Bennett, 203 F. 3d 1293 (11th Cir. 2000).

Weast v. Schaffer, 377 F.3d 449 (4th Cir. 2004), *affirmed sub nom. Schaffer v. Weast,* 546 U.S. 49 (2005).

Wenger v. Canastota Central School District, 146 F.3d 123 (2d Cir. 1998), *cert. denied,* 526 U.S. 1025 (1999).

Wenkart, R. D. (2004). The burden of proof in IDEA due process hearings. *Education Law Reporter, 187,* 817–823.

Winkelman v. Parma City School District, 150 Fed. Appx. 406 (6th Cir. 2005), *cert. granted,* 127 S. Ct. 467 (2006).

Woods v. New Jersey Department of Education, 796 F. Supp. 767 (D.N.J. 1992); 823 F. Supp. 254 (D.N.J. 1993).

Zirkel, P. A., & Maher, P. J. (2003). The statute of limitations under the Individuals with Disabilities Education Act. *Education Law Reporter, 175,* 1–5.

7

Remedies for Failure to Provide a Free Appropriate Public Education

INTRODUCTION

If school board officials fail to provide students with disabilities with the free appropriate public education (FAPE) that they are entitled to pursuant to the Individuals with Disabilities Education Act (IDEA), the courts are empowered to receive the records of administrative proceedings, hear additional evidence at the request of a party, and grant appropriate relief based on the preponderance of the evidence standard (20 U.S.C. § 1415(i)(2); Assistance to the States for the Education of Children with Disabilities, 2006, 34 C.F.R. § 300.516(c)(3)). One form of relief that courts often award is reimbursement of tuition and other costs that parents incurred in unilaterally obtaining appropriate services for their children. Another type of relief, one that is available to parents who financially cannot obtain private services in advance, is compensatory educational services to make up for services that their children were denied. Under the right circumstances, parents are also entitled to reimbursement for their legal expenses. While courts are generally reluctant to award punitive damages against school boards, recent litigation indicates that this attitude is changing.

A great deal of litigation has focused on remedies in special education, including key cases that made their way to the U.S. Supreme Court. Many of the remedies that exist to compensate for the failure of school officials to provide a FAPE are based on case law. Nevertheless, in amending the IDEA, Congress provided additional guidance about the types of remedies that are available to students and parents along with setting forth the circumstances under which they may be granted. In fact, some congressional action occurred in response to judicial interpretations of the IDEA. This chapter provides information on the remedies available to parents and students, including those based on provisions in the IDEA itself as well as those that emerged from case law.

This chapter begins with an overview of the most common remedies fashioned by the courts: tuition reimbursement and compensatory educational services. The next section of the chapter examines situations where parents received awards of attorney fees in disputes with their school boards. Next, the chapter discusses the evolving law of damages. As with previous chapters in this book, the chapter ends with a list of recommendations for practitioners.

TUITION REIMBURSEMENT

According to the IDEA, while administrative or judicial proceedings involving placements disputes are pending, students must remain in their then-current educational placements unless their parents and school board officials or states agree otherwise (20 U.S.C. § 1415(j); 34 C.F.R. § 300.518(a)). Due process proceedings under the IDEA can often take several months or even years. Parents who are concerned that the then-current placements of their children are inappropriate may not wish to have the children remain in those placements for the length of time it takes to reach final settlements. Parents in this situation frequently opt to remove their children from their then-current placements and enroll them in private facilities. Parents who prevail in their placement challenges can, under appropriate circumstances, be reimbursed for the tuition and other expenses associated with the private placements. While case law provided parents with this relief for many years, the IDEA and its regulations now explicitly authorize tuition reimbursement (20 U.S.C. § 1412(a)(10)(C)(ii); 34 C.F.R. § 300.148).

Supreme Court Decisions

The U.S. Supreme Court handed down two important judgments about reimbursement of tuition when parents unilaterally placed their children in private schools. In *Burlington School Committee v. Department of Education, Commonwealth of Massachusetts* (*Burlington*, 1985) the Court affirmed that the IDEA allowed reimbursement as long as the parents' chosen placement was determined to be the appropriate placement for their child. The Court ruled that when Congress empowered the judiciary to grant appropriate relief, it intended to include retroactive relief as an available remedy. The Court reasoned that reimbursement merely requires school boards to pay the expenses that they would have been paying all along if officials had developed proper individualized education programs (IEPs) from the beginning. If reimbursement were not available, the Court explained, then a student's right to a FAPE, the parents' right to participate fully in developing an appropriate IEP, and the IDEA's procedural safeguards would be less than complete. Further, the Court maintained that a parental violation of the IDEA's status quo provision does not constitute a waiver of tuition reimbursement. However, the Court cautioned parents who make unilateral placements that they do so at their own financial risk since they will not be reimbursed if school board officials can show that the boards proposed, and had the capacity to implement, appropriate IEPs.

Eight years later, in a unanimous decision, the Supreme Court, in *Florence County School District Four v. Carter* (*Carter*, 1993), affirmed that parentally chosen placements need not be in state-approved facilities in order for them to obtain tuition reimbursement. In *Carter*, a student's parents, dissatisfied with the IEP that school officials developed for their daughter, placed her in a private school that was not on the state's list of approved facilities. Eventually, a trial court found that since the school board's IEP was inadequate, it had to reimburse the parents for the cost of the private school placement. The Fourth Circuit affirmed, noting that the private school provided an educational program that met the Supreme Court's standard of appropriateness as enunciated in *Board of Education of the Hendrick Hudson Central School District v. Rowley* (*Rowley*, 1982), even though it was not state approved and did not fully comply with the IDEA. The Fourth Circuit asserted that when the school board defaulted on its obligations under the IDEA, reimbursement for a placement at a facility that is not approved by the state is not forbidden as long as the educational program provided at the school meets the *Rowley* standard. The Supreme Court agreed, emphasizing that the IDEA is designed to ensure that all students with disabilities receive an education that is both appropriate and free. The Court added that barring reimbursement under the circumstances in *Carter* would have defeated the IDEA's statutory purposes.

Reimbursement Ordered Under *Burlington* and *Carter*

Tuition reimbursement is frequently awarded when parents can show that school officials failed to offer appropriate IEPs but their own chosen facilities did provide their children with appropriate educational programs.

Courts may deny parental requests for tuition reimbursement awards if they are convinced that school officials offered, and had the capacity to implement, appropriate IEPs. Once courts agree that proposed IEPs are appropriate, they do not need to examine the appropriateness of the parents' chosen placements. Even so, tuition reimbursement is frequently awarded when parents can show that the school officials failed to offer appropriate IEPs but their own chosen facility did provide their children with appropriate educational programs.

Parents' Chosen Placements Must Be Appropriate, Not Perfect

Burlington illustrates that parents can be reimbursed for private school costs when their chosen placements are appropriate and those of school board officials are inappropriate. Recognizing that parents are not experts when it comes to making educational placements, courts do not expect them to make the exact required placements. Rather, as long as hearing officers or courts are satisfied that parentally chosen placements are more appropriate than those proposed by school officials, the judiciary generally awards reimbursement, even when the schools that the parents selected are not identical to those that are finally judged to be appropriate. The courts reach this outcome because they realize that when parents make unilateral placements, they may not have as many options available to them as do school boards. Consequently, the courts do not expect parents to necessarily make exactly the same appropriate placement decisions that school officials might have made. Not surprisingly, courts decided that reimbursement is still an available remedy under these circumstances (*Garland Independent School District v. Wilks*, 1987).

On the other hand, courts do not approve full reimbursement awards under all circumstances. As such, courts have denied reimbursement requests when they thought that parentally chosen placements went well beyond what was required and were more costly than necessary (*Alamo Heights Independent School District v. State Board of Education*, 1986).

The amount of advice and counsel that school board officials provide to parents who seek to make unilateral placements may influence the extent of reimbursement awards. The Eleventh Circuit agreed that a residential placement was required for an autistic child, but was troubled by the fact that the parents had chosen one in Tokyo, Japan (*Drew P. v. Clarke County School District*, 1987, 1989). The court was of the opinion that the parents were entitled to some reimbursement, but it was not convinced that a placement so far from home was necessary. Other courts denied full reimbursement to parents who chose residential placements when private day schools were sufficient to provide their children with an appropriate education (*Board of Education of Oak Park & River Forest High School District No. 200 v. Illinois State Board of Education*, 1988; *Lascari v. Board of Education of the Ramapo Indian Hills Regional High School District*, 1989). Under these conditions, courts generally award reimbursement for students' educational expenses at schools but not the costs of room and board.

Parents have been denied tuition reimbursement for unilaterally obtained placements if they are not appropriate, even when school officials fail to offer appropriate IEPs. For example, the federal trial court in Connecticut declared that a school board's IEP was not appropriate because school personnel committed several procedural errors. Even so, the court denied the parental request for reimbursement because their chosen placement was not appropriate since the school was not staffed by professionals who could deliver the special education services the child needed (*P.J. v. State of Connecticut State Board of Education*, 1992). Similarly, the Second Circuit determined that reimbursement was not warranted where a hearing officer commented that although a school board's proposed placement was inappropriate, the parents' chosen placement was also inappropriate (*M.S. ex rel. S.S. v. Board of Education of the City School District of the City of Yonkers*, 2000).

Courts can order reimbursements for parents under *Carter* if their chosen facility can deliver appropriate services, regardless of its certification level or that of its staff. In such a case, the Ninth Circuit awarded reimbursement to the parents of an autistic student who unilaterally enrolled him in a private clinic that was not certified to provide special education services (*Union School District v. Smith*, 1994). The court acknowledged that school board officials failed to offer an appropriate placement but that the student received educational benefit from his placement at the private clinic. Likewise, the federal trial court in Maryland declared that parents were entitled to be reimbursed for tuition expenses at a private school that was not approved to provide special education services because evidence revealed that the student received an appropriate education at the school (*Gerstmyer v. Howard County Public Schools*, 1994). Further, the Second Circuit affirmed that parents who enrolled their son in a program that was not staffed by certified individuals were entitled to reimbursement because it still offered the child an appropriate education (*Still v. DeBuono*, 1996). The court concluded that the promise of the IDEA would have been defeated if reimbursement were barred when the parentally chosen providers were not certified and the reason the service was not provided by the state was due to a shortage of qualified providers.

In an interesting case, the Third Circuit affirmed a monetary award to compensate a mother for the time she spent providing services to her preschool-age daughter. After the mother requested, but was denied, the addition of Lovaas therapy to her preschool-age daughter's program, she received training to provide it herself and offered the services to her child. A state court posited that because the child's program was inadequate, it had to remand to the hearing officer to consider an appropriate remedy. A hearing officer awarded reimbursement to compensate the parent for the time she spent providing therapy to her child. The federal trial court and the Third Circuit agreed with that award because the services that the mother provided were appropriate and the county's denial of those services constituted a violation of the IDEA (*Bucks County Department of Mental Health/Mental Retardation v. Commonwealth of Pennsylvania*, 2004).

The School Board Must Be Given the Opportunity to Act

In *Burlington* the Supreme Court held that parents who violated the status quo provision did not waive their right to reimbursement. Yet, in post-*Burlington* cases courts agreed that parents waived their right to reimbursement where they made unilateral placements before giving school board officials the opportunities to address their concerns. To this end, parents must notify school officials that they are dissatisfied with the IEPs of their children to afford educators the opportunity to take appropriate corrective action. This case law is now incorporated into the IDEA and its regulations (20 U.S.C. § 1412(a)(10)(C)(iii); 34 C.F.R. § 300.148(d)).

According to the IDEA and its regulations, the cost of reimbursement may be reduced or denied under four circumstances. First, costs can be reduced or denied if at the most recent IEP team meetings that parents attended prior to removal of their children from public schools they did not inform the team that they were rejecting the proposed placements; this notice must include statements of parental concerns and their intent to enroll their children in private schools at public expense (20 U.S.C. § 1412 (a)(10)(C)(iii)(I)(aa); 34 C.F.R. § 300.148(d)(1)(i)). Second, costs can be reduced or denied if at least 10 business days, including any holidays that occur on business days, prior to the removal of children from public schools, parents do not provide school officials with written notice of their intent to do so (20 U.S.C. § 1412(a)(10)(C)(iii)(I); 34 C.F.R. § 300.148(d) (1)(ii)). Third, costs can be reduced or denied if, prior to the parents' removal of their children from public school, educators informed the parents of their intent to evaluate their children, including statements of the purpose of the evaluation that were appropriate and reasonable, but the parents did not make their children available (20 U.S.C. § 1412(a)(10) (C)(iii)(II); 34 C.F.R. § 300.148(d)(2)). Fourth, costs can be reduced or denied if courts find that the actions of parents were unreasonable (20 U.S.C. § 1412(a)(10)(C)(iii)(III); 34 C.F.R. § 300.148(d)(3)).

A case from the Eighth Circuit, although resolved before these provisions were incorporated into the IDEA, is illustrative. The court ascertained that reimbursement should not have been awarded where the parents had not given school officials the opportunity to make changes to a child's educational program (*Evans v. District No. 17 of Douglas County*, 1988). The student regressed and school officials wanted to meet to discuss the situation, but the parents made a unilateral placement change before the meeting could take place. The court asserted that insofar as there was no indication that the educators would have refused to make a change in the student's program, the board was entitled to have the opportunity to modify her IEP and placement. The court emphatically stated that school officials must be put on notice that parents disagree with the educational programs of their children and must be given opportunities to modify placements voluntarily before parents are justified in taking unilateral actions. Ten years later, the same court denied reimbursement to parents who, without any discussion with school personnel regarding possible accommodations to meet their child's needs, removed him from school after one day in the eighth grade (*Schoenfield v. Parkway School District*, 1998).

Courts frequently deny reimbursement awards in situations where parents take unilateral actions before giving school officials opportunities to intervene. Generally, courts reason that equity prevents reimbursement awards from accruing prior to when school officials have had the opportunity to evaluate students and make placement recommendations (*Ash v. Lake Oswego School District*, 1991, 1992; *Tucker v. Calloway County Board of Education*, 1998; *Johnson v. Metro Davidson County School System*, 2000; *L.K. ex rel. J.H. v. Board of Education for Transylvania County*, 2000). Parents may also forfeit their right to tuition reimbursement by failing to cooperate with school officials in the evaluation process (*Patricia P. v. Board of Education of Oak Park and River Forest High School District No. 200*, 2000).

As noted, the IDEA requires parents to provide school officials with written notification of their intent to enroll their children in private schools at public expense if they hope to obtain reimbursement awards. Parents who fail to challenge the IEPs of their children and provide school officials with the written notice required by the IDEA prior to making unilateral placements have been denied reimbursements (*Yancy v. New Baltimore City Board of School Commissioners*, 1998; *Nein v. Greater Clark County School Corporation*, 2000; *Greenland School District v. Amy N.*, 2004; *Ms. M. ex rel. K.M. v. Portland School Committee*, 2004).

Reimbursement May Be Granted When School Officials Commit Procedural Errors

The fact that school officials devised appropriate educational programs for students is not sufficient to preclude reimbursement awards. IEP teams must spell out appropriate placements in properly executed IEPs. Procedural errors are sufficient grounds for awarding reimbursement for unilateral placements because, under *Rowley*, an educational placement is inappropriate if it is not contained in a properly executed IEP. For instance, the Third Circuit ascertained that reimbursement was warranted when a school board proposed an appropriate program but the IEP was defective on procedural grounds (*Muth v. Central Bucks School District*, 1988). Here school officials proposed a placement that was later deemed appropriate, but failed to write an IEP for that proposal. Similarly, the Fourth Circuit affirmed a reimbursement award in deciding that school board officials failed to provide an appropriate education for a child (*Board of Education of the County of Cabell v. Dienelt*, 1988). The trial court had held that the board's program was not appropriate due to procedural defects where school officials failed to conduct annual reviews and involve the parents in the IEP process.

As indicated, school boards must be given opportunities to evaluate students and propose appropriate placements. This means that school boards may be liable for tuition reimbursement if officials do not properly evaluate children. In one such instance, the Fourth Circuit affirmed that parents were justified in making a unilateral placement when school board officials failed to propose an appropriate placement due to an improper evaluation of the child (*Hudson v. Wilson*, 1987). The court maintained that the parents did not waive their right to reimbursement when they removed their child from the public schools before school personnel conducted additional assessments and proposed a final IEP.

The IDEA requires parents to provide school personnel with notice of their intent to place their children in a private facility in order to later qualify for reimbursement. Even so, as reflected by a case from Maryland, parental failure to notify school personnel may be excused if school boards did not follow proper procedures. The federal trial court was of the opinion that parents could not be denied reimbursement because they failed to notify school board officials of their intent where educators failed to provide the parents with notice of procedural requirements as mandated by state law and the IDEA (*Mayo v. Baltimore City Public Schools*, 1999).

As illustrated by a case from Ohio, an improperly written IEP can provide the basis for a reimbursement award. The Sixth Circuit, noting that flaws in an IEP were not harmless technical errors, awarded reimbursement to a parent who rejected an IEP that did not provide an objective means to measure progress and did not adequately explain the services the student would receive (*Cleveland Heights–University Heights City School District v. Boss*, 1998). Along the same line, the Second Circuit approved a reimbursement award to parents who enrolled their child in a private school after school board officials proposed a Section 504 accommodation plan instead of an IEP (*Muller v. Committee on Special Education of the East Islip Union Free School District*, 1998). The trial court had specified that the student qualified for special education as emotionally disturbed. Moreover, the Sixth Circuit awarded reimbursement to parents in concluding that school officials denied a FAPE to a student in predetermining his placement (*Deal ex rel. Deal v. Hamilton County Department of Education*, 2004).

According to the Fourth Circuit, procedural errors must actually interfere with the provision of a FAPE before parents are entitled to reimbursement awards. In this case, the parents sought summer services and school officials failed to give their request proper consideration. The court treated this as a harmless error because the evidence revealed that the student was not entitled to summer services (*DiBuo v. Board of Education of Worcester County*, 2002).

Parental Delays or Failure to Cooperate May Affect Reimbursement Awards

According to a federal trial court in New York, the IDEA does not prevent parents from being reimbursed for tuition costs even if they cause delays in the hearing process (*Eugene B. v. Great Neck Union Free School District*, 1986). The court was of the view that the parents could still be reimbursed because their choice of a private school was the appropriate placement. The parents sought reimbursement, but school officials argued that since the parents caused several delays in the proceedings, they should not have been reimbursed for the period of each of the delays. The court disagreed, stating that the board was responsible for the private school tuition for the entire time period regardless of whether there were delays in the proceedings.

In contrast, other courts interpreted the IDEA as denying parental requests for reimbursement when they engaged in unreasonable delays in requesting hearings. The Third Circuit decided that parents waived their right to reimbursement if they did not initiate review proceedings within a reasonable period of time (*Bernardsville Board of Education v. J.H.*, 1994). In this case, since the parents waited two years before filing their claim, the court observed that waiting this amount of time without a mitigating excuse was unreasonable. Echoing this rationale, five years later the same court affirmed in relevant part that parents who enrolled their children, gifted students who had learning disabilities, in a private school but waited 16 months before requesting tuition reimbursement, were not entitled to recover the costs for the time period prior to their request for a hearing (*Warren G. v. Cumberland County School District*, 1999). It is also worth noting that state statutes of limitations may impose further limits on the time frames within which parents may file reimbursement claims.

As exemplified by cases from California and Wisconsin, frustrating the attempts of school boards to develop IEPs may result in reductions or losses of reimbursement awards. A federal trial court contended that a parent's failure to cooperate fully with school officials who attempted to design an educational program justified the reduction of a reimbursement award (*Glendale Unified School District v. Almasi*, 2000). In Wisconsin, where parents refused a recommended evaluation but later placed their daughter in a residential facility, the school board refused to pay the tuition at the facility because it had not made the placement. The trial court decreed that since the board could not have been faulted for failing to act in the face of parental resistance, the parents were not entitled to reimbursement (*Suzawith v. Green Bay Area School District*, 2000).

Reimbursement for Related Services

> In addition to tuition, courts consistently award reimbursement for the costs of related services. The criteria for reimbursement of related services are the same as for tuition expenses: Parents must demonstrate that the services were required for students to receive an appropriate education.

In addition to tuition, courts consistently award reimbursement for the costs of related services. The criteria for reimbursement of related services are the same as for tuition expenses: Parents must demonstrate that the services were required for students to receive an appropriate education. In the majority of cases, related services are provided at private schools in conjunction with special education services. Courts often award reimbursement for the costs of privately obtained related services when school boards fail to provide needed services along with public special education placements.

Courts have awarded reimbursement for the costs of psychotherapy or counseling services (*Max M. v. Thompson*, 1983, 1984, *sub nom. Max M. v. Illinois State Board of Education*, 1986; *Gary A. v. New Trier High School District No. 203*, 1986; *Doe v. Anrig*, 1987; *Vander Malle v. Ambach*, 1987; *Tice v. Botetourt County School District*, 1990; *Babb v. Knox County School System*, 1992; *Straube v. Florida Union Free School District*, 1992). In some of these cases the therapeutic services were provided to students who were placed in private schools or psychiatric facilities due to emotional difficulties. In others, the counseling services were obtained privately by parents to supplement the services the student received in a public school setting. Regardless of the setting where students receive special education services, parents seeking reimbursement awards must show that their children would not benefit from special education without psychotherapy or counseling.

School board officials must provide transportation, when needed, because students cannot benefit from special education services if they cannot get to where they are being offered. School boards must even provide students who attend private schools at public expense with appropriate transportation. Frequently, tuition reimbursement awards include compensation for other necessary costs such as transportation. Even when tuition reimbursement is not an issue, it may be awarded to parents when school boards fail to provide appropriate transportation. In such a case, the First Circuit permitted a father to be reimbursed for driving his son, who had physical disabilities, to school himself after school personnel failed to make appropriate arrangements (*Hurry v. Jones*, 1984). In another case, a trial court in New York directed a school board to reimburse a care provider for costs associated with transporting a student to an educational facility for children with physical disabilities (*Taylor v. Board of Education of*

Copake-Taconic Hills Central School District, 1986). The award in this case included reimbursement for hiring a babysitter to watch other children while the caretaker transported the child to the center. A trial court in South Dakota awarded reimbursement for transportation for a student who moved into the district with an IEP calling for door-to-door transportation (*Malehorn v. Hill City School District*, 1997). The suit arose after the child's mother challenged the board's denial of her request for special transportation for her daughter. While a hearing officer upheld the action of school officials, the court explained that the board was required to honor the terms of the previous IEP until such time as they could review it and develop a new plan for the child.

Courts award reimbursement for a variety of related services such as occupational therapy (*Rapid City School District v. Vahle*, 1990) and speech therapy (*Johnson v. Lancaster-Lebanon Intermediate Unit 13, Lancaster City School District*, 1991). One court awarded reimbursement for the cost of lodging for a student and his mother that was required because the facility the child attended was not within daily commuting distance of the family's residence (*Union School District v. Smith*, 1994).

The Hearing Officer May Grant Reimbursement Awards

Although the courts granted parental requests for reimbursement cited in this section, parents do not necessarily have to seek judicial review in order to obtain these awards. Hearing officers have the authority to grant reimbursement awards along with other forms of appropriate equitable relief. For example, a trial court in North Carolina ruled that reimbursement was included within the IDEA's provision that a hearing may be held on any matter relating to a FAPE (*S-1 v. Spangler*, 1986, 1987, 1993, 1994). The court also indicated that Congress did not intend to give courts any greater powers of equity than those given to a hearing officer. In that respect, the IDEA and its regulations currently grant hearing officers the authority to confer reimbursement awards (20 U.S.C. § 1412(a)(10)(C)(ii); 34 C.F.R. § 300.148).

COMPENSATORY EDUCATIONAL SERVICES

Courts can grant awards of compensatory educational services when school boards fail to provide an appropriate education for children and their parents lack the financial means to obtain alternate services. Generally, compensatory services are provided during time periods when students would otherwise not be eligible for services.

Courts can grant awards of compensatory educational services when school boards fail to provide an appropriate education for children and their parents lack the financial means to obtain alternate services. Parents are thus forced to allow their children to remain in inappropriate programs while administrative hearings are pending. Consequently, children may lose several years of appropriate educational services during the often lengthy appeals process. Generally, compensatory services are provided during time periods when students would otherwise not be eligible for services. In most cases involving the remedy of compensatory services, the courts apply the *Burlington* rationale in evaluating whether such services are warranted (Zirkel & Hennessy, 2001).

Compensatory Services Granted

The courts agree that they have the authority to award compensatory services because Congress empowered them to fashion appropriate remedies to cure deprivations of rights secured by the IDEA. The courts reason that compensatory services, like reimbursement, merely compensate students for the inappropriate education they received while placement issues were in dispute or school officials failed to act properly. The theory behind compensatory educational services awards is that appropriate remedies are not limited to those parents who can afford to provide their children with alternate educational placements while litigation is pending (*White v. State of California*, 1987; *Lester H. v. Gilhool*, 1990; *Todd D. v. Andrews*, 1991; *Manchester School District v. Christopher B.*, 1992; *Murphy v. Timberlane Regional School District*, 1992, 1993, 1994a). Ordinarily, compensatory services must be provided for time periods equal to the time that students were denied services (*Valerie J. v. Derry Cooperative School* District, 1991; *Manchester School District v. Christopher B.*, 1992; *Big Beaver Falls Area School District v. Jackson*, 1993). Compensatory awards may be granted even after students passed the ceiling age for eligibility under the IDEA (*Pihl v. Massachusetts Department of Education*, 1993; *State of West Virginia ex rel. Justice v. Board of Education of the County of Monongalia*, 2000).

A case from the Eleventh Circuit illustrates the similarity between awards of tuition reimbursement and compensatory services. The court affirmed that an award of compensatory educational services was similar to one for tuition reimbursement in that it was necessary to preserve the student's right to a FAPE (*Jefferson County Board of Education v. Breen*, 1988). The court wrote that without compensatory services awards, the rights of students under the IDEA would depend on the ability of their parents to obtain services privately when due process hearings were pending. The Eighth Circuit reached a like outcome in decreeing that compensatory educational services were available to the parent of a student with disabilities who could not afford to provide appropriate educational services himself during a lengthy court battle (*Miener v. Missouri*, 1986). In granting the award of compensatory education, the court added that Congress did not intend for the entitlements of special education students to a FAPE to rest upon the ability of their parents to pay for the costs of the placement in advance. A third court agreed that if compensatory services were not available, parents would have earned a Pyrrhic victory because the rights of their children to a FAPE would have been illusory (*Cremeans v. Fairland Local School District Board of Education*, 1993).

Students may receive compensatory services even after they earn valid high school diplomas. The federal trial court in Massachusetts awarded compensatory educational services to a student who earned a high school diploma after discovering that the school board officials failed to follow proper procedures (*Puffer v. Raynolds*, 1988). The court reasoned that the fact that the student earned a diploma was not an indication that she had no need for required special education services. Rather, the court treated the student's having earned her diploma as evidence that she succeeded despite the shortcomings of her educational program. The court ordered the school board to provide the student with services equal in scope to what she should have received prior to her graduation. A federal trial court in New York also wrote that a student who graduated was entitled to compensatory educational services while attending college, but not in the form of college tuition (*Straube v. Florida Union Free School District*, 1992). Further, the federal trial court in New Hampshire ordered a school board to provide compensatory services to a student for a period of time when he was denied educational services after he graduated from high school or reached the ceiling age of eligibility (*Valerie J. v. Derry Cooperative School District*, 1991).

Compensatory services awards accrue from the point that school board officials knew, or should have known, that the IEPs of students were inadequate (*M.C. ex rel. J.C. v. Central Regional School District*, 1996; *Ridgewood Board of Education v. N.E.*, 1999). Generally, compensatory services are provided for a period equal to the period of deprivation.

Hearing officers have the power to grant awards of compensatory educational services. As with the power to grant tuition reimbursement, courts recognized that hearing officers may fashion appropriate relief, which sometimes requires awards of compensatory services (*Cocores v. Portsmouth, NH School District*, 1991; *Big Beaver Falls Area School District v. Jackson*, 1993).

Compensatory Services Denied

As with tuition reimbursement, compensatory services are available only when parents can demonstrate that their children were denied the FAPE mandated by the IDEA (*Timms v. Metropolitan School District*, 1982, 1983; *Martin v. School Board of Prince George County*, 1986; *Garro v. State of Connecticut*, 1994). Nevertheless, a federal trial court in Tennessee denied an award of compensatory education in positing that although the homebound program that the student received was inappropriate, at that time neither school officials nor the parents were aware of the existence of an appropriate program (*Brown v. Wilson County School District*, 1990). Insofar as school officials had not taken any actions that resulted in the denial of a FAPE to the student, the court did not think that the board had to provide compensatory services.

The Third Circuit pointed out that compensatory services are warranted only when parents can demonstrate that their children underwent prolonged or gross deprivations of the right to a FAPE (*Carlisle Area School District v. Scott P.*, 1995). Absent such evidence, the court denied an award of compensatory services where an administrative appeals panel ordered additional services included in a student's IEP. In like fashion, the Eighth Circuit affirmed that a student was not entitled to compensatory services absent a showing of egregious circumstances or culpable conduct on the part of school board officials (*Yankton School District v. Schramm*, 1995, 1996). The fact that a student had not regressed as a result of the school board's failure to provide an appropriate program in a timely fashion caused a trial court in New York to deny compensatory services (*Wenger v. Canastota Central School District*, 1997, 1998). In addition, a school board's timely action to correct deficiencies in a student's IEP led the federal trial court in New Jersey to deny a parental request for compensatory services (*D.B. v. Ocean Township Board of Education*, 1997).

Failure to take advantage of offered services may be the basis for denial of an award of compensatory services. In such a case the Ninth Circuit uncovered evidence that school officials offered parents extra tutoring and summer school for their child, but they rejected the proposal (*Parents of Student W. v. Puyallup School District No. 3*, 1994). The court thus denied the parents' request for compensatory services. In a conceptually related case, the federal trial court in Minnesota denied compensatory speech therapy services where parents withdrew their son from his educational program and rejected the services that school officials offered (*Moubry v. Independent School District No. 696*, 1996).

ATTORNEY FEES AND COSTS

Litigation is expensive and many parents, after succeeding in their disputes with school boards, believe that they should be reimbursed for their costs in securing the rights of their children. Many parents sense that they achieve nugatory victories if they prevail in showing that school board officials failed to provide the FAPE their children were entitled to receive under the IDEA but are left with large legal bills.

The IDEA contains one of the most comprehensive mechanisms that Congress ever created for dispute resolution. Litigation is expensive and many parents, after succeeding in their disputes with school boards, believe that they should be reimbursed for their costs in securing the rights of their children. Many parents sense that they achieve nugatory victories if they prevail in showing that school board officials failed to provide the FAPE their children were entitled to receive under the IDEA but are left with large legal bills. Initially, most courts viewed awards of attorney fees as awards for damages (see, e.g., *Diamond v. McKenzie*, 1985).

In 1984 the Supreme Court ruled in *Smith v. Robinson* that recovery of legal expenses was unavailable under the IDEA. Congress responded by amending the IDEA in 1986 to include the Handicapped Children's Protection Act (HCPA) (20 U.S.C. § 1415(i)(3)) within its provisions. The HCPA allows courts to provide awards of reasonable attorney fees to parents who prevail against school boards in actions or proceedings brought pursuant to the IDEA. Awards are based on the prevailing rates in the community in which cases arose. The courts have the authority to judge what is a reasonable amount of time to have spent preparing and arguing the case in terms of the issues litigated. Awards may be limited if school boards made settlement offers more than 10 days before the proceedings began that were equal to or more favorable than the final relief that parents obtained. Fee awards also may be reduced if courts find that parents unreasonably protracted the dispute, an attorney's hourly rate was excessive, or the time spent and legal services furnished were excessive in light of the issues litigated. Attorney fees may be awarded for representation at administrative and judicial hearings but are not available for legal representation at IEP meetings unless such sessions were convened as a result of administrative or judicial orders (20 U.S.C. § 1415(i)(3)(D)(ii); 34 C.F.R. § 300.517(c)(2)(ii)). Interestingly, this change specifically prohibits awards of attorney fees for resolution proceedings.

Hearing officers cannot make awards of attorney fees since this authority is reserved for the courts (*Mathern v. Campbell County Children's Center*, 1987). Yet, parents do not necessarily have to go to court to recover their legal expenses. Agreements may be worked out with school boards for payment of the parents' legal expenses. If parents are required to file court actions to recover attorney fees, and they succeed, they may recover their costs in filing the fee petitions as well (*Angela L. v. Pasadena Independent School District*, 1990). Parents do not need to exhaust administrative remedies prior to filing fee petitions since hearing officers cannot award attorney fees (*J.G. v. Board of Education of the Rochester City School District*, 1986, 1987; *Esther C. v. Ambach*, 1988; *Sidney K. v. Ambach*, 1988).

When Parents Prevail

One of the most often litigated issues under the IDEA is whether parents were actually the prevailing party in litigation. While on its face the issue seems fairly straightforward, unfortunately it is not. Most special education disputes involve multiple issues and parents may have had only partial success. Courts generally define a prevailing parent as one who succeeded on most of the issues that were litigated. Even so, in some situations where the parents have not prevailed on all issues, the courts have granted partial awards.

Full Awards

For the most part, courts grant full awards when parents prevail on the major issues in the litigation even if they did not succeed on some minor points. In the majority of cases, the work performed litigating minor issues is inseparable from that of contesting major issues, is insignificant compared to that required by the major issues, and/or is performed in conjunction with the work completed for major issues (*Turton v. Crisp County School District*, 1988; *Angela L. v. Pasadena Independent School District*, 1990; *Phelan v. Bell*, 1993). Courts ordinarily agree that parents are the prevailing parties when they acquire the primary relief they sought or prevail in the principal issues in their suits (*Barbara R. v. Tirozzi*, 1987; *Kristi W. v. Graham Independent School District*, 1987; *Neisz v. Portland Public School District*, 1988; *Mitten v. Muscogee County District*, 1989).

Parents may receive full reimbursement of their legal expenses even when they do not prevail on all issues. Typically, courts make full awards if the time spent litigating the various issues cannot be easily apportioned on an issue-by-issue basis. In such a case, the Sixth Circuit awarded attorney fees to parents who did not receive the residential placement they requested but succeeded in obtaining additional services (*Krichinsky v. Knox County Schools*, 1992). In other cases, courts permitted parents to receive full fee awards because the matters before administrative hearings were intertwined, could not have been viewed as a series of separate claims, and the parents received most of what they requested (*Moore v. Crestwood Local School District*, 1992).

Partial Awards

Courts grant partial awards of attorney fees when parents do not prevail on the most significant issue in the litigation but succeed on some of the contested matters. In addition, parents may receive only partial awards when they prevail on some of their claims and the issues litigated are distinct enough so that the work done on each can be separated from the work done on all of the others (*Max M. v. Illinois State Board of Education*, 1988; *Burr v. Sobol*, 1990; *Koswenda v. Flossmoor School District No. 161*, 2002).

Requested fee awards may be reduced for various other reasons such as if a court thinks that a requested hourly rate or the number of hours billed was excessive (*Mr. D. v. Glocester School Committee*, 1989; *Hall v. Detroit Public Schools*, 1993; *Troy School District v. Boutsikaris*, 2003) or finds fault with the time sheets submitted by an attorney (*In re Conklin*, 1991; *Smith v. District of Columbia*, 2004).

As reflected by a case from Indiana, a court can make adjustments in requested fee awards. A federal trial court reduced a requested fee amount in recognizing that the parents' counsel unnecessarily protracted the proceedings (*Howey v. Tippecanoe School Corporation*, 1990). Another court decided that an attorney who was not familiar with special education laws could not bill for the time and research expended in getting up to speed with the statutes (*King v. Floyd County Board of Education*, 1998).

Courts do not always reduce awards by evaluating the number of hours spent litigating each issue and reducing awards by the amount of fees charged for unsuccessfully litigating certain issues. Sometimes awards are adjusted in proportion to the parents' overall success and failure in the litigation. When, for instance, the federal trial court in New Jersey found it difficult to apportion legal costs issue by issue, it simply reduced the requested fee award by 50% because the parents had not achieved their primary objective but had succeeded on several other significant questions (*Field v. Haddonfield Board of Education*, 1991).

When Parents Do Not Prevail

Parents cannot recover their legal expenses when school boards are the prevailing party. It should go without saying that parents who do not succeed on any of their claims do not achieve prevailing party status (*Wheeler v. Towanda Area School District*, 1991). As discussed in the previous section, parents may receive limited reimbursement if they prevail on at least some of their claims. Parents will not be awarded attorney fees if their legal relationship with their school boards is not altered as a result of the litigation, even if they received minor victories through their legal actions (*Salley v. St. Tammany Parish School Board*, 1995; *Board of Education of Downers Grove Grade School District No. 58 v. Steven L.*, 1996; *Metropolitan School District of Lawrence Township v. M.S.*, 2004). Parents also are not the prevailing party if the changes that occur are not a direct result of the litigation but are caused by other factors.

As noted, courts sometimes grant parents partial reimbursement of their legal expenses if they obtain some, but not all, of the relief that they sought. If the relief that parents obtained is insignificant, courts may not grant even partial awards. In an illustrative conflict, the Seventh Circuit affirmed the denial of a parental request for attorney fees, even though the parents obtained an order that conferred benefits on their daughter on the ground that the ultimate outcome of the case negated the value of those benefits (*Hunger v. Leininger*, 1994). A federal trial court in Wisconsin also denied a fee request in writing that the relief the parents obtained was minimal in light of their overall objectives (*Linda T. ex rel. William A. v. Rice Lake Area School District*, 2004).

Courts may deny fee awards if they deem that parents unnecessarily protracted proceedings (*Fischer v. Rochester Community Schools*, 1991) or that the problem the parents complained of could have been resolved without resort to administrative or judicial review (*Combs v. School Board of Rockingham County*, 1994). Parents may not receive fee awards if they request administrative hearings before school officials have had opportunities to develop appropriate IEPs (*Johnson v. Bismarck Public School District*, 1991; *Patricia E. v. Board of Education of Community High School District No. 155*, 1995; *Payne v. Board of Education, Cleveland City Schools*, 1996; *W.L.G. v. Houston County Board of Education*, 1997).

Catalyst Theory

In the past, courts awarded attorney fees based on the catalyst theory, even if administrative hearings or judicial actions never took place (see, e.g., *Doucet v. Chilton County Board of Education*, 1999; *Daniel S. v. Scranton School District*, 2000). Under the catalyst theory, courts can award fees if suits, or even threats of litigation, motivate change in the behavior of defendants, causing the termination of proceedings. However, recent litigation appears to have struck down the catalyst theory (Wenkart, 2002).

In a nonschool case, *Buckhannon Board & Care Home v. West Virginia Department of Health and Human Resources* (*Buckhannon*) (2001), the Supreme Court rejected the catalyst theory in deciding that in order to be a prevailing party a claimant must prevail before the courts in a judgment on the merits or through a consent decree (Osborne, 2003). Subsequently, circuit courts have denied fee requests based on the rationale in *Buckhannon*, explaining that the high Court's opinion governed claims filed pursuant to the IDEA (*J.C. v. Regional School District No. 10*, 2002; *John T. by Paul T. and Joan T. v. Delaware County Intermediate Unit*, 2003; *T.D. v. LaGrange School District No. 102*, 2003; *Doe v. Boston Public Schools*, 2004; Osborne, 2005).

Fees for Administrative Hearings

The IDEA provides for the recovery of attorney fees to parents who prevail in "any action or proceeding" brought under its procedural safeguards section (20 U.S.C. § 1415(i)(3)(B); 34 C.F.R. § 300.517(a)). The meaning of the phrase "any action or proceeding" has been in dispute. Many school boards claimed that it refers only to court actions and that attorney fees are not recoverable for work performed at the administrative hearing level. After some controversy, it is now well settled that attorney fees are available for representation at administrative hearings even if disputes are settled without judicial intervention. It is also well settled that parents can file suit solely for the purpose of recovering legal expenses (Osborne & DiMattia, 1991).

The District of Columbia Circuit resolved the leading, and most controversial, case on the topic in 1990 (*Moore v. District of Columbia*, 1990). Initially, a divided three-judge panel decreed that congressional language in the HCPA/IDEA provided for an award of attorney fees only in cases where the losing party in an administrative action appealed to the courts and prevailed in the judicial action (*Moore v. District of Columbia*, 1989). According to that decision, fees could not be awarded to parents who prevailed at the administrative level and brought judicial action only to obtain attorney fees. While this opinion was contrary to the majority of cases from the other circuits, the court granted a rehearing en banc (Osborne & DiMattia, 1991).

On further review, the en banc panel vacated the earlier judgment, declaring that attorney fees were available for administrative proceedings. This time the court concluded that congressional use of the phrase "any action or proceeding" meant to authorize fees for parents who prevailed in civil actions or administrative proceedings. The court added that the legislative history of the HCPA/IDEA supported its interpretation. Later courts unanimously agreed that parents who prevailed at the administrative level could recover their legal expenses (Osborne & DiMattia, 1991).

Settlement Offers

School boards can lessen their liability for fees by attempting to reach settlements with parents before beginning administrative hearings. One section of the HCPA/IDEA provides that fees are not available for legal representation that occurs after school boards make written settlement offers if the final relief obtained by the parents is not more favorable to them than the settlement offers. Settlement offers must be made at least 10 days before the scheduled start of due process hearings (20 U.S.C. § 1415(i)(3)(D)(i); 34 C.F.R. § 300.517(c)(2)(i)(A)).

In order to avoid paying fee awards, school board settlement offers must be deemed to be equal to or better than the final relief obtained by the parents. Settlement offers do not need to be identical to final administrative orders in order to stop the time clocks of attorneys from ticking. Parents are not entitled to awards of attorney fees when the final relief they obtain is substantially similar to the last offers they receive from school boards (*Hyden v. Board of Education of Wilson County*, 1989) or is less favorable than those offers (*Mr. L. and Mrs. L. v. Woonsocket Education Department*, 1992). On the other hand, parents can be reimbursed for their legal costs when they win more favorable terms than their school boards offer

(*Capistrano Unified School District v. Wartenberg*, 1995; *Virginia McC. v. Corrigan-Camden Independent School District*, 1995).

Courts may be called on to consider whether settlement offers were, in fact, more favorable than the final results obtained through administrative hearings. In such a case, a federal trial court in Ohio disputed a school board's claim of a more favorable settlement offer because the offer in question did not include specific details (*Gross ex rel. Gross v. Perrysburg Exempted Village School District*, 2004). The court rejected the board's claims in pointing out that the parents addressed all of these matters with the requisite level of specificity.

Courts have recognized that parents are entitled to collect attorney fees for legal work completed up to the time of settlement offers, even when hearings are canceled because they accepted settlement offers (*E.P. v. Union County Regional High School District No. 1*, 1989; *Shelly C. v. Venus Independent School District*, 1989; *Barlow-Gresham Union High School District No. 2 v. Mitchell*, 1991). In the wake of *Buckhannon*, however, lower courts denied fees when the parties reached settlement agreements before completing administrative hearings (*Brandon K. v. New Lenox School District*, 2001; *J.S. v. Ramapo Central School District*, 2001; *Jose Luis R. v. Joliet Township H.S. District 204*, 2002; *P.O. ex rel. L.T. and T.O. v. Greenwich Board of Education*, 2002; *Algeria v. District of Columbia*, 2004; *Smith v. District of Columbia*, 2004; *Smith ex rel. Smith v. Fitchburg Public Schools*, 2005). At the same time, attorney fees may be awarded for settlement agreements if hearing officers or courts sanction the agreements in some way. Courts agree that incorporating settlement agreements into orders or reading them into the record confer on them the judicial imprimatur that *Buckhannon* required (*D.M. ex rel. G.M. and C.M. v. Board of Education, Center Moriches Union Free School District*, 2003; *Abraham v. District of Columbia*, 2004).

Fees to Attorneys From Public Agencies

Many parents use attorneys from public advocacy agencies in special education litigation because these attorneys provide low-cost or free legal services via sliding scale fee arrangements. Courts agree that when parents who are represented by public agency attorneys prevail in special education actions, the attorneys are entitled to be reimbursed at the prevailing rate in their communities even when it is higher than the one that the agency would otherwise have charged the parents (*Eggers v. Bullitt County School District*, 1988; *Mitten v. Muscogee County School District*, 1989; *Yankton School District v. Schramm*, 1996).

Fees to Lay Advocates and Pro Se Parents

During the early stages of disputes parents frequently rely on the services of lay advocates to advise and represent them in meetings with school boards. Although the services of lay advocates may be beneficial in resolving disputes, because they are not attorneys, advocates may not be reimbursed for legal representation (*Arons v. New Jersey State Board of Education*, 1988). If advocates work in conjunction with attorneys, it is possible that they may be reimbursed for their services as part of the attorneys' costs (*Heldman v. Sobol*, 1994). Even so, representation solely by lay advocates is not reimbursable (*Connors v. Mills*, 1998).

The majority of courts agree that parents who represent themselves may not be compensated under the HCPA even if they are members of the bar (*Rappaport v. Vance*, 1993; *Heldman v. Sobol*, 1994; *Miller v. West Lafayette Community School Corporation*, 1996; *Doe v. Board of Education of Baltimore County*, 1998; *Erickson v. Board of Education of Baltimore County*, 1998; *Woodside v. School District of Philadelphia Board of Education*, 2001). On the other hand, a federal trial court in Georgia decreed that nothing in the language of the IDEA prohibits awards of fees to attorney-parents (*Matthew V. v. DeKalb County School System*, 2003).

Costs of Expert Witnesses

The HCPA/IDEA permits parents to recover other costs in bringing special education suits along with attorney fees (Osborne, 2005). Yet, courts have not agreed over whether parents can recover the costs of expert witness fees. A variety of federal courts declared that parents may include the costs of expert witnesses in their requests for attorney fees awards, reasoning that these expenses were often a necessary part of administrative hearings (*Chang v. Board of Education of Glen Ridge Township*, 1988; *Turton v. Crisp County School District*, 1988; *Aronow v. District of Columbia*, 1992; *P.L. by Mr. and Mrs. L. v. Norwalk Board of Education*, 1999; *Mr. J. v. Board of Education*, 2000; *Pazik v. Gateway Regional School District*, 2001; *Brillon v. Klein Independent School District*, 2003; *Murphy v. Arlington Central School District Board of Education*, 2005). A trial court in Georgia even held that parents were entitled to be reimbursed for the services of an expert who did not testify but who did contribute to the development of the case (*Turton v. Crisp County School District*, 1988). Conversely, the federal trial court in New Jersey refused to reimburse parents for the full costs of an expert witness since it was of the opinion that even though the expert witness was helpful, the expert's presence was not necessary (*E.M. v. Millville Board of Education*, 1994).

Other courts flatly denied requests for reimbursement of expert witnesses. In one case the District of Columbia Circuit denied expert witness fees reasoning that the IDEA did not enable a prevailing party to shift expert witness fees (*Goldring v. District of Columbia*, 2005). On at least two occasions the Eighth Circuit denied expert witness fees reflecting that nothing in the plain language of the IDEA indicated that the courts were authorized to award fees for expert witnesses (*Neosho R-V School District v. Clark*, 2003; *Missouri Department of Elementary and Secondary Education v. Springfield R-12 School District*, 2004). Similarly, the Seventh Circuit declined to award expert witness fees absent specific authorization within the statute (*T.D. v. LaGrange School District No. 102*, 2003). Previously, a federal trial court in North Carolina denied a request for reimbursement of expert witness fees, simply stating that Section 1415 of the IDEA does not provide for an award of expert witness fees (*Eirschele v. Craven County Board of Education*, 1998).

As is often the case, the Supreme Court intervened to resolve the split between the Circuits and to ensure a more uniform interpretation of the IDEA. In *Arlington Central School District v. Murphy* (2006), the Supreme Court, reversing the Second Circuit's earlier order to the contrary, interpreted the IDEA as not permitting parents to be reimbursed for the services of expert witnesses or consultants who assisted them in their disputes with school boards (Osborne & Russo, 2006). Although recognizing that this created the anomalous situation whereby parents who prevailed in their disputes with their school boards could recover attorney fees, but not expenses to cover the costs associated with expert witnesses or consultants who helped them to win their cases, the Court concluded that since Congress was aware of this fact but refused to modify the IDEA accordingly, it saw no reason to rewrite the statute. One practical result of this decision is that school boards should be able to save money by eliminating costs that they might otherwise have had to incur for expert witnesses and consultants.

Fees for Representation in Complaint Resolution Procedures

The IDEA's regulations require states to adopt procedures for resolving complaints filed by organizations or individuals regarding violations of the IDEA (34 C.F.R. §§ 300.151–300.153). Whether fees are available for representation in filing complaints through the IDEA's complaint resolution procedures is unsettled. The Ninth Circuit and the federal trial court in Vermont agreed that fees may be awarded for representation in filing complaints under a state's or the IDEA's complaint resolution procedures (*Upper Valley Association of Handicapped Citizens v. Blue Mountain Union School District No. 21*, 1997; *Lucht v. Molalla River School District*, 1999). Conversely, the federal trial court in Minnesota denied a fee award for an attorney who filed a complaint on behalf of a student with disabilities (*Megan C. v. Independent School District No. 625*, 1999). The court ascertained that the filing of a complaint was not an action or proceeding for purposes of recovering attorney fees under Section 1415. Noting that the IDEA itself does not authorize a complaint resolution procedure, the Second Circuit affirmed that fees are not reimbursable for representation at a complaint resolution proceeding (*Vultaggio v. Board of Education, Smithtown Central School District*, 2003).

Fees for Representation at IEP Meetings

The IDEA specifically prohibits reimbursement of attorney fees for attendance at IEPs meeting unless such sessions were convened as a result of administrative or judicial actions (20 U.S.C. § 1415(i)(3)(D)(ii); 34 C.F.R. § 300.517(c)(2)(ii)). Courts have consistently denied fees for representation at IEP meetings (*E.C. ex rel. R.C. v. Board of Education of South Brunswick Township*, 2001). Still, at least one court did allow reimbursement for the time an attorney spent scheduling an IEP meeting when that effort was the direct result of a court order (*Watkins v. Vance*, 2004).

Awards to School Boards

Although the HCPA/IDEA allows prevailing parents to recover legal expenses, it did not give school boards the right to seek reimbursement for their legal expenses if they succeeded in litigation. Using their general powers of equity, courts have sometimes, albeit reluctantly, awarded attorney fees to school boards when parental claims were frivolous or for unnecessarily prolonged litigation. The First Circuit, for example, concluded that a school board was entitled to reimbursement of legal expenses under Appellate Rule 38 in finding that the parents' suit was "completely devoid of merit and plagued by unnecessary delay" (*Caroline T. v. Hudson School District*, 1990, p. 757). The court commented that the parents engaged in tactics throughout the proceedings that led to undue delays and also failed to cooperate in negotiations to settle the dispute. In another case, a federal trial court in New York denied a prevailing school board's request for attorney fees based on the claim that the parents brought the action in bad faith (*Hiller v. Board of Education of the Brunswick Central School District*, 1990). The court was convinced that both parties proceeded in good faith and should bear their own costs.

The 2004 amendments included a provision that allows school boards to seek reimbursement of their legal expenses when parents file complaints that are found to be frivolous, unreasonable, or without foundation or when the litigation was continued after it clearly became frivolous, unreasonable, or without foundation (20 U.S.C. § 1415(i)(3)(B)(i)(II); 34 C.F.R. § 300.517(a)(1)(ii)). School boards may also obtain awards when parental suits are filed for improper purposes, cause unnecessary delays, or needlessly increase the costs of litigation (20 U.S.C. § 1415(i)(3)(B)(i)(III); 34 C.F.R. § 300.517(a)(1)(iii)). Under these provisions, awards are to be levied against the parents' attorney, not the parents themselves. In light of the courts' past reluctance to award attorney fees to school boards incident to their general powers of equity, even under circumstances similar to those described within the statute, it remains to be seen whether school boards are willing to use this provision to recover some of the costs of litigation.

By the same token, school boards may not continue litigation that is clearly frivolous, unreasonable, or without foundation or engage in any tactics that unnecessarily prolong litigation or otherwise abuse the process. Under the Federal Rules of Civil Procedure, a federal trial court in California issued sanctions against a school board and its attorney for raising frivolous objections, making misstatements, and mischaracterizing facts (*Moser v. Bret Harte Union High School District*, 2005).

DAMAGES

The term *damages*, by its broad definition, typically refers to monetary relief that is awarded to compensate an aggrieved party for a loss (Zirkel & Osborne, 1987). The term, as used in this chapter, is defined in a narrower context. Here the term *damages* refers to monetary awards given to persons who were injured by the actions of others or for punitive purposes (Garner, 1999). For the purposes of this chapter, compensatory awards, such as reimbursements for tuition and other out-of-pocket expenses, are not considered to be damages awards. In the context of special education, courts, especially in recent years, have treated punitive damages as a separate entity from compensation for lost services.

Failure to Provide an Appropriate Education

> In general, courts historically have stipulated that damages are not available under the IDEA unless school boards flagrantly failed to comply with the act's procedural requirements. In recent years, courts have agreed that Section 1983 may be used as a back door to gain damages awards for violation of the IDEA.

In general, courts historically have agreed that damages are not available under the IDEA unless school boards flagrantly failed to comply with the act's procedural requirements (Osborne & Russo, 2001). The Seventh Circuit, in a case where the parents actually sought tuition reimbursement, insisted that monetary awards were not available under the IDEA unless exceptional circumstances existed (*Anderson v. Thompson*, 1981). One of those exceptional circumstances occurs when school officials act in bad faith by egregiously failing to comply with the IDEA's procedural provisions. Although this case involved an award of tuition reimbursement, other courts have either cited it or used analogous reasoning in declaring that damages are unavailable under the IDEA (*Marvin H. v. Austin Independent School District*, 1983; *Powell v. DeFore*, 1983; *Gary A. v. New Trier High School District No. 203*, 1986; *Barnett v. Fairfax County School Board*, 1991).

The Supreme Court specifically struck down the Seventh Circuit's treatment of reimbursement as a damages award in *Burlington School*

Committee v. Department of Education, Commonwealth of Massachusetts (1985). This decision notwithstanding, the legal principle that a damages award is available only when a school board acts in bad faith has survived (*Charlie F. v. Board of Education of Skokie School District 68*, 1996).

The Fifth Circuit asserted that damages awards are inconsistent with the goals of the IDEA and that appropriate relief does not include punitive damages when school officials act in good faith (*Marvin H. v. Austin Independent School District*, 1983). Similarly, the Fourth Circuit affirmed that damages are not available unless parents can demonstrate that school officials acted in bad faith or committed intentional acts of discrimination (*Barnett v. Fairfax County School Board*, 1991). A trial court in New York decided that while damages were allowed for bad faith or egregious failures to comply with the IDEA, they were not warranted when officials made good faith efforts to provide appropriate placements but committed misjudgments (*Gerasimou v. Ambach*, 1986).

On the other hand, a federal trial court in Michigan indicated that when a court thinks that a school board's placement is inappropriate, it is limited to fashioning an appropriate placement (*Sanders v. Marquette Public Schools*, 1983). The court held that damages were unavailable even if parents could show that school officials acted in bad faith or grossly misused their professional discretion. Another federal trial court in Michigan was of the opinion that the recovery of monetary, nonrestitutional damages was impermissible under the IDEA (*Wayne County Regional Education Service Agency v. Pappas*, 1999).

The Fourth Circuit emphatically ruled that awards of compensatory and punitive damages are inconsistent with the IDEA's structure (*Sellers v. School Board of the City of Manassas*, 1998). Reasoning that a claim that a student was denied a FAPE was indistinguishable from one for the all but nonjusticiable tort of educational malpractice, the court emphasized that such damages were simply inconsistent with the IDEA's intent. Two years later, the Tenth Circuit agreed with this rationale, adding that the IDEA may not provide the basis for a Section 1983 claim (*Padilla v. School District No. 1 in the City and County of Denver*, 2000).

Along similar lines, the Second Circuit maintained that a damages award would not only have been inconsistent with the IDEA's goals but would have undercut its carefully structured procedure for administrative remedies (*Polera v. Board of Education of the Newburgh Enlarged City School District*, 2002). Echoing this sentiment, the First Circuit affirmed that the primary purpose of the IDEA is to ensure a FAPE, not provide a mechanism for compensating personal injury (*Nieves-Marquez v. Commonwealth of Puerto Rico*, 2003).

Torts

The purpose of tort remedies is to compensate individuals for injuries that resulted from the unreasonable conduct of others. Torts are civil wrongs, other than breaches of contracts, committed against someone's person or property. Torts may result from either intentional or unintentional acts. In order to receive a damages award, the litigant must show negligence on the part of the person who allegedly committed the torts. Awards may be granted to compensate for the actual loss as well as for punitive purposes (Russo, 2006). In the realm of special education in particular, because the nature of the students' disabilities may increase their likelihood of injury, school officials may have to adopt a heightened standard of care (Mawdsley, 2001).

State courts in Louisiana, California, and Michigan addressed a variety of issues dealing with negligence. The court in Louisiana indicated that school boards are unlikely to be liable for injuries received by students who have been mainstreamed as long as such placements were reasonable (*Brooks v. St. Tammany Parish School Board*, 1987). A court in California held that tort damages were not available under the IDEA for a claim that a student was denied a FAPE (*White v. State of California*, 1987). The court decided that the appropriate remedy for a denial of services would have been an award of compensatory educational services. Similarly, a state court in Michigan observed that damages for negligence were not recoverable under the IDEA for a school board's failure to evaluate a student properly (*Johnson v. Clark*, 1987). The court was unconvinced that Congress intended for the IDEA to serve as a vehicle for a private cause of action for damages.

In related matters, the Sixth Circuit affirmed that the IDEA does not create any right to recover damages for loss of earning power attributed to the failure of school officials to provide a student with a FAPE (*Hall v. Knott County Board of Education*, 1991). Here, the student sued to recover lost wages allegedly resulting from the insufficient education that he received. The same court later remarked that a student could not receive a damages award for the emotional injury allegedly suffered when he was wrongfully barred from participating in sports (*Crocker v. Tennessee Secondary School Athletic Association*, 1992).

Section 1983

Section 1983 of the Civil Rights Act of 1871 (42 U.S.C. § 1983) provides for punitive damages designed to punish and discourage individuals who deprive others of rights, privileges, and immunities secured by the Constitution and laws of the United States. In recent years, courts have agreed that Section 1983 may be used as a back door to gain damages awards for violations of the IDEA (Mawdsley, 2002; Osborne, 2002; Osborne & Russo, 2001; Wenkart, 2004).

In a case from the Third Circuit, the mother of a child who was eventually placed in a special education setting sought damages claiming that school officials persistently refused to evaluate the student and provide necessary special education services (*W.B. v. Matula*, 1995). A trial court denied the motion for damages, but on appeal the Third Circuit reversed. In interpreting congressional enactment of the HCPA as meaning that violations of the IDEA can be redressed in private causes of action under Section 1983 and Section 504, the court ruled that Congress "expressly contemplated that the courts would fashion remedies not specifically enumerated in IDEA" (*W.B. v. Matula*, 1995, pp. 494–495). Even so, the panel cautioned "that in fashioning a remedy for an IDEA violation, a district court may wish to order educational services, such as compensatory education beyond a child's age of eligibility, or reimbursement for providing at private expense what should have been offered by the school, rather than compensatory damages for generalized pain and suffering" (p. 495). Nonetheless, the panel "did not preclude the awarding of monetary damages" (p. 495) and left it up to the trial court to fashion appropriate relief.

Actions under Section 1983 seeking damages for violations of the IDEA's procedural protections may be particularly viable. Accordingly, the federal trial court in Minnesota reasoned that there is an enforceable Section 1983 interest implicit in the IDEA's procedural protections such that a case could be brought under Section 1983 to enforce the procedural rights contained in the IDEA (*Brantley v. Independent School District No. 625, St. Paul Public Schools*, 1996). Trial courts in other states agreed that damages may be available under Section 1983 for violations of the IDEA (*Emma C. v. Eastin*, 1997; *Cappillino v. Hyde Park Central School District*, 1999; *B.H. v. Southington Board of Education*, 2003).

On the other hand, the Eighth Circuit acknowledged that since parents cannot recover damages under the IDEA, they cannot seek damages under Section 1983 for violations of the IDEA (*Bradley v. Arkansas Department of Education*, 2002). Likewise, a federal trial court in California reflected that parents cannot bypass the procedural and remedial scheme of the IDEA by repackaging their claim as one under Section 1983 so that a jury may award them damages (*Alex G. ex rel. Stephen G. v. Board of Trustees of Davis Joint Unified School District*, 2004).

RECOMMENDATIONS

Courts are empowered to grant appropriate relief when school boards fail to provide children with a FAPE as mandated by the IDEA. Under most circumstances, the appropriate relief that courts award is ordering school officials to provide a FAPE in the future. However, many cases have been filed seeking compensation for the past failure of school officials to provide the services that students were entitled to receive under the IDEA. The courts have used their traditional powers of equity to provide students with disabilities with compensation for lost services and their parents' out-of-pocket expenses. Following a great deal of legal controversy, the courts

Figure 7.1   Frequently Asked Questions

Q: Under what circumstances may parents be reimbursed for unilaterally enrolling their children in private schools?

A: Parents must first notify school board officials, in writing, of their dissatisfaction with the current placement of their children and of their intent to enroll them in private schools. If hearing officers or courts later agree with parents that the IEPs offered by school officials failed to provide the students with a free appropriate public education, and the parentally chosen placements are judged to be appropriate, they can be reimbursed. Reimbursement is available even if the parentally chosen facility is not state approved.

Q: Why can school boards be ordered to provide compensatory educational services?

A: The theory behind compensatory education awards is that they are similar to tuition reimbursement awards. In each case, awards are designed to right wrongs. Reimbursement compensates parents for providing appropriate educational services when their school boards fail to do so. Compensatory education awards provide students with the appropriate education services that were denied; the awards are meant to make up for the lost services. Courts often grant compensatory education awards in cases where parents were unable to provide the appropriate services themselves.

Q: Many frivolous cases are filed. Can school boards recover their legal costs when parents file frivolous claims?

A: A new provision of the IDEA allows courts to award attorney fees to school boards when complaints are deemed to be frivolous, unreasonable, or without foundation or when the litigation was continued after it became frivolous, unreasonable, or without foundation. Courts can also grant awards if the parents filed complaints for improper purposes, caused unnecessary delays, or needlessly increased the cost of litigation. Interestingly, the IDEA provides that the fees be assessed against the parents' attorneys, not the parents themselves.

Q: Can school boards be assessed punitive damages?

A: This is an area of special education law that is currently unsettled. Most courts agree that punitive damages are not available under the IDEA. Recently, however, some courts have given strong indications that parents can seek punitive damages under other statutes protecting the rights of students with disabilities, such as Section 504 or Section 1983. Whether courts will allow damage suits under these statutes varies from jurisdiction to jurisdiction. Even so, it is unlikely that courts would assess damages unless it can be shown that school officials acted in bad faith or intentionally discriminated against students with disabilities.

Figure 7.1 (Continued)

Q: Why should school officials make every effort to reach settlements agreement with the parents?

A: Litigation can be expensive, not only in terms of legal fees, but also in terms of time, resources, and aggravation. Litigation, because of its adversarial nature, may also bring about an irreparable breakdown in the relationship between the parents or guardians and school officials. Reaching settlement agreements prior to litigation oftentimes can salvage these relationships. Moreover, recent cases have denied attorney fees to parents who settled their complaints via settlement agreements. It may be much more cost effective for school officials to compromise, and reach settlements, than to continue litigation.

and Congress have provided many guidelines for what types of compensation may be provided to parents when school officials fail to meet their obligations under the IDEA. The recommendations below have been generated from the IDEA and the numerous cases that awarded compensation to parents. Although this is an area that is governed more by federal than state law, as always, readers should consult state as well as federal statutes and regulations.

School officials should

- Take immediate actions to review student IEPs and placement when parents notify school officials of their dissatisfaction.
- Immediately correct any deficiencies found in student IEPs.
- Attempt to settle placement disputes with parents as quickly as possible, thereby reducing any retroactive tuition reimbursement or compensatory education awards that may be imposed.
- Provide parents with information about possible private school placements when they indicate that they intend to make unilateral changes in placements.
- Be prepared to show that the IEPs and placements proposed by school officials meet the requirements for a FAPE.
- Be ready to demonstrate that school board officials followed all of the IDEA's procedural steps in developing student IEPs and making placement recommendations.
- Be prepared to show that parents were notified of their procedural rights at several junctures throughout the evaluation and placement process.
- Be willing to compromise and consider alternative dispute resolution procedures.
- Make written settlement offers to parents throughout litigation; recall that settlement offers that are later determined to be equal to

or better than the final relief obtained by parents can reduce attorney fees awards.

- Agree to pay parents' legal expenses when it is clear that they were the prevailing parties in special education disputes since additional legal action over attorney fees will only incur additional expenses for school boards.
- Always proceed in good faith, carefully following the IDEA's procedures.

REFERENCES

Abraham v. District of Columbia, 338 F. Supp.2d 113 (D.D.C. 2004).

Alamo Heights Independent School District v. State Board of Education, 790 F.2d 1153 (5th Cir. 1986).

Alex G. ex rel. Stephen G. v. Board of Trustees of Davis Joint Unified School District, 332 F. Supp.2d 1315 (E.D. Cal. 2004).

Algeria v. District of Columbia, 391 F.3d 262 (D.C. Cir. 2004).

Anderson v. Thompson, 658 F.2d 1205 (7th Cir. 1981).

Angela L. v. Pasadena Independent School District, 918 F.2d 1188 (5th Cir. 1990).

Appellate Rule 38, Fed.R.App.P. 38.

Arlington Central School District v. Murphy, 126 S. Ct. 2455 (2006), *reversing Murphy v. Arlington Central School District*, 402 F.3d 332 (2d Cir. 2005).

Aronow v. District of Columbia, 780 F. Supp. 46 (D.D.C. 1992), 791 F. Supp. 318 (D.D.C. 1992).

Arons v. New Jersey State Board of Education, 842 F.2d 58 (3d Cir. 1988).

Ash v. Lake Oswego School District, 766 F. Supp. 852 (D. Or. 1991), *affirmed* 980 F.2d 585 (9th Cir. 1992).

Assistance to the States for the Education of Children with Disabilities, 34 C.F.R. §§ 300.1–300.818. (2006).

Babb v. Knox County School System, 965 F.2d 104 (6th Cir. 1992).

Barbara R. v. Tirozzi, 665 F. Supp. 141 (D. Conn. 1987).

Barlow-Gresham Union High School District No. 2 v. Mitchell, 940 F.2d 1280 (9th Cir. 1991).

Barnett v. Fairfax County School Board, 927 F.2d 146 (4th Cir. 1991).

Bernardsville Board of Education v. J.H., 42 F.3d 149 (3d Cir. 1994).

B.H. v. Southington Board of Education, 273 F. Supp.2d 194 (D. Conn. 2003).

Big Beaver Falls Area School District v. Jackson, 624 A.2d 806 (Pa. Commw. Ct. 1993).

Board of Education of Downers Grove Grade School District No. 58 v. Steven L., 89 F.3d 464 (7th Cir. 1996).

Board of Education of Oak Park & River Forest High School District No. 200 v. Illinois State Board of Education, 21 F. Supp.2d 862 (N.D. Ill. 1988), *vacated and remanded on other grounds sub nom. Board of Education of Oak Park & River Forest High School District No. 200 v. Kelly E.*, 207 F.3d 931 (7th Cir. 2000).

Board of Education of the County of Cabell v. Dienelt, 843 F.2d 813 (4th Cir. 1988).

Board of Education of the Hendrick Hudson Central School District v. Rowley, 458 U.S. 176 (1982).

Bradley v. Arkansas Department of Education, 301 F.3d 952 (8th Cir. 2002).

Brandon K. v. New Lenox School District, 2001 WL 1491499 (N.D. Ill. 2001).

Brantley v. Independent School District No. 625, St. Paul Public Schools, 936 F. Supp. 649 (D. Minn. 1996).

Brillon v. Klein Independent School District, 274 F. Supp.2d 864 (S.D. Tex. 2003).

Brooks v. St. Tammany Parish School Board, 510 S0.2d 51 (La. App. Ct. 1987).

Brown v. Wilson County School District, 747 F. Supp. 436 (M.D. Tenn. 1990).

Buckhannon Board & Care Home v. West Virginia Department of Health and Human Resources, 532 U.S. 598 (2001).

Bucks County Department of Mental Health/Mental Retardation v. Commonwealth of Pennsylvania, 379 F.3d 61 (3d Cir. 2004).

Burlington School Committee v. Department of Education, Commonwealth of Massachusetts, 471 U.S. 359 (1985).

Burr v. Sobol, 748 F. Supp. 97 (S.D.N.Y. 1990).

Capistrano Unified School District v. Wartenberg, 59 F.3d 884 (9th Cir. 1995).

Cappillino v. Hyde Park Central School District, 40 F. Supp.2d 513 (S.D.N.Y. 1999).

Carlisle Area School District v. Scott P., 62 F.3d 520 (3d Cir. 1995).

Caroline T. v. Hudson School District, 915 F.2d 752 (1st Cir. 1990).

Chang v. Board of Education of Glen Ridge Township, 685 F. Supp. 96 (D.N.J. 1988).

Charlie F. v. Board of Education of Skokie School District 68, 98 F.3d 989 (7th Cir. 1996).

Civil Rights Act of 1871, Section 1983, 42 U.S.C. § 1983.

Cleveland Heights–University Heights City School District v. Boss, 144 F.3d 391 (6th Cir. 1998).

Cocores v. Portsmouth, NH School District, 779 F. Supp. 203 (D.N.H. 1991).

Code of Federal Regulations (C.F.R.), as cited.

Combs v. School Board of Rockingham County, 15 F.3d 357 (4th Cir. 1994).

Conklin, In re, 946 F.2d 306 (4th Cir. 1991).

Connors v. Mills, 34 F. Supp.2d 795 (N.D.N.Y. 1998).

Cremeans v. Fairland Local School District Board of Education, 633 N.E.2d 570 (Ohio App. Ct. 1993).

Crocker v. Tennessee Secondary School Athletic Association, 980 F.2d 382 (6th Cir. 1992).

Daniel S. v. Scranton School District, 230 F.3d 90 (3d Cir. 2000).

D.B. v. Ocean Township Board of Education, 985 F. Supp. 457 (D.N.J. 1997).

Deal ex rel. Deal v. Hamilton County Department of Education, 392 F.3d 840 (6th Cir. 2004).

Diamond v. McKenzie, 602 F. Supp. 632 (D.D.C. 1985).

DiBuo v. Board of Education of Worcester County, 309 F.3d 184 (4th Cir. 2002).

D.M. ex rel. G.M. and C.M. v. Board of Education, Center Moriches Union Free School District, 296 F. Supp.2d 400 (E.D.N.Y. 2003).

Doe v. Anrig, 651 F. Supp. 424 (D. Mass. 1987).

Doe v. Board of Education of Baltimore County, 165 F.3d 260 (4th Cir. 1998).

Doe v. Boston Public Schools, 358 F.3d 20 (1st Cir. 2004).

Doucet v. Chilton County Board of Education, 65 F. Supp.2d 1249 (M.D. Ala. 1999).

Drew P. v. Clarke County School District, 676 F. Supp. 1559 (M.D. Ga. 1987), *affirmed* 877 F.2d 927 (11th Cir. 1989).

E.C. ex rel. R.C. v. Board of Education of South Brunswick Township, 792 A.2d 583 (N.J. Sup. Ct. 2001).

Eggers v. Bullitt County School District, 854 F.2d 892 (6th Cir. 1988).

Eirschele v. Craven County Board of Education, 7 F. Supp.2d 655 (E.D.N.C. 1998).

E.M. v. Millville Board of Education, 849 F. Supp. 312 (D.N.J. 1994).

Emma C. v. Eastin, 985 F. Supp. 940 (N.D. Cal. 1997).

E.P. v. Union County Regional High School District No. 1, 741 F. Supp. 1144 (D.N.J. 1989).

Erickson v. Board of Education of Baltimore County, 162 F.3d 289 (4th Cir. 1998).

Esther C. v. Ambach, 535 N.Y.S.2d 462 (N.Y. App. Div. 1988).

Eugene B. v. Great Neck Union Free School District, 635 F. Supp. 753 (E.D.N.Y. 1986).

Evans v. District No. 17 of Douglas County, 841 F.2d 824 (8th Cir. 1988).

Field v. Haddonfield Board of Education, 769 F. Supp. 1313 (D.N.J. 1991).

Fischer v. Rochester Community Schools, 780 F. Supp. 1142 (E.D. Mich. 1991).

Florence County School District Four v. Carter, 510 U.S. 7 (1993).

Garland Independent School District v. Wilks, 657 F. Supp. 1163 (N.D. Tex. 1987).

Garner, B. A. (Ed.). (1999). *Black's law dictionary* (7th ed.). St. Paul, MN: West.

Garro v. State of Connecticut, 23 F.3d 734 (2d Cir. 1994).

Gary A. v. New Trier High School District No. 203, 796 F.2d 940 (7th Cir. 1986).

Gerasimou v. Ambach, 636 F. Supp. 1504 (E.D.N.Y. 1986).

Gerstmyer v. Howard County Public Schools, 850 F. Supp. 361 (D. Md. 1994).

Glendale Unified School District v. Almasi, 122 F. Supp.2d 1093 (C.D. Cal. 2000).

Goldring v. District of Columbia, 416 F.3d 70 (D.C. Cir. 2005).

Greenland School District v. Amy N., 358 F.3d 150 (1st Cir. 2004).

Gross ex rel. Gross v. Perrysburg Exempted Village School District, 306 F. Supp.2d 726 (N.D. Ohio 2004).

Hall v. Detroit Public Schools, 823 F. Supp. 1377 (E.D. Mich. 1993).

Hall v. Knott County Board of Education, 941 F.2d 402 (6th Cir. 1991).

Heldman v. Sobol, 846 F.3d 285 (S.D.N.Y. 1994).

Hiller v. Board of Education of the Brunswick Central School District, 743 F. Supp. 958 (N.D.N.Y. 1990).

Howey v. Tippecanoe School Corporation, 734 F. Supp. 1485, (N.D. Ind. 1990).

Hudson v. Wilson, 828 F.2d 1059 (4th Cir. 1987).

Hunger v. Leininger, 15 F.3d 664 (7th Cir. 1994).

Hurry v. Jones, 734 F.2d 879 (1st Cir. 1984).

Hyden v. Board of Education of Wilson County, 714 F. Supp. 290 (M.D. Tenn. 1989).

Individuals with Disabilities Education Act, 20 U.S.C. § 1400 *et seq.* (2005).

J.C. v. Regional School District No. 10, 278 F.3d 119 (2d Cir. 2002).

Jefferson County Board of Education v. Breen, 853 F.2d 853 (11th Cir. 1988).

J.G. v. Board of Education of the Rochester City School District, 648 F. Supp. 1452 (W.D.N.Y. 1986), *affirmed* 830 F.2d 444 (2d Cir. 1987).

John T. by Paul T. and Joan T. v. Delaware County Intermediate Unit, 318 F.3d 545 (3d Cir. 2003).

Johnson v. Bismarck Public School District, 949 F.2d 1000 (8th Cir. 1991).

Johnson v. Clark, 418 N.W.2d 466 (Mich. Ct. App. 1987).

Johnson v. Lancaster-Lebanon Intermediate Unit 13, Lancaster City School District, 757 F. Supp. 606 (E.D. Pa. 1991).

Johnson v. Metro Davidson County School System, 108 F. Supp.2d 906 (M.D. Tenn. 2000).

Jose Luis R. v. Joliet Township H.S. District 204, 2002 WL 54544 (N.D. Ill. 2002).

J.S. v. Ramapo Central School District, 165 F. Supp.2d 570 (S.D.N.Y. 2001).

King v. Floyd County Board of Education, 5 F. Supp.2d 504 (E.D. Ky. 1998).

Koswenda v. Flossmoor School District No. 161, 227 F. Supp.2d 979 (N.D. Ill. 2002).

Krichinsky v. Knox County Schools, 963 F.2d 847 (6th Cir. 1992).

Kristi W. v. Graham Independent School District, 663 F. Supp. 86 (N.D. Tex. 1987).

Lascari v. Board of Education of the Ramapo Indian Hills Regional High School District, 560 A.2d 1180 (N.J. 1989).

Lester H. v. Gilhool, 916 F.2d 865 (3d Cir. 1990).

Linda T. ex rel. William A. v. Rice Lake Area School District, 337 F. Supp.2d 1135 (W.D. Wis. 2004).

L.K. ex rel. J.H. v. Board of Education for Transylvania County, 113 F. Supp.2d 856 (W.D.N.C. 2000).

Lucht v. Molalla River School District, 225 F.3d 1023 (9th Cir. 1999).

Malehorn v. Hill City School District, 987 F. Supp. 772 (D.S.D. 1997).

Manchester School District v. Christopher B., 807 F. Supp. 860 (D.N.H. 1992).

Martin v. School Board of Prince George County, 348 S.E.2d 857 (Va. Ct. App. 1986).

Marvin H. v. Austin Independent School District, 714 F.2d 1348 (5th Cir. 1983).

Mathern v. Campbell County Children's Center, 674 F. Supp. 816 (D. Wyo. 1987).

Matthew V. v. DeKalb County School System, 244 F. Supp.2d 1331 (N.D. Ga. 2003).

Mawdsley, R. D. (2001). Standard of care and students with disabilities. *Education Law Reporter, 148*, 553–571.

Mawdsley, R. D. (2002). A section 1983 cause of action under the IDEA? Measuring the effect of *Gonzaga University v. Doe. Education Law Reporter, 170*, 425–438.

Mayo v. Baltimore City Public Schools, 40 F. Supp.2d 331 (D. Md. 1999).

Max M. v. Illinois State Board of Education, 684 F. Supp. 514 (N.D. Ill. 1988), *affirmed* 859 F.2d 1297 (7th Cir. 1988).

Max M. v. Thompson, 566 F. Supp. 1330 (N.D. Ill. 1983), 592 F. Supp. 1437 (N.D. Ill. 1984), *sub nom. Max M. v. Illinois State Board of Education*, 629 F. Supp. 1504 (N.D. Ill. 1986).

M.C. ex rel. J.C. v. Central Reg. School District, 81 F.3d 389 (3d Cir. 1996).

Megan C. v. Independent School District No. 625, 57 F. Supp.2d 776 (D. Minn. 1999).

Metropolitan School District of Lawrence Township v. M.S., 818 N.E.2d 978 (Ind. Ct. App. 2004).

Miener v. Missouri, 800 F.2d 749 (8th Cir. 1986).

Miller v. West Lafayette Community School Corporation, 665 N.E.2d 905 (Ind. 1996).

Missouri Department of Elementary and Secondary Education v. Springfield R-12 School District, 358 F.3d 992 (8th Cir. 2004).

Mitten v. Muscogee County District, 877 F.2d 932 (11th Cir. 1989).

Moore v. Crestwood Local School District, 804 F. Supp. 960 (N.D. Ohio 1992).

Moore v. District of Columbia, 886 F.2d 335 (D.C. Cir. 1989).

Moore v. District of Columbia, 907 F.2d 165 (D.C. Cir. 1990).

Moser v. Bret Harte Union High School District, 366 F. Supp.2d 944 (E.D. Cal. 2005).

Moubry v. Independent School District No. 696, 951 F. Supp. 867 (D. Minn. 1996).

Mr. D. v. Glocester School Community, 711 F. Supp. 66 (D.R.I. 1989).

Mr. J. v. Board of Education, 98 F. Supp.2d 226 (D. Conn. 2000).

Mr. L. and Mrs. L. v. Woonsocket Education Department, 793 F. Supp. 41 (D.R.I. 1992).

M.S. ex rel. S.S. v. Board of Education of the City School District of the City of Yonkers, 231 F.3d 96 (2d Cir. 2000).

Ms. M. ex rel. K.M. v. Portland School Committee, 360 F.3d 267 (1st Cir. 2004).

Muller v. Committee on Special Education of the East Islip Union Free School District, 145 F.3d 95 (2d Cir. 1998).

Murphy v. Arlington Central School District Board of Education, 402 F.3d 332 (2d Cir. 2005).

Murphy v. Timberlane Regional School District, 973 F.2d 13 (1st Cir. 1992), *on remand* 819 F. Supp. 1127 (D.N.H. 1993), *affirmed* 22 F.3d 1186 (1st Cir. 1994a), *contempt finding* 855 F. Supp. 498 (D.N.H. 1994b).

Muth v. Central Bucks School District, 839 F.2d 113 (3d Cir. 1988), *reversed and remanded on other grounds sub nom. Dellmuth v. Muth,* 491 U.S. 223 (1989).

Nein v. Greater Clark County School Corporation, 95 F. Supp.2d 961 (S.D. Ind. 2000).

Neisz v. Portland Public School District, 684 F. Supp. 1530 (D. Or. 1988).

Neosho R-V School District v. Clark, 315 F.3d 1022 (8th Cir. 2003).

Nieves-Marquez v. Commonwealth of Puerto Rico, 353 F.3d 108 (1st Cir. 2003).

Osborne, A. G. (2002). Can Section 1983 be used to redress violations of the IDEA? *Education Law Reporter, 161,* 21–32.

Osborne, A. G. (2003). Attorneys' fees under the IDEA after *Buckhannon:* Is the catalyst theory still viable? *Education Law Reporter, 175,* 397–407.

Osborne, A. G. (2005). Update on attorneys' fees under the IDEA. *Education Law Reporter, 193,* 1–12.

Osborne, A. G., & DiMattia, P. (1991). Attorney fees are available for administrative proceedings under the EHA. *Education Law Reporter, 66,* 909–920.

Osborne, A. G., & Russo, C. J. (2001). Are damages an available remedy when a school district fails to provide an appropriate education under IDEA? *Education Law Reporter, 152,* 1–14.

Osborne, A. G., & Russo, C. J. (2006). The Supreme Court rejects parental reimbursement for expert witness fees under the IDEA: *Arlington Central School District Board of Education v. Murphy. Education Law Reporter, 213,* 333–348.

Padilla v. School District No. 1 in the City and County of Denver, 233 F.3d 1268 (10th Cir. 2000).

Parents of Student W. v. Puyallup School District No. 3, 31 F.3d 1489 (9th Cir. 1994).

Patricia E. v. Board of Education of Community High School District No. 155, 894 F. Supp. 1161 (N.D. Ill. 1995).

Patricia P. v. Board of Education of Oak Park and River Forest High School District No. 200, 203 F.3d 462 (7th Cir. 2000).

Payne v. Board of Education, Cleveland City Schools, 88 F.3d 392 (6th Cir. 1996).

Pazik v. Gateway Regional School District, 130 F. Supp.2d 217 (D. Mass. 2001).

Phelan v. Bell, 8 F.3d 369 (6th Cir. 1993).

Pihl v. Massachusetts Department of Education, 9 F.3d 184 (1st Cir. 1993).

P.J. v. State of Connecticut State Board of Education, 788 F. Supp. 673 (D. Conn. 1992).

P.L. by Mr. and Mrs. L. v. Norwalk Board of Education, 64 F. Supp.2d 61 (D. Conn. 1999).

P.O. ex rel. L.T. and T.O. v. Greenwich Board of Education, 210 F. Supp.2d 76 (D. Conn. 2002).

Polera v. Board of Education of the Newburgh Enlarged City School District, 288 F.3d 478 (2d Cir. 2002).

Powell v. DeFore, 699 F.2d 1078 (11th Cir. 1983).

Puffer v. Raynolds, 761 F. Supp. 838 (D. Mass. 1988).

Rapid City School District v. Vahle, 922 F.2d 476 (8th Cir. 1990).

Rappaport v. Vance, 812 F. Supp. 609 (D. Md. 1993).

Rehabilitation Act, Section 504, 29 U.S.C. § 794.

Ridgewood Board of Education v. N.E., 172 F.3d 238 (3d Cir. 1999).

Russo, C. J. (2006). Negligence. In C. J. Russo (Ed.), *Key legal issues for schools: The ultimate resource for school business officials* (pp. 83–97). Lanham, MD: Rowman & Littlefield Education.

S-1 v. Spangler, 650 F. Supp. 1427 (M.D.N.C. 1986), *vacated and remanded due to mootness* 832 F.2d 294 (4th Cir. 1987), *on remand* (unpublished opinion), *affirmed sub nom. S-1 v. State Board of Education,* 6 F.3d 160 (4th Cir. 1993), *rehearing en banc, reversed* 21 F.3d 49 (4th Cir. 1994).

Salley v. St. Tammany Parish School Board, 57 F.3d 458 (5th Cir. 1995).

Sanders v. Marquette Public Schools, 561 F. Supp. 1361 (W.D. Mich. 1983).

Schoenfield v. Parkway School District, 138 F.3d 379 (8th Cir. 1998).

Sellers v. School Board of the City of Manassas, 141 F.3d 524 (4th Cir. 1998).

Shelly C. v. Venus Independent School District, 878 F.2d 862 (5th Cir. 1989).

Sidney K. v. Ambach, 535 N.Y.S.2d 468 (N.Y. App. Div. 1988).

Smith ex rel. Smith v. Fitchburg Public Schools, 401 F.3d 16 (1st Cir. 2005).

Smith v. District of Columbia, 117 Fed. Appx. (D.C. Cir. 2004).

Smith v. Robinson, 468 U.S. 992 (1984).

State of West Virginia ex rel. Justice v. Board of Education of the County of Monongalia, 539 S.E.2d 777 (W.Va. 2000).

Still v. DeBuono, 101 F.3d 888 (2d Cir. 1996).

Straube v. Florida Union Free School District, 778 F. Supp. 774 (S.D.N.Y. 1991), 801 F. Supp. 1164 (S.D.N.Y. 1992).

Suzawith v. Green Bay Area School District, 132 F. Supp.2d 718 (D. Wis. 2000).

Taylor v. Board of Education of Copake-Taconic Hills Central School District, 649 F. Supp. 1253 (N.D.N.Y. 1986).

T.D. v. LaGrange School District No. 102, 349 F.3d 469 (7th Cir. 2003).

Tice v. Botetourt County School District, 908 F.2d 1200 (4th Cir. 1990).

Timms v. Metropolitan School District, EHLR 554:361 (S.D. Ind. 1982), *affirmed* 718 F.2d 212 (7th Cir. 1983), *amended* 722 F.2d 1310 (7th Cir. 1983).

Todd D. v. Andrews, 933 F.2d 1576 (11th Cir. 1991).

Troy School District v. Boutsikaris, 250 F. Supp.2d 720 (E.D. Mich. 2003).

Tucker v. Calloway County Board of Education, 136 F.3d 495 (6th Cir. 1998).

Turton v. Crisp County School District, 688 F. Supp. 1535 (M.D. Ga. 1988).

Union School District v. Smith, 15 F.3d 1519 (9th Cir. 1994).

Upper Valley Association of Handicapped Citizens v. Blue Mountain Union School District No. 21, 973 F. Supp. 429 (D. Vt. 1997).

Valerie J. v. Derry Cooperative School District, 771 F. Supp. 483 (D.N.H. 1991).

Vander Malle v. Ambach, 667 F. Supp. 1015 (S.D.N.Y. 1987).

Virginia McC. v. Corrigan-Camden Independent School District, 909 F. Supp. 1023 (E.D. Tex. 1995).

Vultaggio v. Board of Education, Smithtown Central School District, 343 F.3d 598 (2d Cir. 2003).

Warren G. v. Cumberland County School District, 190 F.3d 80 (3d Cir. 1999).

Watkins v. Vance, 328 F. Supp.2d 27, (D.D.C. 2004).

Wayne County Regional Education Service Agency v. Pappas, 56 F. Supp.2d 807 (E.D. Mich. 1999).

W.B. v. Matula, 67 F.3d 484 (3d Cir. 1995).

Wenger v. Canastota Central School District, 979 F. Supp. 147 (N.D.N.Y. 1997), *affirmed* 146 F.3d 123 (2d Cir. 1998).

Wenkart, R. D. (2002). Attorneys' fees under the IDEA and the demise of the catalyst theory. *Education Law Reporter, 165,* 439–445.

Wenkart, R. D. (2004). The award of section 1983 damages under the IDEA. *Education Law Reporter, 183,* 313–335.

Wheeler v. Towanda Area School District, 950 F.2d 128 (3d Cir. 1991).

White v. State of California, 240 Cal. Rptr. 732 (Cal. Ct. App. 1987).

W.L.G. v. Houston County Board of Education, 975 F. Supp. 1317 (M.D. Ala. 1997).

Woodside v. School District of Philadelphia Board of Education, 248 F.3d 129 (3d Cir. 2001).

Yancy v. New Baltimore City Board of School Commissioners, 24 F. Supp.2d 512 (D. Md. 1998).

Yankton School District v. Schramm, 900 F. Supp. 1182 (D.S.D. 1995), *affirmed* 93 F.3d 1369 (8th Cir. 1996).

Zirkel, P. A., & Hennessy, M. K. (2001). Compensatory educational services in special education cases: An update. *Education Law Reporter, 150,* 311–332.

Zirkel, P. A., & Osborne, A. G. (1987). Are damages available in special education suits? *Education Law Reporter, 42,* 497–508.

8

Conflict Management

IDEA Compliance

INTRODUCTION

As this book has demonstrated, a major part of the Individuals with Disabilities Education Act (IDEA) (2005) is designed to ensure that school officials comply with its provisions, which require them to provide a significant array of substantive and procedural rights to students with disabilities and their parents. At the same time, the IDEA's due process provisions created a vehicle for the resolution of disputes regarding the delivery of the free appropriate public education it guarantees for students with disabilities.

The IDEA's due process mechanism is the most elaborate system that Congress ever established for the resolution of disputes between parents and school officials. Unfortunately, although Congress intended for parents and school officials to work together in developing individualized education programs (IEPs) for students with disabilities, there are some situations where the parties simply cannot agree. Aware of the fact that parents and school officials cannot always agree about what is best for children, Congress saw the need to include dispute resolution processes in the IDEA.

This book provides information about many of the literally thousands of cases that have been filed since the IDEA was enacted. These suits involved numerous aspects of the federal special education legislation. Moreover, the deluge of litigation in special education is unlikely to stop in the near future, as the rate of cases continues to increase (Zirkel, 2005).

Special education administrators have been heard to lament that it often seems as though they must be half lawyers to carry out their positions successfully. While having law degrees is certainly not a prerequisite for assuming leadership positions in education, the fact remains that the process for providing special education to students with disabilities is very much a legal one. Successful special education practitioners must therefore be knowledgeable about the law and understand how the legal system operates. The educators who are most successful are those who proactively manage the legal system rather than respond by allowing the legal system to manage their activities. Inasmuch as the purpose of this chapter is to provide information on how and when to access the legal system, it does not end with specific recommendations apart from this narrative discussion.

PREVENTATIVE LAW

The best way to deal with legal challenges is to prevent them from occurring. Even so, in recent years school boards have been forced to budget an increased amount of money for legal fees. It almost goes without saying that few will argue that this money would be better spent on educational programs. This is most true in special education, where litigation has increased faster than in any other area related to schools (Zirkel & D'Angelo, 2002). In addition to their own legal fees, school systems may be required to reimburse parents for their legal expenses when parents are the prevailing parties in litigation.

Aware of the need to avoid unnecessary litigation, many school officials have demonstrated an interest in the area known as preventive law. The goals of preventive law are to eliminate disputes entirely before they can arise and to put school systems in favorable positions should litigation occur. In order to be most effective, educators must practice preventive law on a daily basis by seeking permanent solutions to situations that give rise to conflict in schools. Generally, it is less expensive to find permanent solutions by enacting proactive policies and procedures than to mount what amounts to reactive or after-the-fact defenses in protracted litigation.

The first step in any program of preventive law is for school administrators and special education practitioners, including teachers, aides, and providers of related services, to be knowledgeable about the legal issues in special education. Reading this book and others like it should provide school officials with a basic knowledge of the issues and the results of previous litigation. The law, however, is constantly evolving. New cases that can alter the status of the law are decided daily. Previous chapters cited examples of how these changes have occurred. Thus, school officials must take affirmative steps to stay abreast of new legal developments.

Today numerous sources of information exist about issues and developments in education law. The Education Law Association (ELA), headquartered at the University of Dayton, in Dayton, Ohio, publishes *The Yearbook of Education Law,* which is called simply *"The Yearbook"* and includes a chapter on special education law. ELA also publishes a monthly newsletter, *ELA Notes,* and a reporter, *School Law Reporter,* as well as monographs that provide up-to-date information on school law. In the interests of full disclosure, we would like to point out that we are both Past Presidents of ELA. In addition, we have both worked on the *Yearbook:* Allan G. Osborne has written the chapter on students with disabilities in the *Yearbook* since 1990, and Charles J. Russo has been editor of the *Yearbook* since 1995.

Many special education and general education journals frequently contain articles on legal issues, especially those involving special education. Professional organizations such as the Council for Exceptional Children, the National School Boards Association, the Association of School Business Officials, and ELA generally include sessions at their annual conventions that address legal issues. In addition, the Colleges or Schools of Education in many colleges and universities offer courses on school law and/or the law of special education that can serve as excellent resources for educators. Workshops on special education law should be part of every school system's professional development program. In providing such ongoing professional development for staff, school officials should consider having the board's attorneys join in the presentations so that they can provide up-to-date legal perspectives. At the end of this book are additional helpful resources: Resource B includes the Web sites of all fifty state (or commonwealth) departments of education; Resource C provides a list of helpful special education Web sites along with brief descriptions of what they contain.

Working With Parents

Litigation frequently arises out of misunderstandings or small differences of opinion between parties. A great deal of costly and time-consuming litigation can be avoided if educators keep lines of communication open with parents and are willing to reach compromises when disagreements occur. When parents reject proposed special education placements and/or IEPs for their children, school officials should make every attempt possible to evaluate their reasons for doing so. The rejections may be due to misunderstandings over what proposals entail or disagreements with only minor aspects of IEPs. If school officials do not communicate, or are unwilling to compromise, then litigation is sure to follow.

For school officials, one of the most important aspects of the communication process, especially with parents, is to be active listeners. When parents present counterproposals or make additional demands, school officials must listen and give serious thought to what they have to say. In the spirit of compromise, educational officials should be prepared to make some concessions. If educators cannot meet parental demands, they should take great care in explaining why parental proposals cannot be implemented as they wish.

Another common source of litigation, in addition to conflicts with parents, is the failure of school officials to implement board policy. Put another way, although boards often have appropriate and legally correct policies and procedures in place, their employees fail to follow them in all situations. This means that it is crucial that educational leaders train new employees and conduct ongoing professional development activities to ensure that staff members are aware of all policies and procedures and the importance of following them.

At least three items can help educators to minimize conflict with parents (Russo & Morse, 2004). First, educators should keep parents informed and offer their support by providing parents with information about the disabilities of their children. This includes directing parents to their central office personnel, to local support groups to help them better understand the disabilities of their children, and possibly to useful Web sites such as those in the resources at the end of this book.

Second, educators should recognize that since parents are part of the solution, not part of the problem, it is important to work with them in the best interest of the children with disabilities. Sadly, some educators treat the parents of special education (and other) students as potential troublemakers rather than as valuable partners who can help address the needs of their children. Educators should keep in mind that because, unlike parents, they are temporary in the lives of children, they must work together with parents in the process of designing educational programming that best suits the needs of students with disabilities.

Third, educators should follow the law. Litigation involving special education can be contentious, and expensive, in view of the fact that prevailing parents can recover attorney fees. Thus, one of the most important steps that school officials can take in the realm of preventive law is to conduct periodic legal audits focusing on board policies, procedures, and practices to ensure that they are legally correct. Given that the status of the law is constantly evolving, it is important that legal audits should be completed at least every two years but preferably annually. School board attorneys, especially those who focus on special education, acting as part of teams with directors of special education and other central office personnel, should work together in conducting audits.

DISPUTE RESOLUTION

Unfortunately, despite the best efforts of school officials to prevent it, litigation is a fact of life in today's school systems. Honest disagreements over what constitutes appropriate placements are all but certain to occur between parents and special educators. Insofar as parents, for their own reasons, sometimes make demands or have unrealistic expectations that school officials cannot (and may not be required to) meet, compromise is not always possible. Further, sometimes litigation ensues because school district personnel make errors.

As described in Chapter 6 of this book, the IDEA contains a meticulous system for dispute resolution. Rather than reiterate the key points in Chapter 6, this section outlines steps that school officials should take when parents threaten to initiate or do initiate legal action.

Mediation

Sometimes communications between school officials and parents break down, making it difficult for the parties to sit down to work out their disagreements. Mediation can be helpful in situations such as these because the IDEA now directs states and school officials to offer mediation services at no cost to parents prior to scheduling due process hearings. Mediation is a viable alternative for the resolution of disputed IEPs, but cannot be used to deny or delay parental rights to formal due process hearings. In fact, parents cannot be compelled to enter into mediation if they prefer to go straight to due process hearings.

The parties involved in special education disputes can engage the services of impartial mediators who will attempt to bring them together through negotiation. Several states have provisions in their own special education laws for formal mediation processes prior to litigation, and the IDEA requires states to maintain a list of trained, impartial mediators. Successful mediation depends on the willingness of school officials to compromise. School officials must evaluate any reasonable proposals that are presented by either the parents or the mediator and be prepared to offer specific counterproposals.

There are many advantages to trying mediation before proceeding to due process hearings. The costs involved and the time spent on due process hearings certainly justify the effort to mediate and avoid the hearing stage. Perhaps most important, mediation can salvage the working relationships between parents and school officials. Unfortunately, even though it is not supposed to be so, due process hearings are often adversarial processes that do little to foster positive working relationships between parents and school officials.

Resolution Conference

A new provision in the IDEA calls for a resolution session to take place within 15 days of parental filings of formal complaints about the education of their children with disabilities (20 U.S.C. § 1415(f)(1)(B)).

These conferences are designed to discuss parental complaints and all pertinent facts so that the disagreements can be resolved. In addition to the parents, relevant members of the IEP team should attend resolution sessions. School board attorneys may not attend resolution sessions unless the parents bring their attorneys along. Again, as with mediation, this step is voluntary and does not need to occur if both parties either agree to waive resolution sessions or to proceed directly to mediation.

If parents are willing, school officials would be wise to take advantage of resolution conferences. Many disputes result from misunderstandings or unclear communication, so that resolution conferences provide one more opportunity to resolve parental concerns in nonadversarial contexts. As an added benefit, as with mediation, this process is far less costly than hearings.

Resolution conferences also provide upper-level administrators, such as Directors of Special Education, to become involved in the process of finding solutions to issues raised by parents. Insofar as administrators above the building level are often not involved in developing contested IEPs, they remain unaware of parental complaints until they are filed. There are two benefits to having district-level administrators present at resolution sessions. First, since these administrators often have a broader view of issues in light of their varied experience, they can bring fresh perspectives to disputes. Second, since these administrators frequently have more authority to commit the resources of their school system, they are able to offer options that IEP teams might not otherwise have considered. Thus, it is often possible that complaints can be resolved simply by including persons with greater authority since they bring something new to the table.

Preparing for Hearings

Despite the best efforts of school officials, sometimes due process hearings are inevitable. If school officials have complied with all of the IDEA's provisions in making their placement decisions, they need not fear due process hearings. Even so, there is simply no substitute for proper preparation prior to hearings.

Preparation for hearings must begin long before it is even apparent that hearings are to take place. The key to success in due process hearings is for school officials to have all of the documentation handy to demonstrate that they complied with applicable laws, policies, and procedures. Documentation in this regard includes, but is certainly not limited to, copies of notice letters sent to parents, signed consent forms, copies of IEPs, and any and all other forms of written communication with parents. It is impossible to create the proper documentation after the fact if it does not exist. Accordingly, educational leaders should treat all special education situations as if they may someday culminate in hearings. In other words, educators should begin documentation on the day they receive a request for services or a referral for an evaluation. Simply stated, special education personnel should be trained to make the documentation process part of the routine of providing special education services.

Generally, the chief special education administrator in a school system, typically with the title of Director of Special Education, is responsible for representing school boards at hearings. Insofar as these administrators usually become directly involved in cases only after problems have developed, they could be unfamiliar with the prior history of the children involved. The first task for such administrators, then, is to gather all pertinent information. At the same time, administrators must become familiar with all aspects and details of cases, as the decisions that need to be made throughout the hearing process require thorough knowledge of the students.

In preparing for hearings, it is worth keeping in mind that the requirements and qualifications for hearing officers vary from state to state. In some states, such as Ohio (Ohio Administrative Code, 2002), hearing officers must be attorneys with some knowledge of special education practices. On the other hand, in states such as North Carolina (North Carolina General Statutes, 1997), hearing officers need not be attorneys and are typically faculty members from local colleges or universities who are versed in special education procedures. It would be a mistake to assume that hearing officers have detailed knowledge of a school system's programs or other available options. For that reason educators must inform hearing officers about the positive aspects of the school officials' proposals and any weaknesses in the parents' position.

One of the most important pieces of evidence that school officials must supply at hearings is proof that they complied with all relevant due process procedures. In the event that officials cannot provide this evidence, or have not complied with the procedures, they should acknowledge their errors. While not all procedural errors are fatal to cases, evasiveness or intentional covering up of procedural errors can be very damaging to the cases of school boards as they can weaken their credibility.

During hearings it is important for the representatives of school boards to make complete presentations of the facts. It may be helpful to use visual aids such as charts, diagrams, or other graphic presentations to clarify points made during the oral argument or cross-examination of expert witnesses. Careful advanced preparation of these materials is necessary.

Those who testify or present evidence on behalf of school systems must also be well prepared in advance. This means not only that witnesses should be familiar with the information about which they are to provide but also that they should be prepared by being given sample questions of the type that they are likely to face at hearings. While it is difficult to know in advance exactly what line of questioning the opposition is going to employ during cross-examinations, school board attorneys should be able to prepare all witnesses adequately for what is to come.

The task of school officials during hearings is to show that their proposed programs are appropriate. According to the IDEA, once educators have shown that they have offered appropriate programs, there is no need to examine any alternative proposals. Even so, prudent school officials should be prepared to show why they do not believe that the programs favored by the parents are necessary. Many school boards have succeeded in due process hearings by showing that the program favored by the parents was inadequate.

The importance of school officials and their attorney working together cannot be overemphasized, because their communication is an important ingredient to success. The next section reviews factors to consider when choosing an attorney.

Selecting an Attorney

The party that is in the right in special education litigation is not always the victor. As in any legal contest, the party that presents the better case wins most often. This being the situation, having qualified attorneys may make all the difference between success and failure at due process hearings and/or in litigation. Thus, the necessity of having skilled attorneys in special education suits cannot be overemphasized.

As an area of law, special education has become increasingly important due to the tremendous amount of litigation that has occurred since the IDEA was first enacted in 1975. School officials must be aware that the law in this regard has become so specialized that they cannot rely solely on their regular attorneys to defend them in special education suits. Put another way, as well qualified as school board attorneys are to handle most legal affairs, many may lack the specialized knowledge that is required to litigate special education cases adequately. To this end, school boards should consider retaining separate attorneys to handle their special education litigation. On the other hand, many boards retain the services of large law firms that focus on education law, firms that typically have attorneys on staff who devote significant portions, if not all, of their practices to the law of special education. Under these circumstances, school officials may need to look no farther than their present firms for special education counsel.

If school boards are not represented by large firms with special education divisions or do not have their own counsel on staff, as is common in larger school systems, officials should locate and retain separate attorneys for special education litigation. These attorneys must be well versed in education law in general as well as in special education law and have experience in administrative hearing procedures, since most litigation begins at this level. Further, attorneys should be familiar with educational issues and practices such as evaluation methods, teaching techniques, and various placement options. Naturally, experienced and talented attorneys cost more. There simply is no substitute for experience.

In order to locate qualified attorneys to handle special education suits, school officials should solicit referrals from other knowledgeable parties. Inasmuch as the persons representing school boards in special education litigation may need to confer with the regular attorneys that boards retain, the boards' attorneys would be a logical starting point. At the same time, school board attorneys may have ready lists of qualified special education attorneys. Special education administrators from other districts can also serve as a good source of referrals. Finally, the national or state school board associations, in addition to county or state bar associations, should be able to provide lists of attorneys who specialize in special education litigation.

School boards should identify, and retain, attorneys long before they are needed. The point at which school boards are under the pressure of litigation over a special education dispute is not the proper time to begin looking for qualified attorneys. It is better to retain, and form relationships with, attorneys well before litigation is pending. By adopting proactive approaches, school officials should be able to take the time necessary to make sure the attorneys they hire are the right persons for the job.

Hiring attorneys, regardless of whether they are generalists or specialists in special education, is much like choosing professionals to fill any open positions in school systems. Educational leaders should first focus on the needs of their districts and consider, as many boards are already doing, putting out requests for proposals, sometimes referred to simply as RFPs, for attorneys who are interested in, and meet the qualifications for, the jobs at hand (Bennett & Pole, 2005). Once attorneys have submitted their applications, school officials should examine their credentials, seek references from friends and colleagues in other school systems that have used the attorneys under consideration, and interview the candidates that appear most qualified. Clearly, selecting attorneys is as important as filling any top-level administrative position in school districts. The process should not be taken lightly.

CONCLUSION

There is an old saying in sports that the best defense is a good offense. The same can be said of special education litigation except that, unlike in sports, it is best to prevent a confrontation from occurring in the first place.

The best way to avoid litigation is to be prepared constantly for such an eventuality. School officials can reduce their risk of suits by making sure that all employees are well aware of the law and know and follow proper procedures. Employees who know and understand law should be less likely to make legal errors. This is especially true in the field of special education where procedure plays such an important role.

When inevitable conflicts do arise, they do not automatically mean that litigation must follow since many disagreements can be resolved through more communication between the parties. Parents and school officials can clear up misunderstandings and negotiate compromises. The parties can also rely on formal mediation processes or prehearing resolution conferences to help settle disputes if communication between them breaks down.

Finally, when litigation is inevitable, school officials must not despair. If school employees have followed proper procedures and placement decisions were made in good faith, the school district has little cause for concern. Nevertheless, when entering the legal arena, school officials must come prepared by being able to defend their actions and recommendations while justifying all of their placement decisions. Moreover, qualified attorneys may be the greatest assets that school boards have when faced with the threat of litigation over providing special education to students with disabilities.

REFERENCES

Bennett, K. M., & Pole, K. M. (2005). Legal services: Getting what you need with RFPs. *School Business Affairs, 71*(8), 16–17.

Individuals with Disabilities Education Act, 20 U.S.C. § 1400 *et seq.* (2005).

North Carolina General Statutes, 115C-116(i) (1997).

Ohio Administrative Code, Section 3301-51-08(D) (2002).

Russo, C. J., & Morse, T. E. (2004). Working with parents of special education students. *Today's School: Shared Leadership in Education, 5*(3), 8–9.

Zirkel, P. A. (2005). The over-legalization of special education. *Education Law Reporter, 195,* 35–40.

Zirkel, P. A., & D'Angelo, A. (2002). Special education case law: An empirical trends analysis. *Education Law Reporter, 161,* 731–753.

Resource A: Glossary

Administrative appeal: a quasi-judicial proceeding before an independent hearing officer or administrative law judge.

Administrative law judge: an individual presiding at an administrative due process hearing who has the power to administer oaths, hear testimony, rule on questions of evidence, and make determinations of fact. The role of an administrative law judge in IDEA proceedings is identical to that of an independent hearing officer.

Affirm: to uphold the decision of a lower court in an appeal.

Annual review: a yearly review of a student's progress in a special education program and an examination of his or her future special education needs. An annual review may repeat some of the original assessments for purposes of assessing progress but generally is not as thorough as the original evaluation. The student's individualized education program is revised and updated at the annual review conference.

Appeal: a resort to a higher court seeking review of a judicial action.

Appellant: the party who appeals a decision court to a higher court.

Appellate court: a court that can hear only appeals and so has appellate jurisdiction.

Appellee: the party against whom an appeal is made to a higher court.

Case law: results from court opinions; this is also referred to as common law or judge made law.

Certiorari (literally, to be informed): a writ issued by an appeals court indicating that it will review a lower court's decision; abbreviated as *cert.*

C.F.R. (Code of Federal Regulations): the repository of regulations promulgated by various federal agencies to implement laws passed by Congress.

Civil action: a dispute between two private parties or a private party and the state to enforce, redress, or protect private rights.

Civil right: a personal right guaranteed by the U.S. Constitution or a state constitution or by a federal or state statute.

Class action: a suit brought on behalf of named plaintiffs as well as others who may be similarly situated.

Common law: the body of law that has developed as a result of court decisions, customs, and precedents.

Compensatory damages: a judicial award that is intended to compensate a plaintiff for an actual loss.

Consent decree: an agreement between parties to a suit that is sanctioned by a court and that essentially settles the dispute by mutual consent.

Contract: an agreement between two parties that creates a legal obligation to do or not to do something; a contract can be written or oral.

Criminal action: an action brought by the state to punish an individual who has been charged with committing a crime.

Damages: a judicial award to compensate an injured party; damages can be legal (or monetary), in the form of a payment by the party causing the injury, or equitable (see the definition of equitable, below).

Declaratory relief: a judicial decree that clarifies a party's legal rights but does not order consequential relief.

De facto (literally, by the fact): a situation that actually exists, whether or not it is legal.

Defendant: the party against whom a suit is brought.

De jure (literally, by law): a situation that occurs by sanction of law.

De minimis (literally, about the smallest matter): an item that is small or unimportant, not worthy of a court's concern.

De novo (literally, from new): a trial de novo is a situation where a court hears evidence and testimony that may have been previously heard by a lower court or administrative body.

Dicta (literally, remarks): a gratuitous statement in a judicial opinion that goes beyond the facts and issues of a case and is not binding on future cases; this is also referred to as obiter dictum (literally, a remark by the way).

En banc (literally, in the bench): a judicial session where the entire membership of a court participates in a decision, rather than a single judge or select panel of judges; a rehearing en banc may be granted if a select panel of judges has rendered a decision that is contrary to decisions rendered by similar courts.

Equitable relief: justice administered according to fairness; a form of relief that orders a party to do something or to refrain from doing something when monetary damages are inadequate to make an injured party whole.

Et sequor **(abbreviated as, and more commonly used as, et seq.; literally, and following):** a term generally used in a citation to indicate "and the sections that follow."

Evaluation team: a group of individuals who perform assessments on the student to determine whether the child has a disability and, if so, what special education and related services he or she will require. An evaluation team is composed of individuals such as the classroom teacher, a special education teacher, an administrator, a psychologist, the parents of the student (and in some cases the student), and other specialists. Different states have various names for the evaluation team such as multidisciplinary team, committee on special education, pupil personnel services team, or pupil placement team.

Ex parte **(literally, by or for one party):** an action initiated at the request of one party without notice to the other party.

Expulsion: a long-term exclusion from school, generally for disciplinary purposes; ordinarily, a disciplinary exclusion of more than 10 days is considered an expulsion.

Ex relatione **(abbreviated as, and more commonly used as,** *ex rel.;* **literally, up on relation or information):** a term in a case title indicating that the legal proceedings were instituted by the state on behalf of an individual who had an interest in the matter.

Full inclusion: the practice of educating students with disabilities in a fully inclusive setting with children who do not have disabilities; this has also been referred to as mainstreaming.

Holding: the part of a court's decision that applies the law to the facts of the case.

Independent hearing officer: an impartial third-party decision maker who conducts an administrative hearing and renders a decision on the merits of the dispute.

Individuals with Disabilities Education Act (IDEA): the federal special education law, codified at 20 U.S.C. §§ 1400–1482.

Injunction: an equitable remedy, or court order, forbidding a party from taking a contemplated action, restraining a party from continuing an action, or requiring a party to take some action.

In loco parentis **(literally, in the place of the parent):** a term that is used in situations where school (or other public) officials act in the place of a child's parents.

In re (literally, in the matter of): a situation in which there are no adversarial parties in a judicial proceeding, only a res (thing) for the court to consider.

Judgment: a decision of a court that has the authority to resolve a dispute.

Jurisdiction: the legal right by which a court exercises its authority; jurisdiction also refers to the geographic area within which a court has the authority to rule.

Moot: when a real, or live, controversy no longer exists; a suit becomes moot if, for example, there is no longer any dispute because a student with a disability turns 21.

On remand: when a higher court returns a case to a lower court with directions that it take further action.

Opinion: a court's written explanation of its judgment.

Original jurisdiction: the power of a court, typically at the trial level, to assert jurisdiction at its inception; this is distinguished from appellate jurisdiction, whereby a court may hear only cases on appeal.

Per curiam **(literally, for or by the court):** an unsigned decision of the court, as opposed to one signed by a specific judge.

P.L. (Public Law): a statute passed by Congress; the IDEA was initially referred to as PL 94-142, the 142nd piece of legislation introduced during the 94th Congress.

Plaintiff: the party bringing a suit to a court of law.

Precedent: a judicial opinion that is binding on lower courts in a given jurisdiction; this is also referred to as binding precedent to distinguish it from persuasive precedent (such as *dicta*) which is not binding.

Preponderance of the evidence: the level of proof required in a civil suit; evidence that has the greater weight or is more convincing. Conversely, a criminal case requires proof beyond a reasonable doubt.

Pro se (literally, for self): a person who represents himself or herself in court.

Prospective: looking toward the future; prospective relief provides a remedy in the future typically by ordering a party either to do or to refrain from doing something.

Punitive damages: compensation awarded to a plaintiff that is over and above the actual loss suffered; such damages are designed to punish the defendant for wrongful action and to act as an incentive to prevent similar action in the future.

Reevaluation: a complete and thorough reassessment of the student. Generally, all of the original assessments will be repeated, but additional assessments must be completed if necessary; the IDEA requires educators to reevaluate each child with a disability at least every three years.

Remand: to return a case to a lower court, usually with specific instructions for further action.

Res judicata **(literally, a thing decided):** a rule that a final judgment of a court is conclusive and acts to prevent subsequent action on the same claim.

Reverse: to revoke a lower court's decision in an appeal.

Settlement agreement: an out-of-court agreement made by the parties to a lawsuit to settle the case by resolving the major issues that initiated the litigation.

Sovereign immunity: a legal prohibition against suing the government without its consent.

Special education: instruction specifically designed to meet the unique needs of a student with disabilities.

Standing: an individual's right to bring a suit to court; in order to have standing, an individual must be directly affected by, and have a real interest in, the issues litigated.

Stare decisis **(literally, let the decision stand):** adherence to precedent.

State-level review officer (or panel): an impartial person (or panel of usually three or more persons) responsible for reviewing the decisions of an independent hearing officer from an administrative due process proceeding under the IDEA. The IDEA provides that if administrative due process hearings are held at the local school district level, provisions must be made for an appeal at the state level.

Statute of limitations: the specific period of time within which a suit must be filed.

Sub nomine **(abbreviated** *sub nom.;* **literally, under the name):** a situation in which a case was on appeal under a different name than the one used at the lower court level.

Suspension: the short-term exclusion of a student from school, usually for less than 10 days, typically for disciplinary purposes.

Tort: a civil wrong other than breach of contract; the most common tort is negligence.

U.S.C. (United States Code): the official compilation of statutes enacted by Congress.

U.S.C.A. (United States Code Annotated): an alternate version of the United States Code that includes annotations to federal and state cases, cross-references to related sections, historical notes, and library references.

Vacate: to set aside a lower court's decision in an appeal.

Resource B: Department of Special Education Web Sites, by State

Alabama: http://www.alsde.edu/html/sections/section_detail.asp?section=65&footer=sections

Alaska: http://www.eed.state.ak.us/tls/SPED/

Arizona: http://www.ade.az.gov/ess/

Arkansas: http://arksped.k12.ar.us/

California: http://www.cde.ca.gov/sp/se/

Colorado: http://www.cde.state.co.us/cdesped/index.asp

Connecticut: http://www.state.ct.us/sde/deps/special/

Delaware: http://www.decec.org/index.php

District of Columbia: http://www.k12.dc.us/dcps/specialed/dcpsspecedhome.html

Florida: http://www.firn.edu/doe/bin00014/ese-home.htm

Georgia: http://www.doe.k12.ga.us/curriculum/exceptional/index.asp

Hawaii: http://doe.k12.hi.us/specialeducation/

Idaho: http://www.sde.state.id.us/specialed/default.asp

Illinois: http://www.isbe.state.il.us/spec-ed/

Indiana: http://ideanet.doe.state.in.us/exceptional/

Iowa: http://www.iowa.gov/educate/content/view/574/591/

Kansas: http://www.kansped.org/

Kentucky: http://www.education.ky.gov/KDE/Instructional+Resources/
Student+and+Family+Support/Exceptional+Children/default.htm

Louisiana: http://www.doe.state.la.us/lde/index.html

Maine: http://www.state.me.us/education/speced/specserv.htm

Maryland: http://www.marylandpublicschools.org/msde/

Massachusetts: http://www.doe.mass.edu/sped/

Michigan: http://www.michigan.gov/mde/0,1607,7-140-6530_6598—,
00.html

Minnesota: http://www.education.state.mn.us/MDE/Learning_Support/
Special_Education/index.html

Mississippi: http://www.mde.k12.ms.us/special_education/

Missouri: http://dese.mo.gov/divspeced/

Montana: http://www.opi.state.mt.us/ [click on the "Programs &
Services of OPI" menu in the upper right hand corner of the page, then
scroll down to "Special Education"]

Nebraska: http://www.nde.state.ne.us/SPED/sped.html

Nevada: http://www.doe.nv.gov/edteam/ndeoffices/sped-diversity-
improve.html

New Hampshire: http://www.ed.state.nh.us/education/doe/
organization/instruction/bose.htm

New Jersey: http://www.state.nj.us/njded/specialed/

New Mexico: http://www.ped.state.nm.us/seo/index.htm

New York: http://www.vesid.nysed.gov/specialed/home.html

North Carolina: http://www.ncpublicschools.org/ec/

North Dakota: http://www.dpi.state.nd.us/speced/index.shtm

Ohio: http://www.ode.state.oh.us/GD/Templates/Pages/ODE/ODE
Primary.aspx?Page=2&TopicID=661&TopicRelationID=675

Oklahoma: http://www.sde.state.ok.us/home/defaultie.html [click
on "Site Index" on the left side of the home page, then scroll down to
"Special Education Services"]

Oregon: http://www.ode.state.or.us/search/results/?=40

Pennsylvania: http://www.pde.state.pa.us/special_edu/site/default
.asp

Rhode Island: http://www.ridoe.net/Special_Populations/default
.aspx

South Carolina: http://www.myscschools.com/offices/ec/

South Dakota: http://doe.sd.gov/oess/specialed/index.asp

Tennessee: http://www.state.tn.us/education/speced/

Texas: http://www.mde.k12.ms.us/special_education/

U.S. Virgin Islands: http://www.usvi.org/education/index.html

Utah: http://www.usoe.k12.ut.us/sars/

Vermont: http://www.state.vt.us/educ/new/html/pgm_sped.html

Virginia: http://www.pen.k12.va.us/VDOE/sess/

Washington: http://www.k12.wa.us/SpecialEd/default.aspx

West Virginia: http://wvde.state.wv.us/ose/

Wisconsin: http://dpi.wi.gov/sped/tm-specedtopics.html

Wyoming: http://www.k12.wy.us/se.asp

Resource C: Useful Special Education Web Sites

http://idea.ed.gov/
This is the site of the U.S. Department of Education; it contains updates on IDEA, IDEA regulations, articles, and other general information.

http://www.ed.gov/about/offices/list/osers/osep/index.html?src=mr
This site includes information from the federal Office of Special Education Programs.

http://www.csef-air.org
This is the Web site for the Center for Special Education Finance; it is easy to navigate and is to the point.

http://www.cec.sped.org
This is the Web site for the Council for Exceptional Children.

http://www.ideapractices.org/
This site on IDEA practices provides articles, information, ideas, and links to other sites.

http://www.irsc.org/laws.htm
This site provides Internet resources for special children, as well as links and articles on the law of special education.

http://www.iser.com
This is the Internet Special Education Resources site; it provides links to many other sites.

http://www.napsec.org/
This site contains material from the National Association of Private Special Education Centers, a nonprofit association whose mission is to represent private special education programs and affiliated state associations.

http://seriweb.com This site for special education resources includes Internet-accessible information on special education.

http://www.specialedlaw.net/index.mv This special education law site provides information on the law of special education.

http://www.specialednews.com This site includes current news articles on special education.

http://www.wrightslaw.com/ The WrightsLaw site includes articles, cases, newsletters, and other information about special education law.

Resource D: Useful Education Law Web Sites

LEGAL SEARCH ENGINES

http://washlaw.edu
This Web site contains law-related sources on the Internet.

http://www.findlaw.com
FindLaw is an Internet resource that helps to find any Web site that is law related.

http://www.alllaw.com
AllLaw is another resource for locating law-related Web sites.

http://www.law.cornell.edu/
This is a Web site sponsored by Cornell Law School; it provides research and electronic publishing.

U.S. SUPREME COURT, FEDERAL COURTS, AND FEDERAL GOVERNMENT WEB SITES

http://www.supremecourtus.gov
This is the official Web site of the Supreme Court of the United States.

http://supct.law.cornell.edu/supct/index.html
This Web site contains recent decisions of the Supreme Court. It also has a free e-mail publication to distribute the syllabus of the Court's decisions within hours after they are handed down.

http://thomas.loc.gov/
This Web site was prepared by the U.S. Library of Congress and has links to the Federal Court System.

http://www.uscourts.gov
This is the U.S. Federal Judiciary Web site.

http://www.gpoaccess.gov/fr/index.html
This Web site contains the *Federal Register.*

http://www.ed.gov/about/offices/list/ocr/index.html?src=mr
This is the Web site of the Office for Civil Rights.

http://www.house.gov/
This is the U.S. House of Representatives Web site.

http://www.senate.gov
This is the U.S. Senate Web site.

http://www.whitehouse.gov
This is the Web site of the White House.

http://www.ed.gov
This is the U.S. Department of Education Web site.

http://www.ed.gov/nclb/landing.jhtml?src=pb
This Web site contains the No Child Left Behind Act.

Index

CORWIN PRESS

The Corwin Press logo—a raven striding across an open book—represents the union of courage and learning. Corwin Press is committed to improving education for all learners by publishing books and other professional development resources for those serving the field of PreK–12 education. By providing practical, hands-on materials, Corwin Press continues to carry out the promise of its motto: **"Helping Educators Do Their Work Better."**

DATE DUE

Please remember that this is a library book, and that it belongs only temporarily to each person who uses it. Be considerate. Do not write in this, or any, library book.